Chris Lambrianou was a career criminal from the East End who became reluctantly involved with the Krays. He served fifteen years in prison for helping to dispose of Jack McVitie's body. After leaving prison, he was determined to go straight. He worked at The Ley Community, a drug rehabilitation centre, helping patients who'd got into trouble with the law. He is now retired and lives in Oxfordshire with his wife Helen.

Robin McGibbon, a former national newspaper sub-editor and publisher, has written and co-written twelve books, including the autobiographies of Barbara Windsor, Charlie Kray and Britain's Sixties' playboy boxer Billy Walker. To coincide with the anniversary of the Krays' arrests, he released a boxset of CDs of his conversations with all three brothers, and has self-published a book about his close relationship with Ronnie and Reggie: *The Krays: Their Life Behind Bars*.

McGibbon, who lives with his second wife, Sue, in Kent, is currently working on a sex-crime newspaper novel, based on high-level police corruption in the seventies.

THE KRAY MADNESS

CHRIS LAMBRIANOU
WITH ROBIN MCGIBBON

PAN BOOKS

First published 1995 by Sidgwick & Jackson

This revised paperback edition published in 2016 by Pan
an imprint of Pan Macmillan
20 New Wharf Road, London N1 9RR
Associated companies throughout the world
www.panmacmillan.com

ISBN 978-1-509-82901-9

1 3 5 7 9 8 6 4 2

A CIP catalogue record for this book is available from the British Library.

Typeset by Ellipsis Digital Limited, Glasgow
Printed and bound by CPI Group (UK) Ltd, Croydon, CR0 4YY

Visit **www.panmacmillan.com** to read more about all our books
and to buy them. You will also find features, author interviews and
news of any author events, and you can sign up for e-newsletters
so that you're always first to hear about our new releases.

For Dad, my hero, who was resilient to the end. For Susie, who showed me love, compassion, trust and the real value of Christian friendship. For my children – they are my life and my joy. For Angela, who I wish I could have known better. For Debbie O'Gornic, without whose help with the chapter concerning my daughter Laura Ashley's accident would never have been completed, and Ingrid Connell for having the faith that I could write it. For the man who listens (Jesus) and turns mourning into joy. Stu and Krishnamurti for *Kingdom of Happiness*. Van Morrison for 'Astral Weeks', 'Hard Nose the Highway', 'Snow in San Anselmo' and 'Warm Love'. Elvis for his gospel songs. Pink Floyd for *The Dark Side of the Moon* and *Wish You Were Here*. And for all those who prayed for me in the darkness. For my wife, Helen, who was, and is, an inspiration.

PROLOGUE

One warm summer's day, three years ago, I was walking around the East End with a Hollywood film director, who was planning a movie about the Kray twins. His name was Brian Helgeland and he wanted to get a feel for the world that Ronnie and Reggie supposedly held in such terror.

I took Brian to Pellicci's, the cafe in Bethnal Green where the twins and their so-called 'Firm' of heavies went for breakfast every morning.

I took him to The Blind Beggar pub, in Whitechapel, where Ronnie shot George Cornell dead, one Wednesday evening, in March 1966.

I showed him the house in Stoke Newington, where, one October night, the following year, my younger brother, Tony, and I had taken Jack (The Hat) McVitie, oblivious to the unimaginable horror that would unfold there.

And I showed him the route Tony took, in the silent early hours of a Sunday morning, when he drove Jack's butchered body through the empty streets, to South London, dumping it outside a church, among confetti thrown at the previous day's weddings.

Everything I showed Brian Helgeland that summer's day, everything I told him about the East End of the sixties, had a profound effect and, when I dropped him at his Hyde Park hotel, he was quiet and sombre. He needed to go for a long walk on his own, he said, to ponder on all he had seen and heard.

Those nostalgic hours affected me, too, and I drove home to Oxford, disturbed at waking all the ghosts I'd buried deep in the darkest recesses of my mind.

I'd taken Brian to the key locations he needed to see, but there was one spot I didn't show him – a place hugely significant to me, but not one I thought would interest an Oscar-winning film man, looking only at the wider, bigger picture.

It was a bus stop, a mile or so away, on Cambridge Heath Road, where I'd been waiting, one rainy February night in 1967, when Ronnie Bender drove by and offered me a lift, to my dad's flat, a couple of miles away.

It was a moment that changed the course of my life.

If my bus had come a few seconds earlier, or if Bender hadn't spotted me, I would never have been persuaded to meet Ronnie and Reggie; would never have got caught up in their madness and mayhem.

As it was, I *did* accept Bender's offer of a lift. And my goose, as they say, was cooked.

Fate would lead me from that bus stop to a blood-soaked suburban flat, and a senseless slaughter that would cost me fifteen years of freedom, and bring shame on the one person I adored above all others – my father.

CHAPTER ONE

I was a little cheeky kid in short, grey trousers, and I was standing outside the hotel, in Regent's Park, in the early evening sunshine, watching the guests arrive.

I was wearing a green cap with gold stripes, green round-neck jumper and yellow scarf, with a leather toggle – the traditional uniform of the Wolf Cubs. I was holding a round tin box I'd found on a bombsite and, as another guest walked up to the hotel entrance, I rattled it and smiled. 'Buy a raffle ticket for the Cubs, mister?' I said, chirpily.

The man stopped. 'How much are they, sonny?'

'Sixpence.'

The man smiled and felt in his trouser pocket. He took out a sixpence and dropped it into the tin box. 'And when is the raffle, young man?'

'Very shortly, sir.' I pointed back towards the Marylebone Road entrance to the park. 'At the church.' I put the box on the ground and handed the man a small numbered ticket. Then I went up to the hotel door and opened it. The man was still smiling as he walked through.

Watching him disappear into the hotel lobby, I felt pleased with myself. I jiggled the tin in my hand, feeling its weight: I had not been counting, but it felt like my best evening ever.

I looked at the clock behind the reception desk: 5.15 p.m.

I had been rattling my tin for nearly two hours since coming home from school; now it was time to get back before my mum and dad started to worry.

I went out of the park, crossed Marylebone Road, then ran down Great Portland Street to a bombsite in Cleveland Street. I crept into a wartime shelter and emptied my tin on the ground, then hid it under some rubble, for use the next afternoon.

I put the sixpences in piles of ten, each pile representing five shillings, and was thrilled when I made five piles. I was right: twenty-five shillings was the best evening I'd had since starting collecting ten days before. I wrapped the coins in a handkerchief, stuffed it in my trouser pocket, then hurried down Fitzroy Street, into Howland Street, where I lived with my three brothers, in a two-bedroomed flat at the top of a four-storey house.

A bit breathless, I crept up the stairs and let myself into a toilet on the landing below our flat: in there was a loose floorboard where I hid the money. As I was taking the hand-kerchief out of my pocket, however, I heard my father's broken English, and it made me jump.

'Chris,' he called out from the other side of the door, 'what are you doing?'

'Nothing,' I said.

'Come out, boy,' he ordered.

I stuffed the handkerchief down the front of my trousers and opened the door.

'Where have you been?'

'With my friends,' I said, looking down.

'In your Cub uniform?'

'Yes,' I said. 'We've been doing odd jobs.'

Dad gave me a strange look. 'Come upstairs,' he said. 'I want to talk to you.'

As my dad followed me up to our flat, the handkerchief dropped out of my trousers and fell with an incriminating thud on the stairs. My dad said nothing, just kept walking without breaking step.

'Why have you been wearing your Cub uniform for the last week, Chris?' he said.

I didn't like lying, but I was too frightened to tell the truth. 'I've been doing odd jobs for the Cubs.'

'Don't lie to me, Chris. A little bird saw you buying sweets and toys. He came and sat on my shoulder, and whispered in my ear. Where did you get the money?'

My dad held up my knotted handkerchief. 'What's this? Where did you get it?'

'I found it,' I said, looking down at the floor. My dad lifted my chin with his finger, forcing me to look at him.

'Where?' he said, softly.

I didn't know what to say. I felt so guilty.

'Is there any more of this in the house?' my dad asked, loosening the handkerchief, so that the sixpences fell on the threadbare carpet.

'Yes.'

'Fetch them.'

I left the room and went downstairs to the toilet. I lifted the loose floorboard and pulled out a rag containing thirty-five sixpences, and went back, looking sheepish and near to tears.

'Was there more?' my dad asked.

'I spent it on sweets and toys.'

My dad looked at me for several seconds, puzzled. 'Chris. Where on earth did you get this money?'

I could not look at him or Mum. I didn't want to see the hurt in their eyes. So I looked at the floor as I told them the full story: that there was no raffle; that I'd invented it and dressed in my Cubs uniform because that was the surest way to trick rich people at the hotel into giving me money.

And that I'd only done it so I could get a fishing rod.

My mum and dad didn't say a word until I'd finished. Then Dad said, 'Look at me and Mum, Chris.'

When I did, I didn't see anger in their eyes, just pain and sorrow.

'How can you do this to us?' he said. 'Your mother and me, we love you. We are decent citizens. We do our best for you and try to bring you up decent. Why do you do this and put yourself in danger? Do you want to go away from us into a prison? Do you want to work for the King for nothing?'

I just stared at the floor, ashamed, praying my dad would not belt me.

For a few moments, he didn't speak. There was total silence; my dad was wondering what to do. Finally, he said, 'Go to your bedroom.'

A few moments later, he changed his mind. 'Come with me,' he said.

'Can I get changed?' I asked, wanting the Cubs uniform I'd dishonoured off my back.

But my dad said, 'No, leave it on.' It was as if he felt the dishonour more than me.

He walked out of the room and down the stairs, without saying a word. He hurried up Cleveland Street as though he wasn't with me, and I had to run to keep up with him. At first, I had no idea where we were going, but when we reached the sports shop at the corner of Great Portland Street, I knew. Dad was taking me back to the White House Hotel.

I was filled with dread, and thought of running away. But I had nowhere to go.

We reached the hotel. My dad asked for the manager. As

we waited in the foyer, several people recognized me and said hello, or smiled. Finally, the manager came and my dad talked to him out of my earshot. We were invited into a side office, where my dad explained everything.

The manager listened with undisguised admiration; for someone so young, he said, I'd shown incredible ingenuity and entrepreneurial flair. My dad said he did not see it that way. 'I'm a decent citizen,' he said, proudly. 'I want my children to be decent citizens. It makes me very unhappy that my son is a thief.'

'What do you want to do?' the manager asked.

'We want to give the money back,' my dad replied.

'That will be difficult. I have no way of knowing which of my guests gave sixpence to your boy.'

My dad got up to leave. 'Then we will leave the money here,' he said. 'It is not ours. We never earned it. We have no use for it. It is covered in shame.'

On the way home my dad kept saying, 'I don't want you to grow up no good, a crook, Chris. I want you to be a decent, law-abiding citizen. I want to be proud of you.'

When we got home, he said, 'Go to your bedroom. Take off your uniform and bring it to me.'

I took off my shirt, jumper, yellow scarf and my grey socks, with the green flags in the garters. I folded them all neatly, feeling I was saying goodbye to an old friend I had let down. I went into the sitting room and handed the uniform to my dad.

He went to a drawer and took out a huge pair of scissors. Then, slowly and very deliberately, he cut the uniform to pieces.

'You will never go to Cubs again,' he said, his voice filled with pain. 'We are so ashamed of you.'

I was just nine years old that awful summer's day, when I first brought shame to my family. All my father wanted was for me to be a law-abiding human being, a decent citizen like him. And discovering his eldest son was a common thief shocked and hurt him deeply.

Sadly, I did not learn the lesson he tried so desperately to teach me. It went in, all right, but I hated the poverty we were living in and I wanted to be as far away from it as possible. I saw crime as a way out. I went from bad to worse, conditioned by my environment, the poverty, and the constant moves, the prejudice. I embarked on a ruthless career of villainy – an insane existence that would lead to the dock of Number 1 Court at the Old Bailey and break my beloved father's heart.

CHAPTER TWO

He was Greek, my dad. He came from Lefkara, a tiny village high in the chalk mountains of southern Cyprus, famous for its lace and silverware. But England always had a fascination for him. To a poor boy, who travelled the island with his father, selling lace from a battered suitcase, England was a land of sophistication and good breeding, and the people polite and caring and courteous. It was a land of opportunity, too, where hard work could bring high rewards.

My dad thrived on hard work. He had learned to fend for himself early on, after his father collapsed and died on their way to Vavatsinia. My dad buried him in the mountains and loaded the lace on a donkey and went into Vavatsinia alone. He was about seventeen. The experience scarred him for life, but it made him grow up quickly and want to make the best of himself. My dad adored Cyprus, but he wanted a better life, so, in 1920, shortly before his twenty-first birthday, he packed what few belongings he had and travelled around Albania and Russia selling lace, before going to Egypt where he worked in a consulate. When he was about twenty-five he sailed for England and got a job as a chef, in London's West End.

He worked long hours, but what time he did get off he loved to spend at the cinema. And that's where he developed a sort of hero-worship for Ronald Colman, a British romantic actor, whose good looks and polished manner thrilled audiences for nearly thirty years, starting with the silent films of the early 1920s.

Ronald Colman was the epitome of the English gentleman: a well-dressed, well-bred, jolly good sport who never let down his friends; a likeable, law-abiding chap who always did the proper thing; a decent citizen.

After seeing Colman play Bulldog Drummond, the stiff-upper-lipped amateur James Bond, in 1929, my dad started modelling himself on him. He grew a pencil-thin moustache, started wearing a brown trilby, and spent hours copying the actor's mannerisms and gentle, polite way of speaking. Colman symbolized everything he liked in a man, everything he wanted to be himself. And Christos Lambrianou wanted desperately to be like him.

My mother, Lilian, was one of seven children, and her parents brought the family to England from southern Ireland, during the potato famine there, in the early 1900s. They settled in Consett, a mining town in County Durham, but my mother quickly saw its limitations. Like my dad, she wanted to better herself, and she was prepared to work hard to do so. In 1930, when she was eighteen, she packed her bags and travelled to London, determined to get a job as a waitress. She was taken on at the Lyons Corner House near Piccadilly Circus, where my dad was working.

The two met and liked each other: Lilian was attracted by the gentle foreigner with the strange accent and old-fashioned British manners; and Christos fell for the teenage waitress's natural, down-to-earth charm and zest for life. When Christos invited Lilian to go to the pictures one night, Lilian accepted immediately. They went to the London Pavilion, in Piccadilly, to see the hit film *All Quiet on the Western Front*, and that was that: they fell in love and, after a long courtship, decided to marry.

Mum ran into a storm when she took Dad north to meet the family. 'How can you possibly marry that man, Lily?' her mother fumed. 'He doesn't even come from this country. He's a foreigner. And he's black.'

Mum's sisters were even more insulting. 'He's like a monkey,' they giggled.

All the family were strict Roman Catholics and went to church every day. But they did not have a clue what being a Christian was all about. Happily, their prejudice and contempt cut no ice with my mum, and she married Dad at Camden Town on 24 June 1935.

I was born on Christmas Day, in 1938, the first child of a happy couple, who loved each other to bits.

We were living in a flat in Mornington Crescent, in north-west London, when war broke out the following September. But early in 1941, after my brother, Leon, was born, we were evacuated to the Midlands where my dad was employed, repairing Spitfires, Hurricanes, and other planes shot down by the Germans.

He worked in a massive hangar, on an airfield just outside Ibstock, in Leicestershire, and the rest of the family lived in the town centre, in a corner shop, converted into living accommodation for evacuees from the south. At weekends, my dad would take me to the airfield and I would stare up at the huge, high planes, the wonderful, pungent smell of glue filling my nostrils, imagining myself as a pilot. Sometimes, my dad would lift me into the cockpit and I'd be off into another world, my three-year-old mind filled with all the heroic feats he told me those brave wartime pilots were performing day after day, night after night. No wonder, when people asked me what I wanted to be when I grew up, I'd say immediately: 'A pilot!'

My dad spoke English well, but he had a heavy Greek accent, and, late one night, it led to him being arrested. He missed the last bus from the airfield and was walking home when two air-raid wardens asked him who he was and where he was going. Hearing his broken English, one of them said to his mate, 'I think we've got ourselves a German spy.' One of them pulled out a gun and they escorted Dad to Ibstock Police Station, feeling pleased with themselves. When they took Dad before the inspector, however, they felt rather foolish.

'That's no spy,' he scoffed. 'That's Mr Lambrianou. He works up at the airfield.'

The inspector apologized charmingly to my dad for the embarrassment and inconvenience, and asked if there was anything he wanted. Dad said he would love a cigarette, and the inspector gave him a whole pack, and a lift home.

It was in Ibstock I first felt afraid of death: of course, those daring pilots faced it every time they took off, but my young mind could not come to terms with that; closer to home, and far more frightening, was the local baker, who had died of natural causes.

The word 'died' played on my mind, and when my mum asked me to go to the baker's for some bread, I refused: I was only four and felt, in a weird way I could not comprehend, that death filled the shop and was actually touching the bread. My mum reassured me there was nothing to worry about, but I felt so uncomfortable I would not go there. I'd run errands to every other shop, but not that one!

It was in that pleasant, slow-paced Midlands town, towards the end of the war, that I was lured into crime. Some older kids found out that hundreds of packets of cigarettes and cigars were stored in a train in the sidings at Ibstock railway station, and one afternoon we busted open a carriage door and helped ourselves. I can't remember what we did with them; probably the older boys went to the American airbase nearby and made a few quid out of the GIs. What I *do* recall is being persuaded to have a puff, not only of a cigarette, but of a cigar, too. I was around five at the time and the nauseating experience should have put me off smoking for life. Sadly, it did not.

I was spending a lot of time with older boys, because by then I had another brother, Tony, and Mum was too busy to give me the attention she wanted; I had to find my own amusement.

It was a situation that led to an experience so evil and frightening that it scarred me for life, and destroyed the trust in people my loving parents had instilled.

It also robbed me, at just six, of my innocence.

One Saturday morning one of the engineers at the airfield gave me a most beautifully crafted plywood replica of one of the Spitfires I loved to stare at and touch. Later that day, back home, I wandered off to the park, happy to play with the plane on my own.

I hadn't been there ten minutes when an older boy, of around fourteen, called me over to show him what I was playing with. He enthused over my beautiful plane, but said he had a much better one, and wanted to show it to me.

Innocently, I followed him into some nearby bushes, where another three boys, all about the same age, were waiting. One of them pushed me over and I fell to the ground. Before I knew what was happening, he and the others held me down, and the first boy stood over me, undoing his trousers. I was wriggling and kicking, trying to get to my feet, but the boys were too strong.

Then one of the boys grabbed my head and held it still as the first boy took out his penis and forced it into my mouth. I was spitting and gagging, not knowing what was happening to me, but there was nothing I could do.

Finally, after God knows how many terrifying minutes, they let me go, and I ran home, tears streaming down my face, and told my dad.

He said he would do something. I prayed it was something dreadful; I wanted him to kill them. I needed to believe that they would suffer for what they had done, and, lying in the massive bedroom with my two baby brothers, I kept thinking: If he doesn't kill them, he doesn't love me, and then I'll stop loving him.

But no one came to take him away and I would lie in the darkness, my childish mind wondering over and over: Why? For years it would puzzle me why he didn't do anything. The Greeks have a strong tradition of avenging wrongs done to the family, and I took my dad's failure to act as a sign of weakness.

Dad and I never talked about that terrible day again, but it played on my mind. I didn't want to go to the airfield and look at the planes any more, and I didn't trust anybody.

When we returned to London, soon after, I knew I would have to be more on my guard, and stronger and more violent than anyone else, if I didn't want to be a victim again.

And, even then, I felt I never wanted to be part of a gang.

My dad's head was filled with dreams of making his fortune in business. England, after all, was the land of opportunity. So, when we were settled back in London, towards the end of the war, he invested what money he had saved, or won from gambling in the capital's casinos, in a restaurant in Charlotte Street, in the West End. He soon discovered, however, that not everyone shared his high principles. There were workshy chancers, who saw those troubled wartime years as the perfect opportunity to get rich quick; ruthless black-market racketeers, who preyed on legitimate businesses and did not like 'no' for an answer. An unsavoury little firm tried to sell my dad some bent gear for his restaurant. When he refused to buy, they tried to insist. When he told them to get lost, they burned his restaurant down.

It was a terrible blow that shattered my dad's deep affection for the English way of life. But his spirit was unbroken and, shortly after the war, he teamed up with a Greek pal and opened another restaurant, in Windmill Street, which not surprisingly they called The Windmill. Sadly, this too was doomed, but for different reasons.

One day, a rat suddenly sprang out from the kitchen area onto the counter, a few inches from my mother, who was serving tea from a huge urn. Hearing her screams, my dad killed the rat by throwing boiling water over it. He acted instinctively, to protect his wife, but an RSPCA official was in the restaurant at the time and reported Dad to the police for causing an animal unnecessary suffering. Dad could not believe it. And when he was later charged, he hired a lawyer to fight the case. Why should he be penalized, my dad argued, for killing an animal officially classified as vermin? He lost and was fined £75. But, as well as being a decent, law-abiding citizen, Dad was a stickler for principles and he refused to pay the fine because he genuinely believed the law had got it wrong. That particular principle cost Dad a month in Brixton Prison. And the price of fighting the case, together with his partner's gambling losses, cost him the restaurant. He went back to working as a chef for someone else.

We were living in a flat off Tottenham Court Road then, in Howland Street under the Post Office Tower. Despite the long hours my mum and dad worked, they had found time to have two more children, Jimmy and Nicky, and, as big brother to four little ones, I began to feel a lot of family responsibility. With Leon, the second oldest, particularly, I would have the most awful screaming rows. He would want to do what he wanted, and I would argue because, being older, I knew better.

With Tony, however, it was different. From the moment he was born, Mum made it clear he was my baby, and after school and at weekends it became second nature to me to look after him while she got on with chores around the flat.

One Saturday afternoon, when Tony was coming up to three, Mum asked me to take him out in his pushchair, and something happened that taught me a lesson I would never forget. I was pushing Tony along a cobblestone alleyway, near the flat, when six boys barred my way and tried to take the pushchair away from me. I was scared out of my wits, not only of being hurt, but of what Mum would say if I went back without Tony.

I was only seven and the kids in the gang were a couple of years older. I begged them to leave us alone, but the more I pleaded, the more they tormented us. I didn't know what to do for the best: I could not wade into all six of them, and I couldn't leave Tony and run for help. Finally, I did the only thing I could: I looked around for a weapon and saw half a brick on the cobblestones. I picked it up and hurled it at the biggest boy, the one with the loudest mouth. It caught him on the side of the head and he fell down, crying in pain. Instinctively, I ran towards the others, fists clenched, and they ran away. The biggest kid must have sensed he had taken on too much, because he also got up and fled. I was proud of myself that I had stood up to them, not only for myself, but for Tony, too. It would not be the last time I put his safety before my own. Nor the last time I would use violence to make my point.

Our flat was surrounded on all sides, it seemed, by lively, enterprising people of all colours and creeds: Italians and Indians and Germans and Maltese and Chinese, all living in harmony, all accepted by everyone else for who and what they were, and all allowed to get on with their lives. All these exotic folk seemed cheerful; there was an air of optimism after the war, with everyone looking forward and seeking something better. That West End area, a mile north of Soho, was like a village, and Christos and Lilian Lambrianou, and their five sons, fitted in neatly. We were a mixture of Greek Cypriot and Irish, but no one gave a damn: we were just another family doing the best we could to put the horror of the past five years behind us and get on with our lives. To me, at seven, that small, bustling area of cosmopolitan activity was exciting; every day I'd wake up feeling I was on the verge of a new adventure. More important, I felt accepted and liked by everyone I met.

There was no one more colourful, more exotic, than the tall, broad-shouldered black man, with gold in his teeth, whom everyone knew as Prince Monolulu. We never saw him in a suit; he always paraded around in bright pink, blue or green pantaloons made of some synthetic fabric, a crisply starched white shirt and a huge feathered headdress. He was a legend, not only to us kids who stared in wonder at his outrageous get-up, but to the nation generally. He was pure show business – a flamboyant publicity machine, who became a national celebrity every June when he paraded around Epsom racecourse, claiming he knew who was going to win the Derby. 'I've gotta horse . . . I've gotta horse,' he would shout, and, of course, all the popular newspapers and radio commentators loved him.

Me and my pals were not interested in Monolulu's racing tips, but we certainly looked up to him. He was like a ray of sunshine on a gloomy day, always smiling, always with a kind word for everyone he met, and he loved kids. When he stepped out of his flat in Cleveland Street he was *on* – and would play the part for all he was worth. 'Come here, boy,' he would call out, his big black face beaming. 'I'm Prince Monolulu. Do you want me to tell you what you're going to be?' And we'd all crowd round him, desperate to know what lay in store for us. To me, he said, 'You're going to be the best boxer in the world.' I remember walking away, convinced that was what I was going to be – after all, it wasn't any old toerag who had told me; it was the famous Prince Monolulu.

To millions, that spectacular, stylish exhibitionist was probably a con man. But to me, and to all the other kids, he was a genuinely nice man. And a hero.

Less exotic, but equally memorable, was a friendly bloke who lived in one of the stables at the end of a cobbled mews, a short walk from our flat. He wore an old flat cap, an even older overcoat, with a piece of string for a belt, a knotted scarf and a pair of Wellington boots. He looked like a tramp, but he was a hard-working man, who rode round the streets in a cart, pulled by a lovely, old, grey horse, scouring the bomb sites for anything that might be worth a few bob.

I spent a lot of time down by those stables, watching the huge, muscular blacksmiths at work in a farrier's shed, and one day I saw this man's grey horse pull his cart into the stable.

'What's yer 'orse's name, mister?' I called out.

He probably did not understand my cockney, because he replied, 'My name's Yorkie. And don't you forget it.'

'And what's yer 'orse's name?' I said again.

'I calls her Galloperlightly,' he said. 'She's like a woman. Don't push her, don't shove her – Gallop Her Lightly.'

I didn't have a clue what he was talking about. But I took an instant liking to him, and went back to that stable the next evening and stood watching him strip copper from old dynamos and chuck it into a big tin bath. I went there day after day and he would brew a pot of rich brown tea, often from rainwater, and hand me a cup, saying, in a broad northern accent, 'There you are, lad – have a nice cuppa.' And then he would be off, telling me, with some pride and not a little nostalgia, about Yorkshire and its famous moors. He came from up there, he said; that's why he was called Yorkie.

Sometimes, during the school holidays, I would join him on his travels and he would teach me what to look for on the bombed areas around Euston and Mornington Crescent. 'Go on lad,' he'd say, stopping at a likely looking site. 'Go and see what you can find.' And I'd jump down and rummage around among the debris, returning, triumphantly, to the cart with an iron bar or some other metal I thought Yorkie might want. I spent many hours with Yorkie during that summer of 1946, but then, one day, just before I was due to change schools, he told me he was not able to take me out.

'Why?' I asked, disappointed.

'Galloperlightly died,' he said.

I didn't know what to say. I felt sad for both of them.

'I don't know if I can get another horse,' he said. 'I'll probably have to let the cart go.'

I was really worried for him. 'What are you going to do?'

'I don't know.'

I suppose he talked to me for a little while, but I can't

remember much now, except my sadness that a happy time of my life was over. The next time I went to Yorkie's stable he was not there and I never saw him again. He vanished out of my life as quickly as he had come into it, but I knew I would never forget him – or his lovely old grey horse.

I had been going to St James's Catholic school in Spanish Place, the other side of Marylebone High Street, but, in September 1946, I started at St Patrick's, another Catholic school but closer to home, in Soho Square, and came into contact with a lovely woman who gave me the greatest gift, outside life itself, that anyone has ever given me.

She was an unmarried schoolteacher, named Pamela Franklin, and she taught me to read. At the time, I never realized what a special gift she was giving me; the only reason I was keen to learn was because I wanted to read the words in the comics, not just look at the pictures. Miss Franklin, who seemed ancient in my young eyes, always had time for me and took special care helping me read. I shall always be grateful to her.

Soho was the film capital of England then, and me and my pals would wander up and down Wardour Street in our lunchbreak, gazing in the windows of the studio offices at posters of the famous faces and the films they were in, each of us lost in our own dreamworlds. If the area around Howland Street had been exciting, Soho was exhilarating. Famous people would pass you in the street. Everyone seemed to be in a hurry, all hustling and bustling from one place to another; all, it seemed, with a purpose. To a seven-year-old, it was breathtaking and magical.

The only time the police came into my life was when I found a dead newborn baby in a cornflakes packet, in an old water tank, at the bottom of Charlotte Street. I was just playing around on the way home from school when I kicked the packet and there it was. I put the baby back in the packet and took it to Tottenham Court Road Police Station. The officer who took it was the father of my best friend, David Peterson. I used to envy David for having a copper as a dad. They were people to be respected then and, if you saw them, you had to be very careful.

Shortly afterwards, I found a revolver, with ammunition, and I took this to the police station, too. I was an honest, good boy in that first year at St Patrick's.

The following year, however, I got in with a different crowd and started to learn about crime; not the sort of childish prank I'd got up to in Ibstock – really serious well-thought-out shop-lifting. There were five of us, and we would target the big West End stores, such as Hamleys toy shop, in Regent Street, and Selfridges, in Oxford Street. We were the 1940s version of Fagin's little firm, led by the Artful Dodger, but, unlike them, we never got caught.

Our criminal activities did not stop there. In the evening, we would go to Regent's Park and rob rich kids of their toy guns and bikes. We would watch them playing cowboys and Indians in what seemed mountainous sand dunes, then swoop. Looking all innocent, we would ask to have a look at their guns, then run off with them.

The boys would climb out of the sand and run off in search of their mums or dads, usually bawling their eyes out. But, by the time they came looking for us, we were long gone.

Invariably, the kids would be warned not to go to the park any more, because we were too rough, too tough. I can imagine them being told, 'We can get you another gun, Johnny, but we can't get you another head!' Me and my mates weren't young gangsters, though: those kids were the Indians and we were the cowboy heroes we saw on the screen when we bunked into the Odeon, in Tottenham Court Road – Hopalong Cassidy, Roy Rogers, Tex Ritter, or, in my case, Gary Cooper! He was my favourite and I think I must have bunked in to the Odeon at least thirty times just to see him in the Cecil B. DeMille classic, *Unconquered*. Those little rich kids in those steep sand hills were the bad guys; they had the guns and we wanted them. Why should they have them when we didn't? I was one of the ringleaders of that 'cowboy' gang, but I'd go in and steal a gun or a bike on my own if none of my mates was around. I was fearless. Mind you, if my mum or dad had known where I was, and what I was doing, there would have been hell to pay!

We would have been in trouble, too, if we'd been caught firing staples from elastic bands at prostitutes' legs, as the women stood on street corners, discussing business with potential clients. Some of the blokes chased us, but they had no chance against nimble kids, who knew all the side turnings and alleyways.

We were too young to know what prostitutes were, of course; to us, they were simply pretty girls chatting up guys they fancied. But I did know about sex. For a day out, we would go to a sandy beach by the Thames at Westminster, and me and my pals watched a couple doing it in a cellar, underneath a derelict house, on a nearby bomb site. I saw the couple and wondered what they were doing down there. Then they stripped off and got down to it – and I knew. I was only nine, but I had a strong sex drive and I remember feeling very excited.

It was around this time that I learned about masturbation and I indulged in it often, ignoring warnings that it would make me go blind.

When Father Crook took my first confession, I happily owned up to this, as well as to nicking stuff from Hamleys.

Making that confession gave me such a high. I came out walking on air!

When I was nine, I fell in love for the first time – a short-lived, heartbreaking experience that left me feeling deeply hurt and betrayed.

The object of my affections was a gorgeous golden Labrador puppy my dad bought for me one afternoon in the spring of 1948. I called the dog Rex, and, for several weeks, my world revolved around him. I would rush home from school, eager to play with him, but I would feed him and take him for walks, too. Unlike Tony, who was fascinated by predators, and would bunk into London Zoo and stare for hours at lions and tigers, I always felt there was something very special about a boy and a dog. In a very short time, Rex became the best friend I'd ever had.

And then, one day, I came home and he wasn't there.

'Where's Rex, Dad?' I asked.

Dad found it hard to look at me. 'I'm sorry, Chrissie,' he said. 'He's going to be a very big dog. We couldn't keep him in the flat. It's too small.'

I just burst into tears. I could not believe that I would never see that lovely puppy, my friend, again. At that moment, I hated my dad; I felt he had let me down.

I begged him to get Rex back and he took me to an ice-cream seller at Hyde Park Corner, who had said he might be able to find the dog a new home.

'Mister,' I sobbed, 'can I have my dog back?'

The man was upset by my tears, but he shook his head. 'I'm sorry, son. If I could give you your dog back, I would. But he's gone to a new family.'

I could not stop crying all the way home. I was sure Rex knew how much I loved him, and I honestly felt he would be pining for me as much as I was for him. For weeks, I could not come to terms with my loss; my heart ached so much, I thought it would break. But, one morning, I woke up and I wasn't crying any more. The best pal I'd ever had was gone and I would never forget him, but the loss now was just another feeling I had varnished over, another painful emotion that really didn't matter.

I was only a kid, but somehow, it seemed, I was missing out on the wondrous, magical and carefree age of innocence called childhood. At nine, I should have been soft, malleable, but I was hard and single-minded.

That terrible ordeal in the bushes at Ibstock and the betrayal I felt over Rex were to blame, in part, but, it was the suffocating family environment, and the poverty we endured, that toppled me over the edge into lawlessness.

Up to nine, I can't remember feeling good very often. I'd been the centre of attention, consumed with love by two adoring parents throughout my formative years, but when one, two, then four, babies crowded me out, I began to miss the spotlight and the affection that went with it.

I needed to do something to make me feel important, to convince myself I was capable of doing something on my own that would make me feel good.

That's why I dreamed up that phoney church raffle. It was a doddle. I knew where to buy the tickets. I knew where to find the people most likely to buy them. And, more important, I knew how to make them part with their money.

It was only a fishing rod I wanted that summer. But it was so, so important, because all my friends had one, and I was sickened at always being the one who went without.

My dad's wrath, and the humiliation and shame he made me feel for stealing from those trusting folk, did little to curb my criminal leanings.

From almost the very next day, I became a thief, with not the slightest trace of conscience. My philosophy was: they've got it – I want it. And I got it.

CHAPTER THREE

One afternoon in late October 1949, I came home from school to be told we were leaving Howland Street. Three days of torrential rain had come in through the roof of the flat, making it uninhabitable and my parents couldn't afford any repairs. Now, we were going to another place, south of the river. I was shocked and upset. I was settled at St Patrick's and when I wasn't there, or getting up to mischief with my school pals, I loved messing around on the cobblestones down by the stables. I was happy and secure where I was. I didn't want to go anywhere, least of all over the water: it sounded miles and miles away, like another country. From what I was to experience there, it might just as well have been.

That evening, we all got on a bus, Mum and my four brothers, and headed to a place called Walworth, between the Elephant and Castle and Camberwell. It was dark when we got there, and still raining. We walked down a long road and over a canal until we came to a huge old building, like a hospital. A man took us to a tiny room with a dingy light. There was just a single bed and a cot. I looked around, worried. 'Where are we all going to sleep, Mum?' I asked.

The man told her that the two oldest boys, me and Leon, would have to sleep somewhere else. 'Come with me,' he said. Mum motioned to us to follow him.

The man took us across a cobbled courtyard into another old building. We went through an archway and up a flight of stairs and, as we climbed them, I could hear the sound of coughing, then spitting, from above. We went through a thick wooden door, into a massive dormitory. The gaslights were turned down, but I could make out rows of single beds, with old men in them. The acrid smell of carbolic soap filled my nostrils.

The man showed Leon and me two beds in a darkened corner of the room and told us to get in. The sheets were starched and stiff and cold, and the woollen blankets hard and smelly, from being used by so many people. We lay there in the darkness, afraid. It was the first time either of us had slept apart from the family.

I tried to sleep, but the fear kept me awake. Suddenly I heard Leon start to cry: not loud sobs, just a soft whimpering. I got up and went over to him. I was cold and unhappy and terrified, but I remember thinking I had to be brave for him; not show fear. I was ten; he was only eight.

'It's going to be all right,' I whispered. 'Don't worry.'

But, as I climbed back into bed and pulled the stiff sheets and hard, smelly blankets up over my ears, trying to block out the coughing and spitting, I didn't know if it *was* going to be all right. We had been taken from a place where we were loved and felt secure, and thrown into a cold, unfriendly world, where, it seemed, no one cared – a new and frightening adult world of strangers, where we might be on our own and have to fend for ourselves.

That dark, depressing building, deep in the heart of one of London's grubbiest, poorest areas, was called a workhouse. And the fear I felt there was to prepare me for the horrors, and lonely years, I would experience later in life.

Under the workhouse rules, Dad was not allowed to stay with us, so he moved in with a friend somewhere in the West End. But that did not stop him seeing us. He would pop over during the day and then, at night, when there were few of the staff around, he would creep in and spend another couple of hours with us. He was a real family man and it must have broken his heart to be apart from us.

I was sent to another Catholic school, in East Lane, where there was a market every day of the week. The boys were just as friendly as my pals at St Patrick's and every lunchtime we would wander up and down the lane, looking at the market stalls. Thanks to Miss Franklin, my reading was good and I'd look longingly at the Superman and Batman comics I could not afford to buy. The family's poverty really bothered me: I was deeply ashamed of living in the workhouse, with no money. I was in the basement of life, surrounded by losers and misfits, and all I kept praying for was that, somehow, something would happen to get us all out of it.

After six weeks or so, something did. We were moved to a halfway house in Victoria, a rest centre, where we would stay while waiting to be rehoused permanently. Sadly, Dad was still not allowed to live with us, but, again, he made sure he saw us every day. For some reason, he felt I was a beautiful boy, destined for film stardom, and one day took me for an audition for a part in an Orson Welles movie: *The Black Rose*, which was being shot in London. We sat around for hours, waiting for my turn to audition, but, of course, I didn't get the part. I was not in the least disappointed. I never saw myself as a film star; my young talents were far more suited to earning money for myself.

One of my entrepreneurial activities was carrying suitcases for old ladies, between Victoria railway station and the coach station nearby, a short walk from the new school I'd been sent to with my four brothers. I'd go onto the railway station concourse with Leon after school, and we'd offer to carry a case between us for two bob. A lot of women were happy to see us slave for our money, but others would give us the same money for carrying a handbag. To a ten-year-old, who had nothing, a couple of bob seemed a fortune.

Behind the station, there was a cinema, called the Biograph, and early one evening Mum took Leon and me to see two Westerns. In the interval, a bald-headed man, in glasses, started chatting to Mum, and asked her if she wanted to go home with him. Naturally, Mum said she did not and, when the man wouldn't take no for an answer, she made us all change seats. A few years later, Mum saw the man's face in the papers and told the police what had happened in the cinema.

They took a statement from her, because the man who chatted her up was the infamous John Reginald Christie, who was later hanged for the murders of seven women and a baby at his home in Notting Hill, 10 Rillington Place. Five of the evil man's victims were strangled after falling for his chat-up line and going home with him!

Early in 1950, we were rehoused in a council flat in Hackney, in the East End, where we were to experience the racial prejudice that was making thousands of people's lives a misery.

The war had been over for five years, but foreigners were still being treated with suspicion, particularly in the East End. Anyone with a strange-sounding name was an unknown quantity, an intruder to be distrusted, and the attitude caused acrimony and tension, which boiled over into downright hatred and terrifying attacks on people's homes. We had not been in our flat, in Belford House in Queensbridge Road,

Haggerston, a month when the windows were smashed and the front door set on fire.

It was all down to ignorance. Unlike those enterprising, go-ahead folk in the West End, the people who surrounded us now were less intelligent, subservient types, who relied on others for their livelihood; narrow-minded working-class people, happy with their lot, no matter how meagre it was.

Around Howland Street, I'd been just another kid, one of an exotic cosmopolitan community, welcomed everywhere. Now, I was an outsider, rudely and blatantly shunned by surly bigots, whose racial bitterness was being stirred up daily by the fanatical Sir Oswald Mosley and his evil Fascist black-shirts.

I did not stand a chance. If my name didn't give away my foreign blood, my appearance did. To some, I was Jewish; to others I was Greek.

It was not the kids who made me feel an outsider; it was their parents. If a friend was having a birthday party, for example, I'd turn up with everyone else, only to hear his mother say, 'All of you can come in, but the Greek kid can't.' It happened lots of times.

To any eleven-year-old this would have been hurtful, but to me it went deeper, because I was as English as everyone else. The more I was shunned, the more I began to feel lost, like a displaced, stateless, person, belonging neither to one world, nor the other. I was hardly Greek because I could not even understand my father's native tongue. But to those East End parents I wasn't English either – even though I was as cockney as Bow Bells.

My dad was aware of my problem; he knew I had no conception of the Greek way of life. When he took me to cafes to watch him play backgammon with his fellow countrymen, I'm sure I embarrassed him by not understanding the way

Greeks behaved with each other. Suddenly, in the middle of a game, there would be a lot of shouting and arguing and banging on the table. It was only good-humoured, high spirits, but I was sure Dad's pals were going to attack him, and I'd steam into them, even though I was only eleven. Dad had to pull me off more than once.

In the same way I did not understand the Greeks, the East End mums and dads did not have a clue what I was about. And they did not want to; all that mattered was that I had a weird name and looked different from their kids. To me, it was a cruel world, and I began to rage at the injustice of it all. Part of me inside was screaming: *How can you judge me? You don't even know me. You have never stopped to talk to me. How can you know what I'm thinking? How can you tell if I am any different from you?*

And then, one day, my dad was attacked. And, young as I was, it changed me overnight.

I was invited to a children's party at a house where Mum worked as a cleaner. Dad splashed out on a taxi to Liverpool Street, where we would get the Underground to West Kensington. When we arrived, Mum and I got out of the taxi, leaving Dad to pay the fare. I heard the driver say something about 'bloody foreigner' but did not take any notice. When Dad caught up with us, however, I saw he had the beginnings of a black eye. The driver had never met my dad, but disliked the look of him so much he had got out of the cab and punched him.

The shock of someone hitting my dad affected me more than anything in my life; I felt violated myself. I remember thinking: that is never going to happen to me. And, over the next few months, I started going out of my way to get involved in fights, in nearby Victoria Park, and at local fairs. I hated the racial prejudice, but it was not only that that fuelled my anger; I was still ashamed of our poverty, too. I knew we could not survive without hire purchase, because I'd seen Mum hide behind the sofa when the tally man called for the weekly instalment. Either that, or she would send me to the door to say they were not in. Lying didn't bother me, but the shame of not having enough money did. And it all came out in the form of violence – even at eleven. But I was a tough little kid and could handle myself. I began to look forward to a good bundle.

I could see that you either fought and learned to survive, or you went down. I learned to varnish over the sensitivity, the pain, until I had a very, very tough exterior. Narrow-minded people, cruel, ignorant bigots, might chip away at one layer and then another, but they would not chip through the whole lot, would not get to the real me. I hardened up a lot in my first year in the East End.

How different my life would have been if the family had not been forced to leave the West End: I'd have stayed at St Patrick's, pampered by those caring nuns, and gone on to get a proper job and become a decent citizen. As it was, I was sent to a rough and ready primary school, Schofield Street, and excelled only in fighting. In fact, I was so handy with my fists that an admiring onlooker, a greengrocer, gave me some money and advised me to think about boxing as a career.

The fight began during a gardening lesson on a bomb site facing the school, where one of the teachers had planted a vegetable patch. Another boy, Brian Stephens, was spoiling for a fight and started winding me up. Eventually, he said, 'Do you want to fight me?' I had nothing against him, so I said, 'No, not really.' But he kept on and on until I had no choice. 'OK,' I said. 'After school.'

It was a long-running, straight stick-up fist fight – the sort you see in the movies, where crowds gather and follow the action. It started in a side street, away from the school, and finished up outside a greengrocer's in Haggerston Road. Brian and I were evenly matched: one second he would be down, then he'd get up and catch me with one that sent me reeling. The battle went on and on, up and down the streets, until I smacked Brian with a beauty on the nose and he said he'd had enough.

As I was cleaning myself up, the greengrocer came up to me and said, 'Son, that's the best fight I've seen in ages. You ought to take it up professional.' And, as if to press home the point, he slipped half-a-crown into my bloodied hand. Whatever pain I was feeling eased immediately.

I have fighting to thank for teaching me to swim. There was a timber yard by a canal, near Queensbridge Road, and I used to steal planks of wood for my mum to put on the fire. I would climb over the canal wall, drop down about twelve feet, and push the planks across to a friend on the other side of the canal.

One morning, a pal let me down and I found myself on my own. Having pushed a load of planks across, I saw a kid I did not know pulling them out.

'Oi,' I shouted. 'Leave 'em alone. They're mine.'

The kid glared at me, thinking he was safe on the other side of the water. 'Yeah?' he sneered. 'What ya going to do about it?' And he carried on dragging the wood from the water.

I had to act quickly. I would not have time to climb up the wall and get round to the other side, so I jumped straight into the filthy water. I'd never swum in my life, and the water was six feet deep, but I threshed my arms and legs wildly and made it to the other bank. As I climbed out, soaked to the skin and panting for breath, the kid threw a punch at me, and we started fighting. We were having a right go at each other when a horse appeared on the bank, pulling a barge. A man called out, 'What are you two fighting for?'

'He's trying to pinch my wood,' I said.

'Stop fighting. There's enough for both of you.'

He was right. We stopped knocking each other about and started dragging the wood ashore. After that, we saw each other a lot and became quite good friends. His name was Kemp and I'll always thank him for teaching me to swim!

I had loving parents and four brothers, but I was a lonely eleven-year-old. I liked being out of the flat because, being the oldest boy, I was always being lumbered with odd jobs, or told to look after Tony or my other brothers. But once out, I often had nowhere to go because none of my friends' parents wanted 'that Greek kid' in their houses. I retreated into myself and became a loner, happy with my own company.

Roaming the streets in Bethnal Green on a Saturday evening, I'd see the loneliness in lots of people – lost souls wandering around, or sitting on benches, waiting for the pubs to open. I remember walking past the pubs later, hearing the singing: all the old wartime songs, such as 'It's a Long Way to Tipperary' and 'Roll Out the Barrel' and 'I've Got a Luvverly Bunch of Coconuts'. Saturday night was about forgetting your worries and problems, about packing up your troubles and having a barrel of fun, chucking another pint down your neck and worrying about tomorrow when it came.

To me, those streets were dark and forbidding, but romantic, too, particularly when the rain came and dampened down the dust, making the streets shiny and clean, and when the old lamplighter shuffled along in the gathering dusk, putting a flame to the gaslights with a long pole.

Even then, I knew that London's streets were not paved with gold; money was hard to come by and you had to get it wherever you could. I chose an unlawful way – stealing lead off the mortuary roof, at St Leonard's Hospital, in Shoreditch. I was lured into it by some older kids, who were stealing lead in a big way and selling it to a scrap dealer, in Hackney. Sadly for me, the police were watching him and he gave them our names.

On 4 February 1952, I appeared before Toynbee Hall Juvenile Court, accused of theft and being beyond parental control. I was sentenced to three years in an approved school, and dragged from the court, screaming and shouting and crying. I was a tough little kid, but had never been separated from my family before.

They sent me to Stamford House, a home for wayward boys, in Goldhawk Road, in West London, to await an allocation to an Approved School.

In three weeks I learned little, except to keep away from homosexuals attracted by my baby face. But then I was taken to St Vincent's, an Approved School, in Dartford, Kent – and learned just about all there was to know about juvenile crime.

That school should have put me on the straight and narrow. But all it did in three years was convince me that being a crook was the best and easiest way to earn a living.

CHAPTER FOUR

St Vincent's was a Catholic Approved School in a big, old country house, amid the rolling Kent countryside. It sounds cosy, but it wasn't. The monks who ran the school ruled by fear and violence. If a boy did not make his bed properly he was stripped to his shorts and lashed with a cane. Hard work, discipline, prayers – that was the order of the day. Every day.

St Vincent's was supposed to be a school, but I did not get much education. For the first six months I seemed to spend most of my time on my knees. We were expected to pray first thing in the morning, at eleven o'clock, lunchtime, mid-afternoon, evening, then just before bedtime.

After that six-month initiation, I spent nearly all day in the fields, digging up earth and planting flowers and vegetables. At the back of the school was the main Kent railway line to London and I would listen to the sound of the trains all day long, wishing I could be on one, going home to Hackney and my mum and dad and brothers.

We were allowed home for the day on the first Sunday in every month, but every other Sunday we were escorted on what they called long walks, but which were, in fact, Army-like marches into Belvedere, about three miles away. The shoes they gave me did not fit and, by the time we got back, I'd be hobbling from blisters on my toes and heels. I've still got corns from those marches.

The Sunday home leave was on condition that we had not got into trouble – and, of course, it did not take me long to lose the privilege! I started a fight with another East End kid, called Charlie Olson, who like me was full of himself. We were both given the customary caning and stopped Sunday leave. It struck me as stupid that *both* of us would lose the day off when I was the one who had taken a liberty, so, without saying anything to Charlie, I went to one of the Brothers and appealed to him to let Charlie go home. To my surprise, he agreed. I felt really good about doing that and it went down well with Charlie, too. We put the fight behind us and became good friends.

That was one of the few enjoyable moments. Another was working in a little shed with the school gardener, whose name was Mr Pollie. He would sit there, smoking a pipe, surrounded by scythes and sickles and forks and wheelbarrows, talking to me about football. 'Who did I support?' he asked one day. I didn't know; I'd never even seen a game. I asked the other lads and it seemed most of them supported Arsenal, Chelsea or Charlton. Someone said there was a side that played well and were good to watch, but never won anything. They were called the Spurs and they played at Tottenham, just up the road from where I lived in Hackney. Spurs! There was something heroic about the name; it conjured up a wonderful vision of hundreds of mounted soldiers riding bravely into battle, their spurs jingling, and I liked it immediately. From that moment, I started supporting the Spurs and I couldn't wait to hear their results every Saturday on *Sports Report*, on the radio, or in the classified edition of the *London Evening News*.

You would have thought this new interest would have steered me off the crooked course my life was taking, perhaps made me look up to the great soccer stars of the day. But, sadly, the kids in St Vincent's talked only of villains – and their favourite was one Ronnie Diamond, an East End gang leader, who had become something of a legend after slashing a rival's face. It was Ronnie Diamond, not any of the Tottenham Hotspur players, who became my role model. The more I heard about him and his exploits, the more I wanted to be like him.

One morning, after I'd been at the school for just over a year, the rumble of the trains pulling out of Dartford station proved too much, and I decided to run away. I didn't have any money, but that had never stopped me from taking rides before. I slipped out and bunked on a train to London Bridge. I took the Tube to Bethnal Green and found my way home from there on foot.

My dad was there when I knocked on the door. He was not, in the least, pleased to see me. 'What are you doing here?' he wanted to know.

'I've come to see you,' I said.

'You're not staying here,' he said. 'You're going back.'

He told me to come in, then started lecturing me, yet again, about law and order; how important it was for me to see out my sentence, then come out and get a proper job and do the right things; live a good, decent life. I think it was then, at thirteen, that I took a close look at my father for the first time. I saw him as a lovely man, but a failure. He had worked hard all his life, but had nothing to show for it. What had he achieved? Nothing. He didn't own one single thing, not even the roof over his family's head.

I did not have the guts to tell him this, nor that I did not see work – a proper job, as he put it – as forming part of my life. I just listened, loving him, but not respecting him, and when he told me I had to go back, I knew he was right. I had no choice. He was a stickler for principles, my dad, and he would not take me back himself. He just said, 'You chose to come home, Chris. Now you must go back the same way and face the consequences.' He refused to give me any money, so I had to bunk on the trains again.

When I arrived, Brother John demanded to know where I'd been. I told him what had happened and he did not look the least surprised. He just told me to go upstairs and strip off, because he was going to punish me. I'd heard that orange peel numbed the buttocks, so I found an orange from somewhere and quickly rubbed the peel on my bottom, hoping it would deaden the pain of what I feared would be a severe beating.

In my worst nightmares, I could not have imagined how severe it would be. Brother John took a run of at least a dozen feet to give him extra power with his cane. I stood there, petrified, thinking, praying, that he was not going to go through with it, then I heard him running and I shut my eyes, and clenched my teeth, and tightened the cheeks of my bum, dreading the impact. When it came, the force of the blow literally lifted me an inch or two off the floor. Brother John ran at me with his cane five more times that evening, leaving me with huge, thick welts on my buttocks.

I hated Brother John and his sadistic streak but, ironically, I have him to thank for turning a negative side of my nature into a positive one. One day, he saw me fighting with a kid named Frankie, who was trying to scratch my eyes out with his long nails. Whether Brother John saw some boxing potential in me, or he just wanted to teach Frankie not to fight like a big girl, I don't know, but he said, 'Right, in the ring, you two.'

I had never put on boxing gloves before, let alone fought in a ring, but it did not matter. As with everything else at

St Vincent's, I had to get on with it. Well, I gave Frankie a right going over and Brother John, who ran a boxing club within the school, took me under his wing. He taught me the finer points of the noble art and, as I came up to my fourteenth birthday, I was good enough to represent London in the Amateur Boxing Association's national championships. I saw my name in *Boxing News* a couple of times, which pleased me no end.

After what seemed a lifetime, I left St Vincent's. I was given a suit that was too small, shoes that were too tight and just enough money to get me home. I was fifteen and pleased to be free, but wondered what I was going to do now. Although St Vincent's had not given me any basic skills it had hardened me. I knew what to expect from life.

After three years in a spacious country house, the flat in Queensbridge Road seemed tiny. Worse, I did not know my family any more; they were like strangers.

Within hours of me walking in the front door, my dad was talking to me, yet again, about the need to get a proper job and become a decent citizen.

I could not tell him that all I wanted to be was like Ronnie Diamond.

I did try to earn an honest living, though. Dad talked to a friend, who gave me a job as a presser in his tailoring firm. But I found it too stifling – like living under a blanket – and, in the end, I went to Dad and held my hands up.

'I'm sorry to let you down,' I said. 'But that job isn't for me.' He was very disappointed, but allowed me to leave. I got a job in a veneer factory, but it was only a labouring job, with no challenge, and after a few weeks, sitting around, doing nothing, I quit that, too. After that, I tried three or four other jobs – simple, labouring work – but could not get on with any of them. I didn't even know whether I was suited to work at all.

Far more important was what was happening to Britain's teenagers. It was early 1955 and a moody young Hollywood actor named James Dean had burst sensationally onto the scene, symbolizing mixed-up, restless, misunderstood youth in the film *Rebel Without a Cause*. And he had a dramatic, highly significant, effect on kids throughout the country. For the first time, it seemed, they felt they were entitled to have personalities of their own; they did not have to be seen and not heard. It came out in the form of rebellion and aggression, particularly among the harder, tougher youngsters in the deprived areas of London. The threatening mood was further symbolized by the Teddy-boy look – long, drape jackets with velvet collars and narrow trousers, called 'drainpipes'. To most adults, Teddy boys were not so much dedicated followers of fashion as arrogant troublemakers, and I have to admit I was one of them.

After three years of extremely strict discipline, I was enjoying my freedom, but I was also lost; I did not know my family, I did not know what I wanted to do with my life. I was desperate to 'belong'. I was a perfect candidate for the Teddy-boy set, ripe to join a group of tearaways, who wanted nothing more than to lounge around in cafes and go looking for trouble in dance halls on Saturday nights.

My mate was a real tough kid, known as 'Gravedigger', because he worked in a cemetery. We got a name for ourselves sorting out problems: any grief and we were straight in, no messing. The most popular dance halls were the Royal, at Tottenham, and Barries, in Mare Street, Hackney. The Royal, particularly, was the place to be on a Saturday if you fancied a bundle. The Tottenham tearaways would be on one side of the dance floor and we'd be on the other, sometimes watching the girls dancing, but more often staring at each other, warming up to the battle that was going to follow. And it did follow. Every Saturday night. We fought in the dance hall itself, in the toilets and, finally, in the streets.

Although brawling was my main interest in life, I did start to take an interest in girls. One I really fancied was Sheila Davies, who lived a few doors away, in Belford House, but she would have nothing to do with me. She had a friend, however, named Patsy Hemmings, who saw something in me that Sheila didn't. At first I was not that keen, but the more she showed out, the more I started taking an interest. Gradually, I let my guard down and started falling in love with her and buying her little presents. Patsy felt the same about me; it was love's young dream.

And then, one day, she came to me and told me what her mum and dad had said.

And my world fell apart.

At first, she didn't mention her parents. She just said that she did not want to see me any more. I could not understand. 'What do you mean?' I said. 'Everything was fine yesterday.'

Eventually I got out of her what was wrong. She said it was because of her mum and dad. They had told her not to see me again.

'Why?' I asked.

'Because you're Greek,' she said. 'They don't want me getting serious with a Greek boy.'

I could not believe what I was hearing. I had been away from the East End for three years, but the prejudice was still there. 'Everyone can come in to the party, but not the Greek kid . . .' Nothing had changed. The disappointment and hurt I'd felt all those years before came flooding back, only now the pain was deeper. I was an adolescent now, and in love for the first time. I felt betrayed. I felt rejected, unjustifiably rejected. And I felt angry.

Patsy said she was sorry, but there was nothing she could do. I believed her, but that did not make me feel any better. I knew where the blame lay – not only with her parents, but her brother, too. We had never got on.

So I decided to have it out with them, ask them just why they did not think I was good enough for their daughter. I went round to the family home in Appleby Street, spoiling for a row.

Patsy was in, but her parents were not. I asked to come in. Patsy refused. She said it was best if we just left it. I was too psyched up to walk away and started to rant and rave: 'How could you do this to me? . . . You knew how I felt . . . I didn't want to know you in the first place . . . Why did you force your way into my life?'

And then, when she still refused to open the door, I kicked in the front window and climbed into the house. Patsy's family had treated me with no respect, I reasoned; why should I treat them with any?

Patsy was crying, begging me to leave. But I was too far gone now. I saw a drinks cabinet in the corner of the room. I opened the first bottle I saw and poured some down me. It was egg flip and, minutes later, as I paced up and down, shouting and screaming at Patsy, I threw up all over the floor. It didn't worry me in the least. I was hurt and angry and I just wanted to lash out for being deemed 'not good enough' when I knew I'd done my best.

When my anger subsided, I looked at all the mess and quickly walked out, feeling deeply ashamed. I felt even more like a loser and, worse, I had given Patsy's parents justification for what they had said. She probably thought that they were right in their judgement of me. I certainly had given them good reason to stick to their ban on me.

My dad was still desperate for me to get a job and, thanks to him, I was taken on – believe it or not – as a commis wine waiter. At the Ritz Hotel, in Piccadilly, of all places! The job did not require any qualifications; I just had to bring up bottles of wine from the cellar and take them to the relevant tables, where the wine butler uncorked them.

I met all sorts of famous people at the Ritz. One of them was a TV personality named Gilbert Harding, who had made a name for himself on *What's My Line?*, a popular Sunday evening panel game, hosted by Eamonn Andrews. Harding was a gruff, blunt, headmaster type who did not suffer fools gladly. He was also a stickler for decorum – a lesson I was to learn with considerable embarrassment.

He had chosen to eat at the hotel one evening when I arrived late. I quickly changed out of my velvet-collared Teddy-boy suit and bootlace tie into my Ritz uniform of black jacket and dark trousers, and hurriedly got to work.

When I took a bottle of wine to Mr Harding's table, he was most displeased. Not with the wine – with my shoes. In my haste, I'd forgotten to put on the plain black ones my dad had bought me. I was still wearing the thick, brown, crêpe-soled suede ones we called brothel-creepers. I have to admit they did not go well with my dark grey trousers!

Mr Harding stared at them. Then he looked up at me from behind his glasses. 'You must never wear those shoes in here again,' he ordered. 'You must remember that this is the Ritz.'

I was called before the manager, who informed me there had been a complaint. Luckily, I was let off with a caution.

I've often wondered what would have happened to me if I'd continued at that famous hotel and been taught about wine and etiquette, and got to see more of the other, more genteel, respectable, cultured side of life I'd never been exposed to. Who knows, maybe I would have become a decent, law-abiding citizen.

As it was, my stay at the Ritz was short-lived. One evening, six months later, four mates and I piled into a car and drove to Canvey Island, off the Essex coast, a few miles from Southend.

And what happened there would, once more, split me from my family and put me out of circulation.

We kidded ourselves we were out for a laugh. But we were looking for trouble really – and we soon found it. First, we had a punch up with a group of teenagers in a dance hall, then did our best to wreck a nearby amusement arcade. After a tear-up with some other youngsters, the police were called and two squad cars followed us as we sped away. After a high-speed chase, we found ourselves heading for a road block. Our driver swerved to go round it, but a copper with a lot of bottle ran towards our car and threw a truncheon at the driver's window, smashing it. Bits of glass went in the driver's eye and the car plunged off the road into a ditch, as he lost control. What seemed like a dozen police jumped into the ditch as we clambered out and tried to get away. All hell broke loose, with punches being thrown from both sides, but all five of us were eventually arrested and taken to Southend Police Station.

'What's going to happen?' I asked one of the coppers on the way.

'You're going to be nicked,' he said. 'Then you're up in court tomorrow.'

I wasn't bothered. It wasn't as if I'd seriously hurt anyone. I was hardly likely to get banged up, especially if I pleaded guilty and said I was sorry. I spent the night in a cell, confident I'd get a slap on the wrist from the magistrates and be sent home.

How wrong I was. The bench took a dim view of the charges of house-breaking, shop-breaking, aiding and abetting, dangerous driving and causing actual bodily harm. I was told I was so unruly I needed a short sharp shock to teach me a lesson and bring me into line.

The shock they gave me was not that short. But it *was* sharp. Sharper than I could ever have imagined.

CHAPTER FIVE

They handcuffed me and took me in a van to Campsfield House, a purpose-built detention centre, for up to sixty hard-nosed thugs, just outside the village of Kidlington, four miles north of Oxford.

To a sixteen-year-old whose post-war travel experience had been limited to the northern outskirts of Kent, and the occasional trip to my mother's family in County Durham as a small child, it seemed like the end of the world. And if I felt lonely being driven through the thick steel gates, and across a huge compound, surrounded by high-wire fencing, it was nothing to the frightening isolation I would experience in the next twenty-four hours.

I strutted cockily into the reception area, in the middle of the compound, my mind racing with what I would have to do to make my stay as painless as possible. Someone, I was sure, would mark my card, tell me who was there, what was going on, advise me on what scams I could get into.

But I walked into a deafening wall of silence. It was the first time I had seen a prison officer and there were about six of them, all glaring at me as if I was something the dog had brought in.

I started to ask a question. It was the worst thing I could have done.

'Shut your mouth,' one of them bellowed in a heavy

Geordie accent. 'We don't want to hear from you. You 'orrible little man.'

'Who the fuck are you talking to?' I shouted back. 'I'm . . .'

I never finished the sentence. Geordie threw himself at me and knocked me over. We were wrestling on the ground, a mass of threshing arms and legs, when his mates pulled us apart, and dragged me off to the punishment block. They locked me in a bare concrete cell, about six feet square, then someone threw in a blackened dinner can and a bit of emery paper and some wire wool.

I banged on the cell door. 'What am I supposed to do with this?' I called out.

'Clean it,' someone shouted back. 'Till it's shining like new.'

'Bollocks to that,' I thought.

But, nearly an hour later, after walking round and round the tiny cell, wondering what to do with myself, I decided I might as well start cleaning the tin. At least it would kill the boredom.

When I'd made it as clean as I could, I called out again. 'I've finished that tin. What do you want me to do now?'

A few minutes later the cell door opened. Another ten tins came flying in. And more emery paper. Not a word was said. Then the cell door clanged shut, leaving me thinking, 'Christ, what lies ahead of me here?'

Around five o'clock, someone brought me some tea, which I later learned was called 'diesel', because that's what it tasted like, and something inedible they called food. Soon after, I was told to strip and change into the detention centre uniform, which included boots I could hardly squeeze into. Then, a bed and some blankets were brought in by two officers, who didn't say a word, either to each other or to me.

I found sleep hard, but finally dropped off around two in the morning, assuming I'd be woken at a reasonable hour, given a decent breakfast, and allowed to go back to bed. That's where I was wrong. That's when they gave me the sharpest shock of my life. At five-thirty, the cell door opened and I was brought out of a deep sleep by someone yelling: 'GET OUT OF THAT BED RIGHT THIS MINUTE.' I squinted through sleepy eyes at the door: three huge screws, built like trees, were standing there.

Having not eaten the previous evening I was ravenous. 'What about breakfast?' I said. 'I'll have something to eat now.'

'GET OUT OF THAT BED!'

I clambered out and stood up, in just my shorts. Suddenly I saw something flying across the cell at me. It was a large wooden log.

'Get hold of that,' one of the screws barked.

I caught the log. It weighed sixteen pounds, I learned later.

'Put it behind your neck,' the screw bellowed. 'Crouch down. Now hop like a rabbit. Out onto the parade ground.'

I had to bunny-hop along a corridor, down some stairs, past the showers and out the other side of the building to a yard, where about thirty other boys were already bunny-hopping around in circles with similar heavy logs.

'Join them,' I was ordered.

After three or four minutes, when I felt ready to drop, we were told to stop. A short, powerfully built screw, who said his name was O'Malley, stood in front of us.

'Right, you 'orrible little bastards. We're thugs and we're gangsters and we're Teddy boys, are we? We like coshing old ladies and nicking their handbags, eh? And we like breaking into harmless people's houses, do we?'

He glared at us, each one in turn, it seemed. Then his lip

curled contemptuously. 'I'm going to show you hard cases,' he sneered. 'I'm going to make you strong. Very strong. By the time I've finished with you, you'll be the strongest burglars who ever walked this earth. I'll give you the strongest coshing arm in the business. You'll be able to put those defenceless old ladies right out of the game.'

He paused. His eyes ran over us all again.

'BIG, STRONG MEN?' he roared. 'YOU THINK YOU'RE BIG STRONG MEN? I'LL SEE HOW BIG AND STRONG YOU ARE. PICK UP YOUR LOGS. NOW START HOPPING. HOP, HOP, HOP. FASTER . . .'

For the next sixty minutes, O'Malley put us through it. When we weren't hopping around like Thumper, we were performing all sorts of standing-still exercises that left us gasping. And then, at 6.30, when we thought we had got through it, he ordered groups of five to bunny-hop to the showers. Carrying our logs, of course.

Another, equally tough, screw was waiting for us there – with freezing water running from each of the five showers. We were forced to stand under them for a full three minutes, then ordered to pick up our logs and bunny-hop up the stairs to our cells, make our beds, then get dressed and wait for the governor's inspection.

I was gasping for a fag; I'd been smoking forty a day. But cigarettes were banned at Kidlington. God knows what O'Malley would have done to someone he caught smoking! The beauty – if that's the word! – of the place was that you did not need a smoke. After two weeks of that tough, early morning regime, and what followed it, I was fitter than I'd ever been, and strong enough to fight a lion. And, of course, by the end of each day, I was so tired I was sleeping well. Like a log, in fact!

It was like being in the Forces. The governor, named Elvey, was an ex-army man, who had been in the war, and he stood no nonsense. On his inspection visits, he went through each cell with the proverbial fine toothcomb. If he spotted as much as a tiny cobweb, he would shout, 'CHRISTMAS DECORATIONS, BOY!' And the negligent prisoner was put on report.

Some of the punishments meted out were vicious and cruel, far more sadistic even than Brother John's. One screw, Reynolds, would take a delight, it seemed, in making offenders stand on their toes, with their arms outstretched, for up to three hours on a Saturday afternoon. Try it for ten minutes and you'll see what effect it has on the calf muscles and shoulders.

Another man, Seaton, could kick a football as hard as a professional player – as many of us were unfortunate enough to discover. We'd be running round the Nissen hut that served as a gym and he would drive one ball after another at whoever took his fancy. I saw boys crying with pain after being hit.

From the moment I arrived, Campsfield House was one long, tough slog. When I wasn't humping my log around in the early morning chill, or standing on my toes all Saturday afternoon, I was hardening my muscles on some other strenuous exercise. Some of the gruelling tasks we were given were pointless, but many were useful. Clearly, Governor Elvey's mandate was to maximize the use of the manpower at his disposal and, at the same time, keep all that youthful energy under control.

One thing is certain: O'Malley was right when he said he would make us strong. I was there just three months but when it was time to leave I had not an ounce of fat on me and I felt strong enough to fight anyone or anything. My last job was helping build a road outside the main gate, and I was able to carry concrete posts and bend steel bars with comparative ease.

The day before I was due to leave, Seaton called me over. 'Lambrianou,' he said. 'I want you in the gym.'

I expected a final going over – perhaps a few bruises to remember him by. But it was worse than that – and it had nothing to do with physical pain.

There was a chair in the middle of the gym. Seaton told me to sit on it. 'You're going home tomorrow,' he said, with a sly smile. 'The governor has told me to give you a farewell haircut.'

I thought, 'I don't like the sound of this.'

He draped a towel round my neck and over my shoulders, then proceeded to lop off great chunks of hair. Just when I thought he'd finished, he took a razor and started shaving my scalp. I looked in the first mirror I could find and was shocked: Seaton had left me totally bald, except for a ridiculous little topknot. I looked like a cross between a monk and a Mohican punk. It was the final humiliation, a little gesture to say, 'You won't be going out for a little while after you've left here.'

The next day, I was given a few pounds for my train fare and escorted to Kidlington station. I was put on the London train, not with any word of encouragement or best wishes, but with a cynical, 'Somewhere along the line, you'll be back.'

I had time to reflect on the journey to Paddington. I was deeply ashamed and embarrassed by my appearance, but that was less important than how I felt about the entire three months at Kidlington. It had, indeed, been a 'short, sharp shock'. I'd been subjected to cruel, sometimes vicious, treatment that reduced other boys to tears. But I had come through it unscathed, unbroken. Thinking back on all that had happened, all the gruelling tasks I'd been forced to do, I was filled with anger and resentment. In my own way, I had achieved something, but I knew I could have achieved a lot more with some encouragement. The short sharp shock was fine in theory, but there was no thought of rehabilitation to back up the effects of strict discipline. All I'd gone through was merely tough programming and I came out like Mad Max.

The Ritz had kept my job open for me but about a month after I had gone back, one of the chefs tried to take advantage of me. I wasn't having any of it and chased him round the kitchen with a cleaver. He ran to the manager, who was very good about it; but the chef had been with the hotel longer than I had, so I had to go. He gave me a month's wages and a reference and I got a job at the Berkeley Hotel but the wages were a big drop from the Ritz. I drifted from there to the May Fair, where I got into a fight and was dismissed.

After that I couldn't get another job and before long I was back on the streets. Without a job to go to, it was not long before I was in trouble again.

CHAPTER SIX

I could hear my dear old dad's words of advice: 'Chris, do you really want to work for the King? The wages aren't that good, you know . . .'

Outside, London was basking in a beautiful sunny summer's day. But I had been done for house-breaking, and was now in Wormwood Scrubs, sitting on a hard wooden chair, sewing sackcloth mailbags that smelled of rags. I had to run a long piece of string through a ball of wax and sew twelve stitches to the inch. Each bag took me an hour and I was paid tuppence. Working for the King? Tell me about it.

I was in the Scrubs, waiting to be allocated a borstal. They finally settled on Hollesley Bay on the east coast, and if Dartford and Kidlington had been the junior schools of crime, this tough penal colony, twenty miles from Ipswich, was the university. This was where the 'chaps' were, the real, no-nonsense villains, to whom crime was not so much a way of life as a business. This was where I was to learn what 'tough' really meant.

It did not take long.

A 'firm' of Londoners got the hump with some heavy guys from Liverpool, who were trying to run the place, and one night a little bit of pushing and shoving boiled over into a full-scale battle that spilled out of the dormitories and into the grounds. The London firm steamed in with meat hooks, and one particularly hard guy stabbed a Scouser, then virtually sliced off another one's arm. Connie Whitehead was his name, and he would feature prominently in my life. He and another ringleader, Bobby Collins, were immediately sent to a main adult prison.

The authorities did their best, however, to encourage us to pour our energy into sport. Someone with an ironic sense of humour had divided the borstal into four houses, named after saints – David, George, Michael and Andrew – and there was a fierce rivalry in football, rugby, cricket and weightlifting, when we weren't working in the fields.

To my surprise, I got involved in walking races. I'd always thought it was a cissy sport. The few walkers I'd seen looked damned stupid doing all that heel-and-toe stuff. But I threw myself into it, often on my own, and I loved pounding the Suffolk lanes. I also got a lot out of cross-country running.

After my experience at Kidlington, I should have settled for a quiet existence, just kept out of trouble and got through my three years as calmly as possible.

But, at seventeen, that was not my style. O'Malley and Seaton and co. had failed to knock the rebellious streak out of me, and when a group of eight guys invited me to join their 'escape' party I did not hesitate.

One night, we pounced on the nightwatchman, tied him up in his office, and fled on bikes stolen from the recreation area. We aimed to go into the nearest town, Woodbridge, but it meant crossing a bridge over a river and someone said it would be manned by security guards. Instead, we stripped off, piled our clothes on large, flat boards we found in a shed, and paddled across. We made our way a few miles north to Saxmundham, where we raided a general store, near a railway, and helped ourselves to tea and cakes and biscuits and anything else that took our fancy.

We felt it wise to split up. I went off with a South Londoner named 'Elephant' Johnny Clark, and we spent the night in a partly built new house. Conveniently, the workmen had left some clothes, which suited us perfectly! The next morning, Johnny and I were walking along the railway line when we saw smoke coming from a railway workmen's shed. We found the rest of our team in there, brewing tea from a barrel of rain water. Unfortunately for us, somebody else must have seen the smoke from the fire too, because the next thing we heard was: 'Come out and give yourself up. We've got you surrounded.'

None of us was the type to give up that easily. Someone opened the door and everyone, except me, dashed out and ran off in different directions. Keeping low down, I managed to crawl unnoticed into a cornfield. I thought I'd got away, but suddenly a huge Alsatian bounded over to me. I whacked him on the nose, to scare him away, but his yelping told the police exactly where I was and I was arrested.

Later that day, I was taken before the governor and told I was guilty of absconding, guilty of tying up the nightwatchman and guilty of breaking and entering the general store. I was sent to the chokey block and locked in a small brick cell for twenty-one days; for fourteen of which I was on bread and water. There was a tiny window in the cell, but it was so high I could not reach it to look out. I knew the approximate time of day only from the light that came in that window.

After twenty-one days, the governor came to see me. I was being kept at Hollesley, not transferred, he said, because he felt I had not been totally responsible for absconding and all that ensued; I had been easily led.

I was sent back to David House and set to work in the fields, digging up sugar beet with a pickaxe, then cutting the heads and tails off with an eighteen-inch knife. I worked with a huge Scottish officer, named Gordon, who was not bothered by the bitterly cold weather. I was, though. My fingers and toes felt as if they were dropping off and I dreaded every freezing day we set off to work.

There was a young kid, called Tobin, working in the field with me. One day, I felt I'd had enough and went over to him.

'Do me a favour,' I said. 'I'm going to look away and I want you to smash the back of my knife onto my hand.'

Tobin looked at me as though I was nuts.

'I'm serious,' I said. 'I can't take it any more. If you won't help, I'm either going to do Gordon, or have it away again.'

When he didn't respond, I said, 'Look, I won't yell. And I won't tell. Just fucking do it. Please.'

Tobin said I was crazy. But he agreed to do it. I stretched out my right hand and turned away. Before I had time to even think of the pain, he brought the back of the knife down. Hard. I felt my forefinger snap. For a fleeting second, I thought I was going to pass out. The pain was excruciating for a few minutes, but it gradually eased and I went to another part of the field, where Gordon was standing.

Holding my damaged hand under the other arm, I told him I'd hurt it falling over, and needed to go to the sick bay. 'Very well,' he said, grudgingly.

My ruse worked. An X-ray showed the finger was fractured, and I was given an inside job, sweeping the corridors. It was a doddle. I did the job quickly and played snooker most of the day.

When my hand healed, I was given another lenient task – looking after the horses on a stud farm. I'd give them their breakfast before I had mine, then change their straw. Later, I would curry-comb them down, and harness them to a huge, steel-framed plough, and work the fields. I loved being out with the horses. It was a different way of life and brought back warm memories of happier yesterdays with Yorkie and Galloperlightly and the horses at the blacksmith's.

I joined the boxing club. And, thanks to a fluke punch in the gym one evening, I quickly found myself representing the borstal team. I was messing about with a kid named Sibley when I stuck out a straight left. It was nothing special, certainly not a technically brilliant powerhouse blow, but it was perfectly timed and landed on the point of Sibley's jaw. He went down, out cold, and because he was rated as a skilled boxer everyone thought I must be something special.

I was *not* special, by any means. But I was strong and what I lacked in expertise I made up for in guts – as the crowd at Ipswich swimming baths found out when I fought there a month later. I was nervous and started very slowly, but, by the third and last round, I took control and had the crowd on their feet. I won easily on points.

A few weeks later, I was selected to fight at a nearby US airbase, and what happened there almost certainly changed my life.

Being second on the bill, I decided to watch the first fight to gauge what sort of opposition the Yanks were putting up. I was impressed: a tall, well-muscled young airman, with fancy boots and 'ROY FRY FROM COLORADO' emblazoned on the back of his dressing-gown, made short work of the borstal boy. Within minutes, it seemed, they announced: 'The second bout of the evening will be between Christopher Lambrianou, from Hollesley Bay, and Roy Fry, from Colorado.' 'Blimey,' I thought, 'the guy's so confident he's fighting back to back, without stopping for breath!' But, by a weird coincidence, it was a different boxer with the same name. He was black and, for a change, I experienced racial prejudice in my favour. Some of the crowd were actually standing on their seats, yelling for me, as I started to give as good as I'd been getting in the first half of the fight. My bravery did not get me the decision. The Colorado kid won on points. But I did get something that, although painful at the time, proved most beneficial later. It was a perforated eardrum.

My never-say-die spirit and toughness earned me a place in the borstal's rugby team, as a prop forward in the scrum. What an experience that was. We had fifteen super-fit, hard, mean-looking guys who gave no quarter and expected none, who revelled in being able to dish out some – controlled – violence in the name of sport. We had some heavy tear-ups in and out of the scrum in most matches, none more so than when we played the police. There were a few scores to be settled on both sides!

Most games were at Hollesley Bay, but sometimes we travelled away. One match was at a naval training school, at Shotley, near Ipswich, in Suffolk, and an experience afterwards affected me deeply. We were being shown round the establishment when we came to the swimming pool where eight- and nine-year-olds were being taught to swim.

Whenever a kid tried to get out, the instructor pushed him back in with a long pole.

I was horrified. 'Hey, what are you doing?' I asked angrily. 'Those kids are drowning.'

The instructor could have told me to mind my own business, but he reacted calmly and sensitively. 'It's the quickest way to teach them to swim,' he explained. 'One day, swimming may save their lives.'

I would be reminded of those words thirty years later when I was at breaking point in prison, fearing I might not have the will to survive. But, at that naval school, coming up to my nineteenth birthday, I had a more pressing, and somewhat irritating, matter on my mind.

The Army.

CHAPTER SEVEN

I had only one week at home before I had to report for duty. I knew I was not cut out to be a soldier. And within an hour or so of me joining the Pioneer Corps, in Wrexham, the Army knew it, too.

I was queuing in the stores with hundreds of other National Service recruits when a timid little kid in front of me approached the counter, smoking a cigarette. The sergeant was not impressed. 'Put that out, you 'orrible little creature,' he roared.

'Christ,' I thought, 'what a liberty, putting the frighteners on a little kid like that.' I deliberately lit a cigarette of my own. And when it was my turn to approach the counter, I blew clouds of smoke arrogantly into the air.

It had the desired effect. The sergeant stood up and glared at me, his eyes narrowing with loathing. 'You disgusting, 'orrible little man,' he screamed into my face.

I pulled him towards me and gave him a right-hander to the chin, sending him reeling. I wanted to give him another dig, but a couple of other kids I'd made friends with stepped forward and held me back.

Another sergeant came running in to calm things down. 'All right, all right,' he said to me. 'You're just in the door. You don't understand what it's about. Just leave it alone. There will be no further action taken at this point.' He turned towards the other sergeant, who was rubbing his chin and staring at me. 'That OK, Sergeant Page?'

Sergeant Page nodded; he did not look too happy. But I was elated. I'd made my mark.

We all gathered in the gymnasium for a briefing, and, although I was not mentioned by name, I was given a warning: 'Those among you who like hitting sergeants doing no more than handing out kit will not be tolerated. You're in the Army now. The sooner you learn to behave the better it will be for you.'

I had no intention of behaving. Indeed, the reverse was true. I planned to rebel, so that they would see it was a waste of time keeping me there.

I quickly discovered that, if you had the inclination, you could slip quietly into Wrexham town centre by crawling under the wire perimeter fence of a tennis court behind our billet. I did not waste any time doing so, particularly as my dad had sent me some money. I had got out unnoticed, and was heading towards the town, when I saw a lovely looking blonde girl. She was about eighteen, with an eye-catching figure, and I started chatting her up. She did not want to join me for a drink, or even a coffee, but she agreed to go for a walk.

'Where shall we go?' I asked.

She pointed towards the main gate of the barracks, but, of course, I could not risk being spotted. In the end, we went back towards the tennis court and ended up having frantic stand-up sex in a shed.

After that I crawled under the tennis court fence nearly every night to see her. She could not wait to see me. She was extremely highly sexed.

And she was the sergeant major's daughter!

Whenever he was putting us through it on the parade

ground, I used to take great pleasure thinking, 'If only you knew!'

Mind you, she was not the only Welsh lass to fall for my rough-edged cockney charm. My lusty adventures with the local talent nearly rebounded on me with nasty consequences, however. One Saturday evening, I went to a dance organized by the local miners and got involved with a young beauty, who gave me the impression she was after the same thing as me – a quickie at the back of the dance hall. I got her round there all right, but she didn't want to know. We went back inside and she told her brother that I had tried it on with her. Suddenly these twelve burly Welsh miners converged on me and a black pal, named Roy.

'What's the problem?' Roy asked them, completely unfazed.

'Keep out of it, you black bastard,' one said. He pointed at me. 'We've got an argument with him, not you.'

'You've got an argument with me?' I questioned, as sarcastically as I could. Then I smashed an empty beer bottle on a table and tore into them, before jumping over a balcony and running out the door. Thankfully, Roy had the good sense to follow me, and we got away. I didn't like running, but odds of 12/1 did not strike me as favourable.

At just nineteen, with a hard life behind me, I was not afraid of anyone, as an equally tough Scotsman, named Lochlan, discovered. I'd seen him when I arrived. He was loud, heavy and decidedly tasty; he looked the part. 'I could have problems with you,' I thought.

Over the first few weeks, we eyed each other up warily, but neither of us said anything. And then, one evening, we found ourselves in The Horns pub, and the confrontation that had been threatening from day one was unavoidable.

I did not notice him until I was in the pub; he was sitting

in the corner, obviously drunk, but he had seen me come in and was staring at me. It was too late to nip back out – even if I had wanted to, which I didn't – so I just stared back at him and walked to the bar. It was like looking into the eyes of a lion; I had to be equally ferocious. I ordered a pint of lager and lime and turned back towards him. He was still staring at me, so I stared back.

He slammed his own pint glass heavily on the table and shouted, 'Who the fuck are you looking at, Cockney?'

'I'm looking at you,' I said, not taking my eyes off him. 'And if you do start anything, it'll be the last thing you do start. And probably the worst mistake you'll ever make.'

We stared at each other for a few seconds. Then, slowly, he smiled. He knew. And I knew. We did not need to do anything more. It was a stand-off. A few days later, I met him at the barracks and we started chatting. He said, 'I knew you weren't frightened of me. I looked at you and knew you didn't care. About me or the situation we were in. You didn't have any fear one way or the other.'

He was right. I didn't care. I didn't want to be in the Army. And the sooner I was out of it, the better. Any place was going to be an improvement.

Lochlan and I became friendly and, because I'd fronted him out, all his Scottish mates in another part of the barracks included me in the rackets they were operating, like nicking coffee and tea, and meat pies, from the kitchen and selling them back to the NAAFI.

I continued to try to work my ticket out of the service by rebelling violently at the slightest provocation. I got the reputation of being 'unmanageable', a nutter who wouldn't take crap from anyone, and the top brass were so concerned they sent me to a psychiatrist to try to find out what made me tick. Sensing there was a chance of a discharge, I told him about my perforated eardrum, and started playing up the pain it was giving me. I was sent for an examination.

One freezing February night – just after the Munich air crash, in which many Manchester United footballers were killed – I was in the mess with Lochlan when two thickset Geordies came in and started throwing their weight around.

They came over to the fire where Lochlan and I were sitting, having a beer and a pie. 'Come on, mate,' one said to Lochlan. 'Move it. You've been round that fire long enough.'

'Leave it out,' said Lochlan.

The reaction was just what the Geordies wanted; they were spoiling for a row. As fists started flying, I grabbed a chair and bashed one of the Geordies on the head, knocking him spark out. The other one ran for his life.

'Let's get out of here,' I said to Lochlan.

'I'm not going anywhere,' he said. 'I haven't done anything.'

'You'll get nicked.'

'No, I won't,' he said. 'Nobody will pick me out.'

I thought he was mad to hang around, but there was no time to argue. I scooted out.

The next thing I heard was that Lochlan had been carted off to the gaolhouse – and was facing a court martial, accused of grievous bodily harm.

I didn't know what to do. I wanted to help, but couldn't without dropping myself in it. The last thing I wanted was to be on a charge myself when I was doing my best to get out of the Army. It played on my mind, though; Lochlan had been all right to me. I didn't want him taking the rap for something I'd done.

I was still playing up my perforated eardrum and seeing the medical officer regularly. On the way for yet another visit, I heard the sound of gunfire. A black guy, named Johnson, was holed up in his quarters, threatening to shoot anyone who went near him.

I knew Johnson. He was a very religious man and, on the few occasions we had spoken, we had treated each other with the utmost respect. I thought that if anyone could talk to him, I could.

'Don't be crazy,' the officer dealing with the crisis said. 'He's got a .303 rifle in there.'

'He won't harm me,' I said. 'I don't think he wants to harm anybody. I've spoken to him. I think he's on the verge of a breakdown. I think he's just had enough.'

They let me go in.

Johnson seemed relieved to see me. He just wanted someone to talk to. I sat on the bed with him and he broke down in tears, floods of tears. 'Man, I've had enough,' he sobbed. 'I can't do the Army. The Army's not for me. I can't be away from my family. I can't . . .'

My heart went out to him. I knew he had a wife and kid, hundreds of miles away. I knew he was one of only a few black guys in the regiment. And I knew about the racial prejudice. I started talking to him gently, sympathetically, telling him I understood. 'You can't stay here, my friend,' I said, quietly. 'They don't know what to do. They may do something to you out of fear. Let me take the rifle. Let me get you out. Let me tell them what it's all about.'

He listened, sobbing loudly. And then he handed me the rifle and it was all over.

In prison, you always get to know the outcome of an incident, but in the Army you never do: there is no grapevine. All I heard was that Johnson was taken to the hospital. I never knew what happened to him after that.

What I never discovered either was whether my action with Johnson altered the Army's view of me. But something happened a few days later that made me think it probably did, albeit in a small way.

I was ordered to see the psychiatrist again. He said the Army had two choices: they could discharge me on medical grounds, or they could try to capitalize on the more positive sides of my personality and train me as a military policeman. Because of my background, he said, I knew about discipline. And because of my physical presence and hard attitude, I knew how to command respect.

That psychiatrist was speaking a lot of sense. But I was not buying it. I did not want the Army; I didn't need it. I saw my future in crime. I wanted to be out of uniform and back on the streets, where I could earn more from one good blag than a military copper earned in a year.

They could not force me to take the MP course, so I went before the Army Medical Board, which decided that my perforated eardrum was enough to end my military career. I could not wait to get on the London-bound train and put the whole nasty business behind me, but there was something I had to do before I left. I went to see the adjutant and said I wanted to make a statement, telling the truth about the mess incident that led to Lochlan's arrest. There was no question of me being charged; the Army was glad to see the back of me. But I was told I would be recalled to Wrexham at a later date to say my piece at the court martial. I did do that. I related everything the way it had happened, hoping it would get Lochlan off the hook. I never found out if it did, but I was happy with myself that I had done the right thing, done my bit, as it were.

Shortly after I returned to London, a registered envelope arrived at Belford House, addressed to me. Inside was £200 in cash and a letter from the Army, saying it was for my uniform and equipment they had bought back from me. The cash came as a pleasant surprise. I'd been told I'd be getting something, but not as much as 200 quid. I'd never seen such an amount.

It was March 1958. I was just nineteen. I had been in the Army for just three months – a waste of time for them as much as me. Now, I was back where I thought I belonged, the only place I felt secure and able to look after myself: the streets of London. Not to get a proper job and become a young man my dad would admire, but to duck and dive anywhere that promised an easy few quid. Within a day or two, I bumped into two guys, slightly older than me, who were getting up to all kinds of skulduggery in and around Highbury, in North London. One was Eddie Greenfield; the other a well-liked, laugh-a-minute, decent sort of bloke, who was always seen in cafes and pubs in Seven Sisters Road. His name was Jack McVitie. And because he was going prematurely bald, and was rarely seen without a trilby, he was known by everyone as Jack The Hat.

I was moving in a very sleazy world, drinking every night, sleeping with different girls and getting up to any bit of villainy that promised a few quid. Doing an honest day's work never crossed my mind. Not once.

I was always a heavy drinker, but at a party in Bethnal Green one night I had an exceptional amount and fell into an armchair. Within seconds, a girl I didn't know sat on my lap and started talking to me. It was all I could do to hold a conversation, let alone anything else, but she seemed keen to get to know me.

The next thing I heard was a guy saying, 'I want to see you outside.'

Never one to turn down a fight, I eased the girl off my lap and got, unsteadily, to my feet. I made my way past other partygoers to the door, assuming the guy had gone outside. But he was standing against a wall, and as I passed, not recognizing him, he said, 'I'm here.'

I turned. And spewed all over him.

Seconds later, someone had turned me round and run me out of the house, onto a bomb site. I could hardly see, I was so drunk, and I fell over onto a load of rubble. I felt a brick hit my shoulder. Then another. I could vaguely make out a group of about four guys. They were, it seemed, intent on stoning me to death. Then girls started screaming, and a young Irish guy ran out of the house, yelling, 'You fucking cowards. You'd never dare do that if the kid was on his feet and sober. You're bloody liberty-takers.'

I didn't know the guy. I didn't know anyone at the party. I didn't even know how I got to be there. I'd been in a pub and someone had invited me along.

Somehow, don't ask me how, I got off that bomb site and back into the house. Then two young girls called a cab and took me home. The following day, bruised but sober, I took some friends to the house, found out who was mainly responsible, and sorted him out. I don't think he ever picked on a drunk again.

A few days later, I met those two caring girls on a bus, going to the West End.

'Whereabouts are you going?' I asked, innocently.

'Oh, one or two clubs,' they said.

The girls were teenagers and very pretty. They seemed naive, too.

'You be careful,' I warned. 'There are lots of funny people around. They'd want to get hold of a couple of good-looking young girls like you and put you on the streets.'

They both giggled. It was me who was naive. They were brasses themselves and they were on their way to work.

It was odd I didn't pick them out as working girls, because at that time I was involved with a pal, named Frankie Shea, in rolling prostitutes' punters. Three girls who went by the names of 'Bubbles', 'Blonde Vicky' and 'Mary French', lured clients back to a room in a house in Paddington where either Frankie or I was hiding behind a wardrobe. The punter would be encouraged to put his clothes on a chair beside the wardrobe and when he was naked and doing what he'd paid for, we would take his wallet and steal whatever money was inside. They never realized they had been done until they were out the door, by which time it was too late.

Frankie and I were making some good money, but decided to quit after one particularly unsettling incident, involving me and one of Mary's clients.

I was behind the wardrobe, waiting for Mary's faked, theatrical moans to increase when I made a noise.

'What's that?' I heard the punter say.

'I didn't hear anything,' Mary said.

'I'm sure someone's behind the wardrobe,' the punter said.

I had to think quickly. Obviously, if he looked behind the wardrobe, I could whack him, lay him out and scarper. But that would cause grief to Mary; he would be bound to call the police.

As I heard the bed creak and the punter get off, I swiftly undid my trousers. And when he looked behind the wardrobe, there I was, looking sheepish, holding my willy in my hand.

'Please don't hit me,' I whimpered. 'Oh, please don't hit me. I can't get satisfaction with a woman any other way. I have to watch other people doing it.'

And I pretended to break down in tears.

The punter was furious. And unsympathetic. 'Get out,' he ordered. 'Get out of this room, you dirty beast.'

Then he glared at Mary. 'You're getting money from me *and* him. I hope I'm going to get a discount on this!'

He was raging. And, as I did up my trousers, and went out of the room, so was I. I didn't get his wallet!

Mary and I got away with it. But it was a close shave and we all decided to knock it on the head after that.

One day, my brother Nicky was sitting on the back balcony at Belford House when he saw a man walking a greyhound up Queensbridge Road.

'Is it any good?' Nicky called out.

The guy, who said his name was Ray, told him the dog was called Fifty Bob, which told you a bit about its ability. But he gave Nicky a tip for a race at Hendon the next night, which came up and earned us all some good money.

Ray obviously knew what he was talking about, so I tracked him down and asked him if he had any more tips. A few days later, he came to the flat and asked if I could get hold of £500, because he had some inside information on the Puppy Derby, which was being run at Wimbledon later that week. I said I couldn't, but I could borrow £100.

Two days later, I went with Ray to the track, in south-west London, with my £100. He had £500, of which he laid off £200, backing the odds-on favourite, called Centurion, to win the race.

As far as the experts were concerned, Centurion was never going to be beaten in a million years. But Ray had been told the dog had been drugged and was going to lose by a mile.

Ray gave me his remaining £300 and told me to put it – and my own £100 – on Centurion to lose.

The first bookie I approached didn't want to know for £400. The most he would take was £50, at odds of 7/2.

I went to another, wanting to place £350 on Centurion to lose. 'Are you crazy?' he said.

'No,' I said. 'I just don't fancy it.'

He took just £100, at 7/2.

I then found a bookie who took £200 and another for £50, then settled back to watch the race.

Poor Centurion. A young kennel girl, at Hendon dog track, had given him the drug, Tuinal, to slow him down and he never stood a chance. Shortly after coming out of the trap, he hit the rails, bounced into another dog, and trailed more than twenty yards behind the winner.

Now it was time to collect our winnings.

The first bookie said I'd had an inside tip, but he paid up, no problem. That was £175, plus the £50 stake. The next one was not too happy and we had a few words. But I was a big lump, quite menacing, and he obviously thought I'd wreck the place if he didn't pay up. So that was another £350, plus the £100 stake.

When I went to the third bookie, to collect £700, plus my £200 stake, he had a bit of a face.

'You bastard,' he said. 'You've nicked my money off me tonight.'

'I don't want to argue with you,' I said. 'You took my money. Now I want my winnings.'

I had a tool with me. And I was quite prepared to use it to get what I was due.

'You knew something about that dog,' he said. 'Why didn't you tell me? Then we could all have got something.'

I looked him straight in the eye. 'I didn't know nothing, mate.'

But he knew I was lying. Centurion had been a red-hot 7/2 odds-on favourite for days and no one in their right mind would have backed £200 for it to lose.

The bookmaker, and the fourth one, paid up, albeit reluctantly, and Ray and I got out of Wimbledon fast. He gave me a good drink for my part in the little coup and we embarked on a brief, but lucrative, partnership where we cashed in on his dog-doping knowledge.

One evening, at Clapton dog track, I met a heavy punter, in his early fifties, named Ernie Simmons, who got most of his gambling money from thieving and any other dodgy move that could earn a few quid. We hit it off immediately, mainly because I could match him drink for drink, and he invited me to join him on a few of his 'jobs'. They were quite successful and, at weekends, we'd spend some of the proceeds on a pub crawl, finishing up at a boozer in St Paul's Road, Dalston, where another local villain, Ronnie Knight, drank with his mistress, an up-and-coming actress, named Barbara Windsor.

The real action, however, was not in the East End; it was in Notting Hill, a volatile area of West London, where prostitution and gambling was rife, where nightclubs were regularly being blown up and guns were always on hand.

I would drive over there in my MGB sports car most afternoons and, one day, I met a guy in the Key Club, who introduced me to a bit of villainy new to me − nicking log books and insurance certificates from car showrooms, as well as motors themselves. We would drive the cars to lock-up garages he owned in various parts of London, or park them in railway station car parks until we found buyers. A couple of cars a night came to a tidy sum, and with the odd piece of bent jewellery I was moving around, I was earning a nice few quid.

I was only twenty, but I was a tall, well-built, impressive figure, who was gaining the respect of renowned underworld characters. Having chosen crime as a career, I was climbing the ladder fast and felt it only right that I should have a chauffeur – a former lorry driver, named George, who had been sacked for dishonesty – and a hairdresser, named Brian, who came to Belford House every week to cut my hair.

CHAPTER EIGHT

Although I was just a common thief, I wanted to have the nice things in life, so I traded in my MGB sports car and bought an American Chevrolet. I knew that the big Yank jobs were associated with gangsters, but that was not my motive; I just felt it was impressive and proved I had a touch of style.

I wanted a break from London and, with money in my pocket from various bits of villainy, I got George to drive me and a beautiful girl, named Wendy, to Blackpool. We spent a couple of days there, then went into Manchester and rented a room in Moss Side from a gentle-mannered black man – coincidentally named Johnson, like the soldier I'd helped. I had said nothing to my parents about going up north, but I was not missed. They never knew when, if ever, I'd be home and had given up worrying.

In Manchester, trouble did not take long to find me.

As me and Wendy and George were walking to a cafe in a bus station, a load of geezers ogled Wendy and made suggestive comments. I ran towards them and they scarpered. I chased one of them and cornered him at the back of the cafe. I pulled out a knife, intending to teach him a lesson he'd never forget, but suddenly thought it wasn't worth it, and gave him a dig instead.

We went in the cafe, thinking that was the end of it, but,

halfway through our meal, we were surrounded by police and arrested. I told them neither the girl, nor my driver, had anything to do with my actions.

'All right,' said one copper. 'Give us the knife and we'll let them go.'

I handed it over; if I was going to be banged up, I was going to need someone on the outside, helping me.

When the police questioned me, I gave a false name and tried to convince them that I was a decent chap, who had been led astray by the two they had let go. It seemed to be working, but then a fingerprint check revealed my real name – and a long list of previous convictions. I was kept in a cell overnight and, the next day, sentenced to one month in the Young Persons section at Strangeways Prison, plus a £90 fine. If I didn't pay, I would have to serve three months.

I needed help, if only to tell my mum and dad where I'd be for the next three months. But my bird had flown, with all the money I'd given her, and George seemed to have had it away back to London, in my Chevvy.

What happened a couple of days later reminded me of a lesson I'd learned early in life: never look for help where you expect it – often, it comes from the most unexpected people.

A screw knocked on my cell door and told me I had a visitor. The only people I thought knew I was there were Wendy and George, but my visitor was Mr Johnson, who had rented us the room: obviously, either Wendy or George had told him what had happened.

Mr Johnson was a kind, Christian-minded gentleman, and he kept in touch over the next few days. But then something happened that landed me in front of the prison magistrates and off the visiting list.

One Saturday morning, me and some other guys were told

to shift a mountain of coal. When we had done it, the screw in charge of the operation told us to move it back again.

I was not having any; it was a pointless exercise.

'The others can move it back, if they like,' I said. 'But I'm not. I've had enough.' I offered him my shovel. 'Take me in.'

'Are you refusing to work?' the screw asked.

'Yes, I am,' I replied.

'Stand over there,' he ordered.

Another guy, a heavy geezer named Flood, who I'd had a tear-up with, chimed in, 'I'm not having it, either. You're taking the piss out of us.' He put down his shovel and walked over to join me.

Another con said, 'I agree with those two,' and dropped his shovel as well.

'Anyone else want to join them?' said the screw.

One by one, the other prisoners put their shovels down and came over to join us.

The screw was fuming. 'You *will* work,' he shouted. 'That's an order.'

But we all just stood there, defiantly, and he was forced to summon other screws, who marched us back to our cells.

Early the following Monday morning, each of us was handed a telegram, charging us with mutinous behaviour. I was outraged. I thought mutiny only happened at sea: Captain Bligh and the *Bounty* and all that. I was wrong. The beaks considered it a serious offence indeed, and we were all given two weeks in the chokey, with only bread and water every third day.

After twelve days, a screw came to my cell at 8 a.m.

'Get your stuff together,' he ordered.

I couldn't understand it. I still had two days to go of my punishment.

'You're going,' he said. 'Somebody's paid your fine.'

Mystified, I got dressed and followed the screw to reception. I thought the only person who could have paid the fine was Mr Johnson, but when I walked out of the gate it was not him waiting to greet me – it was my dad. Mr Johnson had contacted him through the police.

Poor Dad. What a shock it must have been for him. He had had no idea where I was – let alone in gaol!

Mind you, Mum felt sure something was wrong. She was very superstitious and when an owl flew out of the trees opposite the flat and smashed against the kitchen window, she had treated it as a warning. 'Chris is in trouble,' she had told Dad.

That was bizarre, but even stranger was what happened after me and Dad left the prison. Since we had several hours to kill before the coach left, he suggested going to a cafe run by some Greek friends, who also ran a spieler upstairs. Imagine my amazement when I found myself back in the same cafe where I'd been arrested! The owner was equally surprised and said that, if he had known who I was, he would have spirited me away before the police arrived.

I didn't want to stay at the cafe or the spieler all day, listening to people talking in a language I didn't understand, so I told my dad I was going off on my own for a while.

'Don't go getting into any more trouble,' he warned.

There was no danger of that. All I wanted to do was go back to Moss Side, thank Mr Johnson, then go to the pictures.

After spending an hour with him and his wife, I walked along Oxford Road and found a cinema, showing Anthony Newley in *Idle on Parade*. It was a comedy – and perfect for my mood. After all the dramas I'd been through, I needed some light relief.

*

That awful month in Manchester affected me deeply. I'd gone there for a fun-filled jaunt, and my stupid arrogance had put me behind bars, once again hurting the people I cared for most. I took a critical look at myself: I would be twenty-one at Christmas, but I'd achieved nothing; I hadn't even held down a proper job. For the first time in my life, I felt a great need to give up the villainy and go straight, so I went for a job, bottling drinks and watching a conveyor belt, at a company called Barnett and Fosters in Hackney.

I felt the job would be good for me and honestly thought I'd get it. I built myself up so much that when I was turned down, it knocked me sideways. I should have started looking for something else, while my appetite for work was strong, but I didn't: I took the soft option and looked for easier, crooked, ways to earn a few quid. It was a recipe for disaster. And, within a month of coming out of Strangeways, I was back in prison for causing an affray, outside a restaurant in Cable Street, Stepney.

Me and my old mate, Charlie Olson, had left without paying the bill. A Maltese mob, who knew the owners, surrounded our car and Charlie and I got out and sorted them with starting handles. It was a brief skirmish, but the penalty wasn't. Me and Charlie were sentenced to six months each in the Youth Section of Stafford Prison.

We were a strong combination and quickly made our mark as tobacco barons, operating a clever operation through a contact in the library. But, after a couple of months, Charlie was transferred, and certain 'faces' started taking liberties with me, thinking I was vulnerable.

I began waging a one-man war against a little firm trying to take over the business, and it blew up one day when they forced my library contact to hand over all the tobacco orders. I would not have minded so much if they were muscling in on just a part of the operation, but they wanted it all, leaving me with nothing. I gave one of the guys a severe seeing to and was put behind the door, amid all sorts of threats from the gang about what I'd get when I came out. Unfortunately for the leader, named Stephenson, a new screw did not know I was not allowed out of my cell, and opened it. I flew across to Stephenson's cell and gave him such a terrible beating that I was taken down to the 'strip cell'. I was left there, virtually naked, until the next morning when the chief prison officer told me I was too violent to remain in the unit with young prisoners and was being transferred to the chokey in the men's prison.

There was a lot of sympathy for me among fellow Londoners, and I smashed the glass of the Judas eye in the cell door, so that they could pass tobacco, bits of food and magazines into the cell.

After a couple of days, I ran out of cigarette papers. I asked the guy in the adjoining cell if he had a Bible, because I'd discovered long before that the paper was extremely thin and ideal for roll-ups.

He arranged for a few pages to be slipped through to me, then told me the person who had been in my cell before was 'Mad' Frankie Fraser, who was a legend among cons and screws alike for the trouble he had caused in prison, and the number of governors he had assaulted.

Apparently, my cell was without a Bible because Frankie had thrown it at a screw, saying he didn't need it – he was going to do his sentence the hard way.

I came out of Stafford a couple of weeks before Christmas 1959, still workshy, and made a New Year resolution to find something that would get me some serious money, but not put me back where I'd just come from.

I found it, or rather *him*, in the Notting Hill area, in late January. He was a safe-blower, named Tony, and when he asked if I wanted to do a few jobs with him I jumped at the chance. A couple of weeks later, we blew a safe in a railway office, in Borehamwood, Hertfordshire, and pulled out £500 – serious money, indeed. I couldn't wait to do more. Over the next couple of months I did another five or six jobs, either with Tony, or other top men in the gelignite business, who offered me work because of my track record. Most of the safes we blew produced a £200 or £300 reward, but we came undone a couple of times. In one safe there was just a packet of stale sandwiches; in another, a set of photographs of a young lady – probably the boss's mistress – minus her bra and knickers!

That spring of 1960, I had money in my pocket and love in my heart. For I had gone to the 58 Club, in Notting Hill, in the early hours, and seen the girl of my dreams – a waitress with long, dark, silky hair and bewitching green eyes, named Carol.

We got talking, more by luck than any skilled planning on my part. Having failed to pull a bird at the club, I was standing on a corner, looking for a taxi, when I heard raised voices. I saw Carol having an argument with a foreign-sounding guy, who it turned out had followed her from the club and was trying to persuade her to go somewhere with him.

When I asked the guy if he knew Carol, he told me to bugger off, because it was none of my business.

'The lady doesn't want to know you,' I said. 'If you don't get going now, I'm going to splosh you over the pavement.'

'You splosh me?' he said, not understanding.

'That's right,' I told him. 'Now, on yer bike.'

'I am wanting this woman,' he said.

'This woman is not wanting you,' I said. 'She was waiting here for me.'

The guy wouldn't have it, so I gave him a right-hander, then stopped a cab and told the driver to take us to Streatham, in South London, where Carol lived. We found an all-night cafe and chatted over coffee. By the time I got a cab back to the East End, it was nearly 4 a.m., and I was head over heels in love, eager to see Carol again.

Over the next few months, we became lovers, but during the summer, a 'gelly' raid went disastrously wrong and I found myself in court, facing another prison sentence.

I loved Carol. But, like my mum and dad, she was just another beautiful flower in the garden of my life that I was hellbent on destroying.

It was a bad omen when me and my safe-blower pal, Tony, discovered our detonators were too damp to blow up the safe in a Stoke Newington post office. We cleaned the place up, promising to return with new detonators the following night, but Tony cried off for some reason. I was greedy for money, however, so I decided to go it alone.

I went to the safe behind the counter, squashed some gelignite into the keyhole, and packed some empty mailbags round the safe to deaden the noise of the blast. I lit the detonator, then ran inside a phone booth on the other side of the room to wait for the bang.

But nothing happened: again, the detonator was too damp.

Cursing the bloody thing, I went over to the safe, pulled the mailbags aside, and replaced the duff detonator with another, drier, one. I went back inside the phone booth, fingers crossed.

Three or four seconds later, there was the most almighty explosion and mailbags flew all over the place. I stepped outside the phone booth, almost choking on the dust and smoke, and went over to the safe. To my amazement, it was only dented, not blown open, and would need another blast.

I was putting the gelly in when I heard a shout from outside: 'We can see you in there. Come out. We've got you surrounded.'

Leaving the gelly and detonators where they were, I quickly climbed through a hole I'd made in the ceiling to get in. I ran down some stairs to the back entrance, but turned back when I saw what seemed like dozens of Old Bill milling around outside. I could hear them on the roof, too, so there was no point climbing up there.

I decided my only chance was the element of surprise. With the coppers concentrating on the rear exit and roof, no one would expect me to go out the front. I'd been taking speed and dropping purple heart tablets like sweets, so my adrenalin was pumping fast. I was fearless – so I ran at the massive, square window, rolled myself into a ball, and hurled myself sideways through it, feeling no pain. The police were so stunned, they didn't react immediately and I was able to get up and run off. Then I had my first bit of good fortune that night: a bus was just pulling away after picking up some passengers. I ran after it and jumped on, chased by half-a-dozen uniformed police. Less than half a mile later, the bus was stopped by a patrol car. I jumped off and made a run for it, but a constable spotted me and brought me down with a rugby tackle. Seconds later, other officers piled on top and I knew my safe-blowing days were over for a while.

A few weeks later, on 24 August, I was sentenced to two years at Verne Prison, in Portland, Dorset, charged with possessing explosives, damaging government property and trying to evade arrest.

'Would Carol be waiting for me when I came out?' I wondered.

She did more than that. She travelled down to visit me several times, and the regime at the prison was so relaxed I was allowed out for a lunchtime drink or two – among other pleasures.

I could not see myself being happy with anyone else, so I asked Carol to marry me. She agreed, and we tied the knot, at Shoreditch Register Office, in East London, the following August, during a weekend home leave.

When I was finally released, a week before Christmas, however, the newlyweds had nowhere to live.

Mum and Dad came to the rescue, agreeing to let us move into a spare room at Belford House. It was not ideal, but me and Carol were young and in love and, at that time, nothing mattered as long as we were together under the same roof. You might think that, having recently finished not one, but three gaol sentences, I would have wanted to find a job to help me buy or rent a home of our own. But the thought never occurred to me. I needed money, of course, but the only way I ever considered getting any was by one bit of villainy or another. I honestly didn't care who I had over, as long as there was a few quid in it for me and I didn't get caught.

In the first part of 1962, I was quite successful and got together enough cash to rent a little flat, off New North Road, in Hoxton. Carol and I had been happy enough at Belford House, and were grateful to Mum and Dad for helping us out, but we were relieved to have our own place. Sadly, it did not last long. We had been in the flat less than a year before I had to ask Mum and Dad to bail us out again. And I have my own arrogance and laziness to blame for it.

It all began when Carol fell ill and Mum suggested she moved back into Belford House, while I stayed on at the flat. Everything would have been fine if I had stayed there and continued to pay the rent. But I didn't. Money was not the problem; I was ducking and diving all over the place and had plenty. It was just that I preferred to sleep at Belford House and never bothered going to the landlord's office to keep the rent up to date. And, because neither me, nor Carol, had a bank account, I couldn't send a cheque.

I had the flat rent-free for nearly three months, ignoring the landlord's warning letters, before I bothered to drive to the rent office. I explained to a young girl clerk that my wife had been ill, apologized for not turning up with money sooner, and promised it would not happen again. Then I plonked down a wad of notes that covered all the arrears.

The girl thanked me and went off to look through a ledger. When she came back, she shook her head.

'I'm sorry, we can't take your money,' she said. 'The flat has been re-let.'

'It can't have been,' I said. 'All our stuff is there.'

'I'm afraid it isn't,' the girl said. 'When we didn't hear from you, we assumed you had left and weren't coming back.'

'Where's all our furniture and the rest of our gear?' I demanded to know.

'The furniture was sold at auction a couple of weeks ago,' she said. 'All your clothes and other personal items were put in bags and left at a builder's yard next door.'

I stood there, staring at the girl in shock. I couldn't believe it. Then my shock turned to fury. I'd spent most of my young life nicking other people's money and property without giving a monkey's about their feelings, but now that it had happened to me, I was gutted.

And when I went to the builder's yard and saw all Carol's lovely clothes screwed up, covered in dust, I was ready to kill.

A few weeks later, I arranged for the landlord to have a very nasty accident. I was out of order and didn't get any satisfaction out of it, but I felt he had taken a right liberty and needed to be taught a lesson.

It was the first time I'd been on the receiving end – and it had a profound effect on me. After that, I cared even less about people and made a promise to myself: no one, but no one, was ever going to have me over again.

And then, early in 1963, I accepted an invitation to go for a drink in a club off Shaftesbury Avenue, and saw for myself what little help the underworld is prepared to offer its own.

I was sitting talking with a pal, Peter Metcalfe, when a strange-looking guy came over to our table and started talking to us. He was a real mess: his arms had been broken and were back to front, elbows at the front. He said he was on the run from Nottingham Prison and had been offered help by the Kray twins, who were into protection. They had sent this guy to the club to see the owner, Eric Mason, who they said would be able to help him. But the poor bloke had been sitting in the club for seven hours and Mason had barely spoken to him. As he had no one to turn to, I took him to some brasses who had a flat in Hornsey, and they let him sleep in a spare room overnight.

The guy left early the next morning, asking the girls to thank me, and I never heard of him again.

My gesture went down well with Mason, and he always made me and my friends welcome at his new West End club, the Brown Derby, which he opened in the autumn of 1963. It's funny how life turns out. If I hadn't helped that escaped prisoner, I'd never have got close to Mason and met a likeable Jewish long-firm expert, named Kenny Bloom.

Kenny and I met in the Brown Derby when I stepped in to sort out a row he and a friend were having with a guy who had insulted some girls. He took to me and, early in 1964, invited me up to Solihull, just outside Birmingham, where he had rented a lovely big house from a doctor. It was my first trip north since my disastrous visit with Wendy and George, and I'll never forget it. Kenny was a big spender, well respected on the Northern club scene, and he took me round, introducing me to all the different 'faces', not only in Birmingham, but in Manchester and Liverpool.

I was a big lump, about fourteen stone, and could have a row. But it was not only my physical presence he liked: I could take care of business, tidy things up. And I could be trusted. I was worth having on the Firm.

Kenny introduced me to something else, too: shotguns. He gave me a couple, saying, 'People will do anything if they've got a shooter up their nose.'

Those shotguns helped shape our lives spectacularly that summer of 1964.

Me and Carol – and my brother Tony and Peter Metcalfe – were in Liverpool for a wedding when we got a message to ring Eric Mason at a house in Blackpool.

When I called, one of Eric's mates, Teddy Fleming, said excitedly, 'Get up here right away. We're having the most amazing time. It's the bloody business up here.'

I persuaded Carol to stay at her parents' home, on the outskirts of Liverpool, then drove up the newly opened M6 to Lytham St Annes with Tony and Peter. Despite the mild weather, we deliberately wore Crombie overcoats for effect, and when we climbed out of the car, outside a house owned by two well-known dancers, I'm sure it looked as if we'd just flown in from Sicily. Our arrival caused a stir; we were obviously expected. People were hanging out of windows, looking at us, and we played up to them. I'd taken the shotguns to Liverpool to shoot water rats along the river banks, near my in-laws' home, and they were still in the boot. Casually, I took them out and put them on the ground, where everyone could see them. I picked up a suitcase, slung the guns over my shoulder, then walked slowly into the house.

It was like something out of *The Godfather*.

The first thing me and Tony and Peter wanted to sort out was money. It was understood we wouldn't drop everything and go up there for nothing. We were not there to walk along the sea front with Kiss-Me-Quick hats: we were there to razzle-dazzle. And that meant money. Someone had to be holding the readies.

'Don't worry about dosh,' Mason told us. 'This is our town. You won't have to pay a penny.'

Mason had fled north after being badly beaten and slashed by Frankie Fraser and, like Kenny Bloom, had turned his attention to Northern clubs, particularly those with gambling licences. He had made his mark quickly. Wherever we went, no one wanted any money; the bill was always already paid.

Mason was a great manipulator: I'd never met anyone who could use a situation, or people, better. I knew he'd invited the three of us up there to impress – and frighten. After our arrival, the whisper went round Blackpool's show-business circuit that some London gangsters were in town, heavily tooled up, to do somebody. And Mason did not enlighten them.

The Kray twins were never mentioned, but everyone knew they were powerful London gangsters, and the only ones capable of sending hit men that far north. Since we, too, were from the East End, everyone assumed we were part of the Kray Firm. None of us had to confirm or deny anything, because no one had the front to mention the twins. We just let them play around with their own imaginations, and pick up the tab for our enjoyment.

All the club owners were happy to do that. We were good

for business: there was an air of mystique around us, an element of anything could happen, and, if it did, it could be dealt with.

We were feted wherever we went. Mason was a charismatic character, always with two or three girls on the go, always calling the waiters for more Bollinger, always revelling in the spotlight. Through him and the gangster image we portrayed, we were treated like film stars. Sometimes even big showbiz names did not get the five-star treatment we did.

The guns, as much as Mason, played their part, and one day an odd-looking gift-shop owner took me into the back of his shop and opened some drawers, containing all sorts of weapons – Lugers, Mausers, tiny pistols.

'I'm a member of a gun club,' he said. 'I can get you anything you want. Big or small.'

I was impressed and bought a couple of pieces on the spot. I never knew when I'd need one; also I liked to have a spare, should a friend ever want one.

My latest purchases, like my supposed connection to the Krays, quickly buzzed around town, boosting my unsavoury reputation.

Over the next couple of months, our reputations grew and we got into every kind of skulduggery you can imagine. If someone had a grudge they wanted settling, we'd do it, in return for a handful of readies. Once, somebody had some grief with a garage owner and we went along and pulled four petrol pumps over with chains.

Kenny Bloom, who was at the Old Bailey facing a long prison sentence, asked me to empty the rented house in Solihull and give all his belongings to a girlfriend. While up there, I met Don Giles, one of the finest long-firm fraudsters in the country, who was looking for two guys who could pass for genuine businessmen for a scam he wanted to set up in London. I knew the ideal guys – two pals from Manchester, named David and Neville – and Don set them up in offices behind the BBC, with smart phones and even smarter secretaries.

Within a few weeks, David and Neville had established lines of credit with several major companies and were ordering thousands of pounds' worth of goods – from frogman's flippers and plimsolls, to hairdryers and radios – which we knocked out cheap to swag shops, who sold on to wholesalers and market stallholders.

For three or four months we all earned good money, but then came the time to do a runner before the companies supplying the goods started pressing for their money.

Before folding the company, we decided to have a final fling on August bank holiday. Me, Don and Tony went to an outfitter's, where we had a credit account, and got suited and booted, in fashionable new gear, saying we had to attend an important conference abroad. Then we went to Alfred Dunhill, the famous store, off Piccadilly, and picked up some expensive cameras and cigarette lighters. We didn't have credit there, but we persuaded staff to accept a company cheque. What they didn't know, of course, was that, by the end of the following week, the company wouldn't exist.

I had decided to spend the holiday weekend at Margate, on the Kent coast, with a gorgeous girl named Honey, who was black.

'Hire me a Mark 10 Jaguar for the weekend,' I instructed one of our secretaries. Then, because I had no licence, I asked Tony to come too.

When he heard I was taking a black bird, he flipped and said he didn't want her to come. Tony wasn't a racist by any stretch, but felt her colour might provoke racial aggro, and he knew I wouldn't stand by and see her embarrassed: he wanted a quiet weekend away without any tear-ups. I tried to make him change his mind, but he was adamant she wasn't coming and I had to give in, because I needed him to drive.

I've always regretted not pulling rank on Tony over that – because we had the most miserable, expensive weekend and ended up having a fight after he pulled a bird, whose mate was a real dog.

Honey came off best. She resumed a relationship with an up-an-coming rock 'n' roll singer.

Mick Jagger.

When I went to the office on Tuesday morning, I got a shock: David and Neville were sitting behind their desks, their faces black and blue. Also in the room was a guy I'd never seen before.

'What the fuck's going on?' I demanded to know.

'Never mind, Chris,' David said. 'It's nothing to do with you.'

I told them it had everything to do with me, because I had introduced them to the firm, and brought them down to London.

Reluctantly, he and Neville told me what had happened. They, too, had wanted to hire Jaguars for the weekend, but Hertz had only a Ford Anglia and a Morris Countryman left. They felt that, if anyone should have Jaguars it should be them, because they were doing the day-to-day work for the company. Apparently, they were so upset they had threatened other people in the long-firm fraud that they were going to contact Hertz and tell them the company was crooked, and the hire charges would not be paid. Unfortunately, they had threatened the wrong people: while the rest of us had been trying to enjoy ourselves over the weekend, David and Neville had been beaten up and tortured.

They were playboy types from the provinces and not part of the London underworld culture: they were more suited to women and gambling and didn't understand the rules of the game. Feeling responsible for what had happened, I got them out of the office and I asked them what they wanted to do. They didn't want any grief, but I could not ignore what had happened.

'I've got shotguns,' I told them. 'Let's go and have a problem with who tortured you.' But they were too terrified. All they wanted was to get back to Manchester where life was quieter and the people less aggressive.

In less than eighteen months, David and Neville would read that one of their torturers was dead – gunned down in a pub, called The Blind Beggar, in London's East End.

CHAPTER NINE

One night, in the middle of the following February, Peter Metcalfe and I found ourselves squelching across a muddy field behind a quietly spoken Scotsman in a flat cap and a raincoat. He was a sophisticated burglar, named Jock, and his speciality was robbing large, rambling country houses.

Jock had picked us up in his car at 6 p.m. and taken us on a mystery tour. We did not know where we were going or what we would do when we got there. We knew it was a bit of villainy, but we'd been told not to bring any equipment, except a pair of gloves. It was all very baffling, but exciting, too, because Jock was an expert in his field and had invited us to help him on a job.

We trudged across to a barn and sat down among half-a-dozen horses. I went to light a cigarette, but Jock told me to put it out. He motioned to a large house, about a hundred yards away. 'Don't want anybody to see the light,' he said.

We sat in the barn for two hours – watching the house. 'I had the upstairs a couple of months ago,' Jock said. 'Tonight, it's the downstairs.'

Around midnight, the downstairs' lights started going out as the owner and his family, and servants, went to bed. We waited another hour until all the upstairs lights were out, too, then Jock said, 'Right, boys, in we go.'

I now realized why we had been told not to bring any

tools: everything we needed was there in the barn – an iron lever to jemmy the back door and a dozen horse's feed sacks to carry the gear we were about to steal.

We crept to the back of the house and Jock wrenched open a patio door. We followed him silently along a narrow hallway and he pointed to about a dozen little boxes. 'Snuff boxes,' he whispered. 'Put them in the sack.'

I pointed at various other items I thought worth nicking, but Jock shook his head. Then he opened a drawer. 'Right,' he said, as if he knew what he was going to find. 'There are the silver plates. Load them up.' We filled the sack and took it outside, then went back into the house with two more.

'We're going to the kitchen now,' said Jock.

'Christ,' I thought. 'He's got a nerve. He's going to have a bite to eat, or make a cup of tea.'

As we started searching the kitchen, there was a noise upstairs, as someone got up to go to the toilet. The three of us went into the nearest room and hid behind a sofa. My heart was racing; I was terrified. If that person had come down the stairs and found us, I would have run. Fortunately, he or she didn't, and Jock led us towards the kitchen.

He opened the pantry door and, with a sense of triumph, whispered, 'That's what we've come for, boys.'

There was an arched, church-like door, built into the wall. It looked like a food cupboard, but Jock knew better. 'That's the safe,' he said.

It was a very primitive safe, with only a padlock. Jock wrenched it off and told us to look inside. We couldn't believe our eyes. It was like an Aladdin's cave, filled with more silver plates, snuff boxes, ceremonial garments and swords, rare stamps, foreign cash, a coin collection, jewellery and watches.

'Start loading all of it,' Jock commanded.

All the stuff we pinched from that pantry was obviously of

great sentimental value, but I didn't give a monkey's. I didn't give it a thought really, I was just doing a job – nothing more than that. I felt a bit like Robin Hood, stealing from the rich to help the poor – me! It wasn't as if the people who owned the stuff were going to lose out financially: they would be covered by insurance.

No, my only problem that night was dragging the swag back the way we had come, through fields, ankle deep in mud. We managed it, though – all ten sacks! – and drove back to London, dreading a pull from the Old Bill.

Jock said he would find a buyer, but I didn't trust him. We were inexperienced, naive amateurs and he was a polished professional. He could have taken us to the cleaners. I felt that if *we* found the buyer, we would have some control over what happened, so I insisted that the selling would be down to us. Jock didn't like it, but he had no choice. I was tough and what I said went.

What I quickly learned was that the weight of our treasure did not reflect its financial worth. Even so, what we did sell fetched more money than I'd seen recently, and I couldn't wait to go to the country again with the flat-capped Scot.

Over the next few months, we pushed Jock to do another four homes. We felt we had found a gold vein and were greedy for more and more money. He, however, was a family man, nearing fifty, and he wanted to slow down. He was also worried: he had a couple of coconuts on board, who were likely to fall on his head.

One bit of work needed a key man and I introduced Jock to an expert I knew as 'Jewish John'. The job had to be abandoned because the Old Bill were sniffing around, but I learned later that Jock and John had gone back on their own, leaving the two coconuts out of it.

When it got back to me that John was quite flush I wanted

to get hold of him, but had no idea where he lived. I knew Jock lived in Harlow, in Essex, however, and that he drove a Ford Corsair.

I asked Peter Metcalfe to drive me to the A11, so that we could watch for Jock's car travelling east. He thought I was crazy. After we'd been there every night for two weeks without seeing it, I began to think so, too. But I could not give up. We'd been double-crossed – and I didn't like it. I wanted to get hold of Jock, give him a slap for taking a liberty, then get what I felt was mine.

My patience finally paid off. After nearly four weeks' waiting, Jock's car came into view – and, lo and behold, Jewish John was in it, too. Two for the price of one! Peter pulled out, put his foot down, and drove the Corsair into the side of the road. I jumped out, wielding an iron bar, and whacked John on the shoulder. I didn't want to harm him, just let him know I meant business.

Jock explained that they had dropped us out because four was too many, but they were looking after our corner. I told him we would drive to his house in Harlow and get it. We didn't get the full wedge, I'm sure, but it was better than nothing.

Although I'd accepted many free drinks from club owners who thought I was part of the Kray Firm, I did not meet the notorious twins until one Thursday night in April when they threw a party to celebrate the opening of their new club, the El Morocco, in Soho.

Three weeks before, on 6 April, Ron and Reg had walked free from the Old Bailey after being cleared of demanding money with menaces from a club owner, named Hew McCowan: they were said to have threatened him with violence unless he gave them a percentage of the takings of the

Hideaway Club in Gerrard Street. After the case, the landlord of the premises, Gilbert France, promptly handed over the club to the twins, who renamed it the El Morocco, and arranged a star-studded opening night for 29 April.

I'd climbed a long way up the criminal ladder by then, and two eminent 'faces' – Jimmy Nash and Richie Anderson – got me an invite to what turned out to be an exciting, intriguing evening. The Kray Firm told everyone they could that various famous personalities – including the Beatles – would be there, and their propaganda worked: the place was packed and one could hardly move.

The moment I walked in, I felt an electric-like atmosphere I'd never experienced in any club before. I'd heard so much about the twins and their henchmen, and what they got up to, I found myself looking into every face, wondering, 'Is that Ron or Reg? Is that one of the Firm?'

It was only idle curiosity: I wasn't interested in knowing anything about them – I was interested only in getting hold of money and, from what I'd heard about the Krays' set-up, the only way to get any was *away* from them. It was common knowledge among my friends and acquaintances that the twins never nicked anything themselves – they waited to hear that somebody had got a touch, then steamed in and frightened them into handing over a percentage. I'd heard that the Krays were not liked; that whenever they walked into a pub, everyone else walked out. But I'd also heard that both of them commanded a lot of respect, and when I saw them, that April evening, I understood why. They had a chillingly confident air about them – a powerful presence that left you believing they were capable of anything.

Jewish John was coming up to forty-five. He had never been inside, and didn't want to. But now he was involved with a professional burglar, and two reckless hooligans taking almighty risks, and he was as worried as Jock. One day he told me he was too long in the tooth to be tramping through fields in the dark, and waiting around in draughty barns, and he was going to chuck it in and go back to robbing houses in towns, on his own.

I didn't believe him and asked him to prove it to me by taking me on one of his jobs. At first, he didn't want to, because, he said, he preferred to work alone. But I said, 'I'll make it easy. You open up the houses, then I'll go in and do the business.' He liked that. And for the next few months, we earned some real money, doing huge homes in Golders Green, Finchley and other posh areas of London, as well as holiday flats on the south coast.

In the second week of August, however, money was suddenly unimportant.

Me and my brothers hadn't seen Mum's family since visiting them in the north-east, when we were children. But, that summer, they came down to stay with us for a few days. After a while it started to bother me that Mum was rushing around, bending over backwards to please them, when it was clear they did not give a toss. Worse, she was trying to impress them by going on and on about her 'lovely boys', when we all knew what we were like.

One day, I could stand it no longer and let out all the hurt and bitterness I'd been storing up over the years. 'Don't embarrass yourself, or us, Mum,' I said. 'You don't need to have their approval. Tell them we've been up to all sorts of trouble and have been in prison. Where were they when we needed them?'

My poor mum just looked at me, sorrowfully, and said, 'Oh, Chrissie, please don't.'

'Mum, stop being a hypocrite,' I shouted.

She ran towards me, angrily. I pushed her away, in disgust, and she fell on the floor.

'Come on,' I said, not thinking she was hurt. 'Get up. Don't put it on for them.'

Then I turned and walked out.

When I went back the following evening, I learned that Mum had gone with her family to their home, near Newcastle. I was sad that she had left on such a bad note with me, but was pleased for her; she could do with a break from us, and London, generally.

However, the next day, Dad got a telegram: 'Come up immediately. Lilian in hospital.'

My brother Tony was in prison at the time, but that night my dad, Carol and me, my brothers Nicky, Jimmy and Leon, and their wives, drove up north. We arrived at the house in the morning, expecting to go on to the hospital, but were told that Mum had died from emphysema in the early hours.

I assumed her body would be in the hospital's chapel of rest, but when we went into the front room, there she was – in a coffin, surrounded by about a dozen people I didn't know, all drinking beer or tea. I hit the roof.

'What are all you lot doing here?' I demanded to know. 'My mother is lying dead there and you're all acting like she's very much alive.'

My dad got hold of me. 'Chrissie, this is the way the Irish are,' he said. 'This is what they do. It's their custom. It's called a wake.'

I didn't like it at all.

That night in bed, Carol held me close as I sobbed my heart out. For my mum. And for myself. I was racked with guilt, remorse, self-loathing, you name it, for causing the row just two days before.

None of us was allowed to lift the coffin: it was carried by official pallbearers, selected by the Catholic church. As they carried Mum out of the room the next afternoon, one of them accidentally knocked the coffin against the door. I grabbed hold of him. 'If you as much as touch anything again, I'm going to really, really hurt you,' I said. And I meant it.

After a beautiful Catholic service, in a church where Mum had worshipped as a child, we went to a nearby cemetery and buried her in the family plot, next to her crippled brother, James, whom she had loved deeply. As her coffin was lowered into the grave, I took a rose from one of the many wreaths and threw it in – a beautiful flower, like my dear mum, dropping into the darkness of eternity.

Her death, at just fifty-three, left me not believing in a God that could take a mother so young away from a loving husband and her five boys. Anything that stood for right was not for me.

After the funeral, I went off and wandered around on my own for a full twenty-four hours. When I finally went back, the next afternoon, filthy dirty and wet, everyone wanted to know where I'd been, and what I'd been doing.

But I couldn't tell them. I didn't know. Those twenty-four hours were a blank.

We returned to London, but there was an emptiness to the flat that only a mother could fill, and sadly me and my brothers found excuses not to go there. We should have done, for the old man's sake, but it held too many sad memories and we didn't think it was the place to be.

Dad stayed there, sitting alone, lost and unhappy. His beautiful flower, his beloved Lily, had gone, and all he wanted now was to devote himself to his five boys. We were all he cared about, really.

*

One day in September, Jewish John came to me and said he was going to jack it in. Again, I didn't believe him. I thought he had seen the serious money we were getting and felt he didn't need me any more. I needed him, and his keys, badly, but this time, his mind was made up. He was getting out of the business before he got nicked.

The more I told him he was kicking me into touch to go solo, the more he protested. Finally, he said, 'Tell me what you want and I'll do it. If you're worried about me, I'll sell you my set of keys and you can do the business on your own.'

I couldn't believe it. 'How much do you want for them?' I asked, excitedly.

'Fifty quid,' he said. 'And I'll even show you how to work them.'

Considering how much those twelve keys had earned, it was a very reasonable price, and I accepted it on the spot.

Over the next few weeks, I started thinking it would be better if I had a female accomplice: if spotted walking up to a door, a young couple would be less suspicious. At that time, I was having an affair with a bird in Ilford, called Ivy, and she had a mate, Jill, who was ideal for what I needed: she was married with kids, but loved the excitement of breaking into homes. It gave her a sexual thrill. She had more bottle than anyone I'd met – and she liked money.

Having checked that the occupants were out, we would break into a house and do rooms separately. We'd come away with paper bags filled with cash or diamond rings or expensive necklaces. I still didn't have a conscience: I was very hard-nosed about it. The people I was robbing had what I wanted. I would pay the price if I got caught. They would pay the price if I got away.

After one successful 'touch', Jill and I went back to Ivy's house. While they had a cup of tea, I went upstairs and tipped the night's haul into the bath: there was a ring worth at least £1,000, the same amount in fivers in a carrier bag, plus more cash and other bits and pieces. Jill had also brought away a fur coat.

I was in the middle of dividing the stuff into equal shares when both girls poked their heads round the door. Jill was all right, because she was getting her corner, but Ivy's eyes came out on stalks – green with envy. It did not help when I put £50 in her hand and said I had to go. Although I said I would be back around 2 a.m., she was peeved that I'd be spending the evening with my wife – and that Carol would be getting more than £50 from the night's work.

Ivy obviously made some phone calls, because when I pulled up outside her house in the early hours, a guy came out the door and walked up to my car, brandishing a knife.

'What do you want?' he growled.

'I've come to see Ivy,' I replied.

'She's my girl,' he said.

'Fair enough, mate. I don't want to fight over your girl.'

'Go home. And stay away from her.'

I thought, 'That suits me fine.' Ivy was beginning to be a headache and I'd been wanting to get rid of her, anyway.

I was fuming at the guy's attitude, but knew he would use the knife, so I drove away, letting him think he had frightened me off. I didn't think that would be the end of the matter, however. And I was right.

When I got home the next evening, after a job with Jill in Brighton, Carol was looking worried.

'Three men have been round here for you,' she said. 'They wanted to know when you'd be back. One of them had a scar on his face.'

I reassured Carol everything was all right, but said I had to deal with it. I drove round to my brother Jimmy's house, talked to him for a few minutes, then asked if I could use his toilet: he had no idea I'd hidden a loaded shooter in the cistern. I took the gun out, dried it and put it inside my belt. Then I left and drove to Ivy's house.

As I pulled up outside, the guy who had threatened me before ran out, followed by four others. He was wielding the same knife.

'You'd better use that this time,' I told him.

'I'm fucking going to,' he said.

'Then you'd better have some of this,' I said.

I pulled out my gun and fired two shots at him. He fell to the ground. I fired three more times at the others running down the path, then pumped a sixth into the guy on the ground. If I'd had another bullet I'd have shot him in the head.

As it was, I drove away not knowing whether he was going to live.

I went to see Frankie Shea – whose sister, Frances, had married Reggie Kray after the El Morocco opening – and told him what had happened. Frank knew the guy I'd shot and felt sure he wouldn't go to the police, but he suggested I got out of town until things cooled down.

That evening, Carol and I drove up to her parents' home, near Liverpool. They saw me as nothing more than a layabout, and we'd never got on. But their house was the perfect bolt-hole for me.

Mind you, the tension and bad atmosphere was hard to stomach at times. I'd be sitting down, minding my own business, and Carol's dad would suddenly rustle a newspaper and tell me about a painter being wanted here, or a decorator needed there. He'd really get up my nose. I'd think, 'What's this prat going on about? I can pick up more in ten minutes than he can earn in a month! Why do I need a job as a fucking painter?'

When he told me off for speaking to Carol in a certain tone, I'd jump down his throat, yelling, 'She's my wife. Her loyalty is to me. You're nothing now.'

That would set him off on his hobbyhorse: the fact that he had been the cook on Captain Scott's second expedition to the South Pole, aboard *Discovery II*.

'I will always be something,' he'd say. 'I was on *Discovery II*.'

Christ Almighty, that used to wind me up. He never let anyone forget about his one claim to fame.

Still, I had to swallow it until Frankie Shea told me it was safe to return to London.

Eventually the tension got me down and I persuaded Carol to move down to Birmingham, where I got a job minding a club, and rented a little flat.

Having heard nothing from Frankie, I was on my toes and always carried a .38 Webley pistol. The guy I'd shot was well connected and I expected a revenge attack. I wasn't scared, just alert. If anyone came to shoot me, I was going to make sure I didn't go down on my own.

Birmingham was home from home for me. There were loads of Londoners up there, all doing crooked business. Anything I could buy in London, I could buy cheaper up there and, soon, I was wheeling and dealing in all sorts of merchandise and making money. I didn't miss London in the least; there was nothing there for me. Birmingham was far better value and it was only an hour or so up the M1.

I felt the city was there for the taking – particularly in the entertainment field – but, for the first couple of months of 1966, I couldn't get my act together. I was still feeling a terrible, crushing guilt over my mother's death and would drive along, tears streaming down my face, as I remembered that terrible last night when I pushed her down. I started drinking heavily, often downing a bottle of vodka a day and jumping from one woman's bed to another.

One of these was a lovely bird, named Susie Edge, who I met in a club when me and an ex-commando pal, Davy Clare, were looking for girls to slip into gambling clubs as croupiers.

Susie was sitting at the bar and I asked her what she would like to drink.

'I don't know what I fancy,' she said.

'You'd better have a Scotch and Coke,' I said, and ordered her one.

Susie became hooked on that drink, and I became hooked on her. She was a free spirit, a lively girl, with an infectious sense of humour, who was liked by everyone who met her. I called her Squirrel, because of her red mop, and she loved me to bits.

I was a selfish, arrogant, pig-headed lump, however, incapable of love, of feeling anything for anybody at a real emotional level, and I began to dislike the person I'd let life make me. I had no principles, no values, no standards. I was not a very nice person to know.

Gradually, I came to terms with Mum's death and started putting myself about. As in Blackpool, with Eric Mason, club owners assumed I was part of the Kray set-up and this opened many doors. I never had to confirm or deny the Kray association; it was enough that I always carried a shooter and was forever zooming backwards and forwards to the East End.

Early that spring, one of these trips landed me in a police cell, accused of having stolen gear. But it could have been a lot worse: I was carrying a gun at the time.

I was travelling with Brian Hood, the brother of the club owner who had employed me as a minder, when I was flagged down by police. I was concerned about some ladies' leather coats in the boot, which had been stolen as part of a long-firm racket, but more worried about my .38 Webley, which I kept hidden behind the car's accelerator and brake pedals.

At Barnet nick I convinced a detective that Brian knew nothing about the coats, and they should let him take my car to my dad's flat to tell him what had happened. They allowed him to come to my cell, giving me the chance to ask him to get rid of the shooter.

I was only on a receiving charge, but the police objected to bail because, they claimed, I was involved in a Birmingham club protection racket, and would intimidate witnesses. So, I was banged up until 22 June when I appeared in court and was given three years' probation.

I owed Brian a favour and had a chance to repay him when he discovered his wife was having an affair with a club owner I knew. But Brian said he would sort it out himself, without violence. I was disappointed; I'd lost my 'pension' for protect-ing the club and would willingly have had the owner over.

Every two weeks, I'd travel down to London to see my dad and some old mates, and, one rainy evening the following February, I'd arranged to buy some US dollars from Connie Whitehead, one of the Kray Firm, who I knew from my borstal days. We were due to meet in The Blind Beggar at 7.30 p.m., but he hadn't arrived by 8 p.m., so I left. As my car was being serviced in a local garage, I walked to Cam-bridge Heath Road, to catch a bus to my dad's flat.

I was standing at a bus stop, wondering what had hap-pened to Connie when a car stopped. Behind the wheel was Ronnie Bender, who'd worked as a barman in Stoke Newing-ton after coming out of the Army. I hadn't see him for years.

'Hi, Chris,' he said. 'Want a lift?'

I accepted gratefully and we started chatting about what I was doing.

'Are you getting a few quid?' he asked.

'I'm getting a *nice* few quid, thanks, Ron,' I said. 'What are you up to?'

'I'm driving for the Krays,' he said.

I was shocked; he didn't seem the type. 'Make sure you leave me out,' I said. I meant it. I was doing my own thing up the road and didn't want to get involved. I'd heard the rumours about one of the twins shooting George Cornell in The Blind Beggar, and wanted to stay well clear.

Ronnie dropped me off at my dad's flat, but a couple of hours later there was a knock on the door, and Ronnie was standing there.

'Don't think I've put you in it, Chris,' he said, almost apologetically. 'But the twins want to have a word with you.'

I thought he was just saying that to nip me for a few quid, and I offered him some. But Ronnie shook his head.

'I don't want any money. They've asked me to fetch you. You've got to come.'

'I told you to leave me out,' I said. 'I'm not interested.'

Ronnie looked me straight in the eye. 'I think you'd better. Tony's down there.'

'What!' I was shell-shocked. My brother Tony had been released from prison in December and I knew he was living in London. But I had no idea he was in the Kray Firm.

'All right, Ron,' I said. 'I'd better come. How is he?'

'He's OK. No problem down there.'

Ronnie drove to the Widow's pub, in Bethnal Green. It was packed, mainly with young men in expensive suits and patent-leather shoes, and although the atmosphere was convivial, with everyone chatting and smiling, I felt all eyes on me as I walked in. I felt I was being weighed up.

I saw Tony talking to someone and acknowledged him with my eyes. I also saw Connie, but he just nodded and turned away.

Ronnie bought me a drink and we stood at the bar, chatting. The twins were sitting down at separate tables, each talking to two or three people. I sussed it immediately: it was all part of a power game. They had summoned me to see them, but they were going to make me sweat it out.

Finally, after fifteen minutes or so, Ron Kray came over and introduced himself. We shook hands.

'We understand you're up the road,' he said, in a quiet voice. 'What you doing up there?'

I told him a little about what I was doing, then he asked me who my friends were, and who I mixed with. It was like an interview.

A few minutes later, Ron's brother came over to us.

'Hello, Chris,' he said. 'I'm Reggie. How do you do.'

He spoke so quietly, I had to bend forward to hear him. 'It's nice to meet you. We've heard about you.'

'We're opening a new club in Leicester,' Ron said. 'Our brother, Charlie, is up there now, sorting it out. Do you think you could introduce some people who might spend a few quid? If you do that, we'll put you in for your corner.'

I told them I saw it as no problem. I knew half-a-dozen big spenders who would like to have a good night out and meet one of the Kray family. The arrangement would not do me any harm, either.

I liked some of the things I saw in the Widow's that rainy February night. If someone was skint, for example, it didn't mean he couldn't drink all night long. Those with money, including the twins, stuck pound notes and fivers – even tenners – in a glass on the bar and each round was taken out of there. It seemed like a good system to me.

I was impressed with the courtesy and politeness of Ron and Reg, too. There was, I felt, a sense of honour and decency and straightness about what they were doing.

But I didn't see a lot of respect among their so-called henchmen, only fear. I saw a lot of Jack-the-Lad stuff going on, too, and it made me think again that I didn't want any part of it. The people I mixed with were quite capable of going out and getting a shilling, but, by the sound of it, the Kray Firm were not. They were taking it off thieves, who were too terrified of the Kray reputation to refuse.

That night, I wanted to believe there would be something in it for me if I got my contacts to spend money in the Krays' club in Leicester. What I didn't know was that their world, their tightly controlled empire, built on fear, was crumbling.

And my future, like theirs, was doomed.

CHAPTER TEN

At that time, I wanted to go straight and, in the Midlands, I could see endless possibilities. A car-dealer friend, John Hunt, had the brilliant idea of opening a chain of car supermarkets, where people could sell cars – and have their vehicles washed – on three floors. He also saw a future in golf driving ranges which were proving popular in America. He wanted me to get involved in either venture, or both, but I had no money to invest: my only income was from a gambling protection racket, run by a Corsican gang, who had invited me into their operation, thinking I was connected to the Krays. I had not told them I was, but they knew I was always going back and forth to the East End, and they made the leap that I was close to the twins. Again, I saw no reason to enlighten them. Although it was a long trek from Birmingham to Leicester, I'd made the effort to take some acquaintances to Charlie's club, and had got very friendly with him. When I asked him if he wanted to get involved in a business venture with me, he jumped at the chance, and I introduced him to John, who lived in a spectacular, Spanish-style ranch house with underground car-park, stables, Roman baths and even a hairdressing salon, which he bought from a peer's wife, with whom he had had an affair. The house in Measham, near Leicester, was called Ponderosa, and it took Charlie's breath away when I took him there in the spring of 1967.

One day, when I told Charlie I was off to spend a couple of days in the East End, he got edgy.

'If you see the twins, don't tell them what we're working on, whatever you do,' he kept saying.

'Why's that, Charlie?' I'd say. 'We're doing nothing wrong. They're part of it anyway.'

'I know,' Charlie would say. 'But you don't know them. They'll want money before we've even earned it.'

Charlie was right. The first time I saw the twins after that meeting at Ponderosa, they made a point of seeking me out.

'What's going on up there?' Ron wanted to know.

'You're not getting any money without telling us?' Reggie would enquire.

I wasn't afraid of the twins, but they did worry me, I must admit. I'd always worked with people where one had an input and everyone involved saw the common good, but, from what Charlie had said, the twins' greed often messed things up. I didn't like being dishonest, but I had to heed Charlie's warning: he was their brother; he knew them better than me. And, anyway, I'd heard enough of what the twins had got up to – shooting George Cornell, for example – to suspect that they were not the professional outfit they liked to portray.

So I just looked the twins in the eye and shrugged: 'We're working on a few things that look promising. But we can't rush them.'

The people I took over to the Kray club in Leicester were genuine big spenders, who, if they liked a place, would go back time and again. But Charlie's pal, Tommy Cowley, was too dense to appreciate that. He went in and nipped them for a few quid for himself, without any thought for the club's future.

'Er, I'm a bit short at the moment,' he'd say. 'Couldn't lend me fifty quid, could you? I'll see you right when I next see you.'

My friends were decent, straight folk and they'd hand over the money, thinking it was a short-term loan that would be repaid. But, of course, it never was.

When I heard what Cowley was doing, I told Charlie it mustn't happen. Not only were my friends good for the club, but they were possible investors for the businesses we were exploring. Charlie was a man you felt you could trust, and I wanted to do business with him. But, sadly, he didn't seem to have the vision either, and he never warned Cowley about his senseless 'nipping'.

One day, early that summer, I got a call asking me to drive to London to see the twins: I wasn't afraid to say no, but didn't want the aggravation that might follow if I did. So, the next weekend, I met up with Ronnie and Reggie and they told me they wanted to help a good friend who'd done them a lot of favours while in prison.

'Who is he?' I wanted to know.

'Roy Shaw,' Ronnie said.

I'd met Shaw briefly in the Scrubs when we were both teenagers. He was a former schoolboy national boxing champion, born in Stepney, and he was serving eighteen years for armed robbery. He had recently been transferred from Parkhurst Prison on the Isle of Wight, to Broadmoor because of his 'uncontrollable temper.'

'What do you want me to do?' I asked.

'Someone's been taking a liberty,' Ronnie said, quietly. He drew hard on his Player's cigarette. 'We want you to do him.'

'What? Give him a hiding?'

Ronnie shook his head. 'No. We want you to shoot him.'

Ronnie explained what had been going on, and I respected Roy and wanted to help him out. When I agreed to do it, Ronnie gave me a fully-loaded Luger and told me they guy I had to shoot was a street trader who ran a stall at Romford

Market. I was to link up with Albert Donaghue who would take me there and point him out.

Shortly before the proposed shooting, I heard on the grapevine that the twins just wanted the guy shot in the legs. Then, on the day we were due to go to the market, Albert met me in Pellicci's cafe and said it was off: for some reason, Roy had decided he didn't want anything done to the guy at all. But the twins wanted to see me at the Grave Maurice pub at seven that night.

When I arrived, they were sitting in a corner. They called me over, and we greeted each other.

I never found out the truth behind it all, but was pleased I'd been prepared to do the right thing by Roy. I was pleased, too, that if the twins merely wanted to know if I had the bottle to shoot someone, I'd shown them they could trust me.

Ronnie was clearly delighted with me. After I'd given him back the Luger, he took off a solid gold watch he knew I liked and handed it to me. 'I would like you to have this,' he said, smiling.

After that, the twins would always invite me to join them for a drink whenever I was down at weekends. By this time, Tony was fully accepted in the Kray circle, and on the pay-roll, a fully paid-up member of their Firm, and my younger brother Nicky had also been drawn into the web. The three of us would drink regularly with Ron and Reg at a number of different pubs, and violence was always bubbling under the surface.

I'd just left one pub with Tony when five blokes walked in and stood drinking a few yards away from Nicky and the twins. Sensing trouble, Reg went over and asked who they were and what they wanted. One of guys said they were taxi drivers and had popped in for a drink on their way home. But Reg recognized a couple of brothers, named Webb, and suspected they were there to front them up. Moments later, it all went off, with the twins and Nicky cutting the gang very badly. It really wasn't a good idea to try to take on the twins on their home ground, no matter how much you outnumbered them.

They were a real handful, at any time, but when Ron was drinking, having not taken his medicine for his mental condition, he was an uncontrollable, powerful lunatic. Even people he knew well were terrified out of their wits, because they never knew what he was going to do. Unlike his twin, Ron did not like to be one of the boys: he wanted to control them. He was very intense, always on the edge of his seat looking for an angle. Reg, on the other hand, wanted to be one of the boys. He was laid back and able to communicate; you could have a chat and a laugh with him.

One evening in September, I got a message that Nicky had been cut in a fight and was in hospital. I went flying down the M1 and me, Tony and a couple of other guys went round the East End, battering down doors to find out who had done it. We finally found out it was a little thief from Bethnal Green. Apparently he'd gone out for a drink with Nicky and things turned nasty. The kid had smashed a pint glass and cut Nicky down the cheek. I was in a rage, determined to avenge my little brother.

Me and Tony got the geezer in the back of a car; Nicky was in the front. I pulled out a shooter and held it against his head.

'What do you want me to do?' I asked Nicky. 'It's entirely in your hands. You tell me and he's dead. Do you want it?'

I held the gun steady, waiting for Nicky's answer. Part of me was dying for him to say, 'Do it.' But he didn't.

'No, Chris,' he said. 'Don't. I don't want you to do it. He's my friend.'

Disappointed, I put the gun away and settled for giving the bloke a slap. At the time, I was disgusted with Nicky for showing what I felt was great weakness, but, in retrospect, I'm pleased I didn't go through with it. I don't think I could have lived with murdering a guy in cold blood. It wasn't even my row.

It had become a regular thing to team up with Tony every couple of weeks and go out for a few drinks, either in the East End or up West. One Friday, about six weeks later, we decided to end the night with a meal and a nightcap or three at a club in Stoke Newington called the Regency, a familiar haunt of the Kray twins and their Firm. We arrived at around 1 a.m., and roughly an hour later Jack McVitie walked in, followed shortly afterwards by Reggie Kray. After the usual pleasant-ries, Reggie told Jack he wanted to have a chat in private, and they went to the end of the restaurant, where it was quiet.

I couldn't hear what was being said, but it looked friendly enough, if intense. Twenty minutes or so later, Reggie got up and walked down the restaurant towards me and Tony.

'Have your meals been paid for?' he asked.

'No,' I said. 'But we'll sort it out. Thanks, Reg.'

He shook his head. 'No. I'll take care of it.' Then he turned to McVitie. 'Have you eaten Jack?' he asked. Jack shook his head. 'Get what you want,' Reg said. 'I'll sort it out.'

By then, Reggie's wife, Frances – my old pal Frank Shea's sister – had killed herself with a drugs overdose and Reggie was beside himself with grief. Since her death in June, he'd been drinking heavily and taking more and more speed, which made him aggressive and angry. I wasn't party to what he said to Jack McVitie that night, but in his twisted cage-like mind I'm sure he knew that the meal he bought that night was Jack McVitie's last supper.

CHAPTER ELEVEN

Ronnie and Reggie were in great form that Saturday night, laughing and joking in the Marquis of Cornwallis on the corner of Vallance Road and Bethnal Green Road. It was their mum Violet's birthday and they were throwing a party: a typical, old-fashioned East End knees up. A jukebox in the corner of the long, L-shaped bar belted out the hits of 1967: the Beatles, the Stones, Dusty Springfield, the Everly Brothers. Members of the Firm were there, suited and booted, all drinking, with smiles on their hard faces. The wives and girlfriends were there, too: all dolled up and smelling nice. Most of us had chucked a £10 note into a pint mug on the bar, and the drinks had not stopped flowing for two hours or more. Ronnie and Reggie were lapping it up. Violet looked happy: she liked nothing more than to see her twins, the apples of her eye, enjoying themselves.

I was on top of the world as well. I was with my brother Tony and two pals from Birmingham, Ray and Alan Mills, and we'd started drinking around seven in Wapping. The vodka and lemonade was going down well and, now, the speed I'd been taking was making me buzz. We'd popped in to introduce our friends to the twins and to pay our respects to their dear old mum. But now that we'd shown our faces for a couple of hours, I was anxious to move on.

'Come on, let's go to the Queen's,' I said to Tony.

The Queen's Arms on Hackney Road was a lively pub, fashionable among East End villains, and Tony was all for it. We said our goodbyes and piled into my huge American convertible. As we pulled away from Bethnal Green, I thought no more of the Krays. I was still living and working in Birmingham and saw them once in a blue moon and, anyway, they were Tony's buddies, not mine.

We had a couple of drinks in the Queen's, but, around eleven, the speed began to make me hyper and I wanted a change of scene again. I wanted to go to Leicester Square, to a bierkeller, where there were a lot of nice people I'd got to know over the past few months.

I pulled Tony to one side. 'I'm going on to the Best Cellar,' I said.

Tony shook his head. 'No, don't go up there. Let's go to the Regency.'

'I'm not going there, Tone,' I said sharply. 'You know what it's like on a Saturday.'

The Regency was a tatty little club-cum-restaurant, three miles further north, owned by two brothers who paid protection money to the Krays. It was OK for a quiet drink after hours in the week. Local villains felt safe there, knowing nearly everyone who walked through the door. But Saturday night was a different matter. Then the place attracted young Jack-the-Lads who didn't know the score, would-be tough guys who liked getting tanked up and having a fight to impress their birds and the Old Bill. The Regency on a Saturday was a place any self-respecting gangster avoided.

Tony knew this as well as me. But he was keen to go there. I told him he could go on his own – I was going to the West End. He nodded to our two pals. 'Ray and Alan have never seen the Regency,' he said. 'Let's go there for one drink. Then we'll go up town.'

He kept on and on and, in the end, I found myself agreeing. But as soon as we walked into the Regency, I knew I'd made a mistake. The place was jam-packed with people I didn't know and I didn't feel comfortable. I'd come out for a good old Saturday night, and I wasn't going to get it in the Regency. I thought about walking out, but Tony was getting the drinks in.

Suddenly a face I *did* recognize came towards us, beaming from under the familiar brown trilby. It was Jack McVitie.

McVitie was a loner, a fun-loving guy who liked nothing better than to get drunk, jump on a table and start stripping off. But when he got involved in selling amphetamines, and started taking them himself, he lost his common sense and started challenging the twins. He probably never gave a thought to what he was saying but, as I was to learn, to them he had become a nuisance.

'Hello, Chris,' Jack said, smiling. 'How's everything? Haven't seen you in a while.'

'What you talking about, Jack?' I said. 'I saw you in here last week.'

'Oh,' he said. 'That's right. I remember now.' And he laughed.

I bought Jack a lager and introduced him to Ray and Alan Mills. Tony had disappeared, but I was more concerned at having beer spilt on my new suit than wondering where he was. I assumed he had gone to the toilet.

Noticing he was not around, McVitie said quietly, 'You know something, Chris? I don't trust your brother.'

I was shocked. 'Come on. Jack,' I said. 'He's as right as rain.'

McVitie shook his head. 'I dunno, Chris. I don't trust him.'

'I've lived with him an awful long time, Jack,' I said. 'He's all right. Believe me.'

A few minutes later, Tony was standing beside me. 'There's a party at Blonde Carol's,' he said. 'Plenty of birds and all the rest of it. Let's go there.'

I knew Carol Skinner. She was a nice girl, a friend of Ivy's, and we'd mixed in the same circles, at dances and clubs, over many years. She was not mixed up in any skulduggery.

I looked at Ray and Alan. 'It's only round the corner. Do you want to go?'

They were all for it. So was McVitie who liked a good party.

We battled our way through the throng and walked downstairs, then out into Rectory Road. It was a few minutes after midnight and I was relieved to be out of the place. I suggested taking my car, but it was blocked in.

'No problem,' said McVitie. He pointed further along the road. 'Mine's on the next corner. Let's take that.'

We all piled into the blue Ford Zodiac, me in the front passenger seat and Tony with the Mills boys in the back. McVitie pulled away and headed towards Evering Road. He was laughing and joking; he couldn't wait to get to the party. McVitie knew where Blonde Carol lived. He parked in a side road opposite and we all strolled across Evering Road to No. 97. We walked up half-a-dozen steps and I knocked on the front door.

It was opened by Ronnie Hart, who led us along a narrow corridor and down some stairs. Jack was first, still eager to get to the party, followed by Tony, then me and the Mills brothers. There was a basement room leading from the stairs. Jack strolled in there, laughing, 'Where's the party, then? Jack's here.'

The moment I walked in the room and saw a group of guys – no more than a dozen and no women – I sensed something was wrong. And I was right. There was no fun and games waiting for Jack McVitie, only a trap. Seconds after he walked into that room, I saw Reggie Kray half run towards him and put a gun to the back of his head. Reggie pulled the trigger. But the gun failed to fire. He pulled it again. Nothing.

I was staring into the room from the stairway. I could not believe what I was seeing. This can't be happening in front of all these people. I went to say something, but no words came out. I was in shock.

It hit me that I had been part of something I'd known nothing about, and I reacted angrily. 'What the hell's going on?' I shouted. 'I want nothing to do with this.'

And then it sunk in that, for the first time in my life, I was confronted with something I couldn't control, something terrible and frightening, and I couldn't handle it.

And I sat down on the bottom stair and put my head in my hands and started to cry.

Connie Whitehead came over to me. 'What's the matter, Chris?' he said.

'I didn't come down here for this,' was all I could say.

Ronnie Kray, who was in the room with Reggie and Hart and half-a-dozen others, came out. 'What's the matter with Chris?' I heard him ask in that quiet, slightly effeminate, voice that chilled so many people.

Connie said, 'He didn't know nothing like this was going to happen. He wants no part of it.'

'Take him home,' Ronnie said, matter-of-factly.

I got to my feet and walked up the stairs, my mind whirling. I told Connie to take me to Queensbridge Road, a couple of miles away. All the way there, he was begging me not to go back to Evering Road.

I kept saying, 'But what about Tony? I've got to go back for him.'

'Forget Tony,' Connie said. 'He'll be all right. You stay out of it.'

'I can't. You know that.'

But Connie was desperate for me to leave it out, and when we pulled up outside my dad's ground-floor flat, he turned off the engine and looked me directly in the face.

'Chris,' he pleaded, 'we've known each other a long time. We've even done time together. I beg you, stay away. Please. No good can come of you going back there.'

'I can't, Connie,' I said again. 'I have to go back for Tony—'

'Chris,' Connie interrupted, 'give me your word you will stay out of it.'

I moved to get out of the car. I sighed. 'All right. You've got my word.'

But, as I watched Connie turn round and drive off, probably back to Evering Road, I knew I was lying. Tony was my kid brother. All our lives, since those far-off days when we were kids in the West End, long before we moved to the East End, I had always looked out for him. I wasn't going to turn my back now, not when he could be the next one on the list for two dangerous men with a taste for murder.

I skipped over a low wall and ran across the lawn leading to the back of my dad's flat. None of my brothers or me ever went in the front. We always used the rear balcony door, which was always unlocked.

It was getting on for one o'clock, but Dad was up, sitting in the lounge, reading his Greek papers. He was a quiet man and that's what he liked to do most nights. Mum had been dead only two years and it was a lonely life for him. That Saturday, he'd have got the ten o'clock bus home from a club where he played backgammon. He'd have made a pot of tea, then settled down to catch up with news of his beloved Cyprus.

I greeted the old man as though nothing was wrong. I couldn't tell him anything. He might have been small and gentle, but he was fearless where his sons were concerned. If he'd known Tony was in trouble, he would have wanted to come with me to help him. I went into the kitchen, poured myself a cup of tea, and took it through to the lounge.

I tried to pass the time of day with the old man, but he was engrossed in his newspaper and my mind was somewhere else. All I could think of was collecting what I needed, then getting out of the flat without the old man asking any questions.

After ten minutes or so, I got up and sauntered into my bedroom. I reached up to an air vent and took out two guns – one a Webley pistol, the other a shotgun. I always kept two guns, oiled and ready, in that bedroom for emergencies.

I looked at both guns for several seconds, thinking about what might be waiting for me at Evering Road. Finally, I put the shotgun back in the air vent and loaded the pistol and slid it inside the top of my trousers. I did up a button of my suit jacket, hiding the gun, and went back into the lounge.

'Just popping out again, Dad,' I said.

He barely looked up from his newspaper.

I let myself out through the balcony door, past the roses my dad had pruned for the winter, then hurried across the lawn, my heart racing from the effects of the booze and speed and tension.

I picked up a taxi almost as soon as I left the flat. Queensbridge Road is a busy thoroughfare and, late on a Saturday night, the place was crawling with them.

Thankfully, the driver was the quiet type. Whether he sensed my mood or not I don't know, but he said nothing during the seven- or eight-minute drive to Stoke Newington. It was just as well; he would have got nothing out of me. My head was filled with too much confusion and apprehension to exchange banal chit-chat.

The whole scenario did not make sense. From what I'd seen, it looked like Reggie Kray had meant to kill Jack McVitie. But that did not add up to what I'd seen in the Regency the previous Friday when Reg and Jack had had a talk in the restaurant. There had been no table-thumping or shouting, nothing to indicate any aggro. It had all been very amicable. And, surely, if Reggie had really wanted to kill Jack, he would not have done it in a flat filled with people. If you wanted to knock somebody off, it was madness to invite a load of eye-witnesses to watch you do it.

And the gun not going off. What was that all about? Maybe it was never meant to go off; maybe it was part of an elaborate plot, just to scare McVitie. But why? Like a lot I'd heard about the Kray twins, it didn't seem to make much sense.

Then there was McVitie himself. If the whole thing was a set-up, to give him the fright of his life, what was he going to think of Tony and me for the part we'd played in it? For luring him to the supposed party?

That led me to think of Tony. Was he part of the plan? Did he know what was waiting for McVitie in that basement room? I didn't want to believe that. But the facts made it look that way. I hadn't wanted to go to the Regency in the first place. It was Tony's idea; he'd insisted. And him disappearing when we got there. Where had he gone? Who had he spoken to? Who'd told him there was a party at Blonde Carol's? I hadn't asked; I'd just gone along with it, taken it all at face value.

Just like McVitie.

I'd get answers to all the questions soon enough. First, I

had to get my kid brother out of that flat. And McVitie if I could.

The taxi turned into Evering Road. I told the driver to stop outside No. 97. I paid him and walked up the path to the front door. The whole building was in darkness. I put my hand in my waistband and felt the Webley. I knocked on the door, not knowing what to expect, but prepared for anything.

Ronnie Bender opened the door. He was shaking.

'Where's Tony?' I asked.

'He's not here,' Bender said.

'What do you mean, he's not here? Where is he?'

'He's gone.'

'What do you mean, gone?'

'They've all run away.'

'Where're the twins?'

Bender's face was pale; he was sweating. 'They've gone, Chris.'

'Where're the others?'

'They've gone, too. Everybody's gone.'

I stood on the doorstep, just staring at Bender. None of it was making any sense.

'Who's here then?' I asked.

'Me,' Bender said. His voice cracked as he added, quietly, 'Me on me own.'

'What?'

'They've left me to get rid of the body.'

'What body?'

'Jack's.'

'Jack's?'

'They've killed him!'

I couldn't believe it! I said, 'No, you're kidding.'

'Chris, they've killed him. He's downstairs. He's dead.'

'Where're the twins?' I asked again.

'They've run away. They told me to get rid of the body. To throw it over onto the railway line, so a train would mash it up. So there'd be no marks. Like the train done all the damage.'

I stared at Ronnie Bender, as if in a trance. I couldn't take in what he was telling me.

Finally, I said, 'Ron, I'm going, mate. I want nothing to do with this.'

And then, as if by magic, there was Tony walking up to the door. He must have been waiting in a side street, knowing I'd come back.

Before I could say much to him, Bender was pleading with me, 'Chris, please help me. I don't know how to deal with this. I don't know what to do. I didn't know anything like this was going to happen. I walked right into it. I only came here for a quick drink with them.'

I looked at him. He was as innocent as the day was long. I thought, 'You poor bastard. You've been well and truly dropped in it.'

I wanted to go. It wasn't my problem. But, at the same time, I was thinking, 'What sort of guy am I if I run away like the rest, leaving poor Ronnie Bender to sort it all out?'

My mind was spinning with all kinds of thoughts. One thing was sure: with a dead body lying in the basement, I had to act lively.

I am the sort of person who loves being led – if the leader knows what he's doing. If he doesn't, then I'm happy to take charge: I'll always know what to do. That night, poor Ronnie Bender didn't have a clue what he was supposed to do. He was only a driver on the Kray Firm and had only come out for a social drink. Now, it had all turned upside-down and the poor geezer didn't know if he was on his head or his backside.

So I heard myself saying, 'OK, Ron. Let's go and have a look, mate.'

McVitie was lying on his back in the middle of the basement flat, blood all around him. He was still wearing his smart, brown pinstripe suit and tie, but not his hat. That was lying a few feet away.

His face was grey, almost white, but for some reason I did not think he was dead. In my imagination, I'd killed a few people, seen them dead in my mind, but the only body I'd actually seen was my dear mum's. I stared at McVitie, lifeless amid his own blood, thinking he was going to get up any moment. Finally, I said to Bender, 'Go and get all the glasses and wash 'em.' I looked at Tony. 'You help him.'

We found some socks in a drawer, which we put on our hands so that we wouldn't leave any fingerprints. Then I went upstairs to where Blonde Carol's two small children were sleeping. I lifted an eiderdown gently off them and went back downstairs.

I found a dustpan and brush, and a bucket, and started sweeping up the blood around McVitie's body. God knows what the man had gone through. From what I swept into the bucket, it was clear his liver had been skewered out. Fighting to keep myself as detached as possible, I was walking up the stairs to a toilet on the ground-floor landing when Blonde Carol came through the front door with her boyfriend, George Plummer.

She stared at me, then at the bucket. Before she could say anything, I said, as gently and calmly as I could, 'Carol, love, there's been a bit of a fight downstairs. There's nothing to worry about. You and Georgie go in the room with the kids and we won't disturb you. But don't come out till we've got it all sorted.'

'All right, Chris,' she said.

As she and George went into the bedroom, I said, 'Carol, please don't come downstairs.'

When I heard a door close, I emptied the bucket down the toilet, then went back to the basement to organize the more difficult job: getting McVitie's body out of the building.

Fortunately, the eiderdown was huge. I laid it across the floor and told Bender and Tony to help me lift McVitie onto it. We rolled him over and twisted both ends of the eiderdown, like a sweet wrapper, so that he would not fall out. Then we carried him to a corner of the room and pulled up the bloodstained carpet, which I'd decided would have to go out with the body.

I looked around the flat and noticed bloodstains on a wooden fire surround. I told Tony to remove it and burn it in the fireplace, while Bender and I went through the whole room, wiping away every scrap of evidence of the slaughter.

By 2.30, it was as clean as it had ever been. Bender and Tony looked to me for what to do next. I'd decided we had to get McVitie into his own car and take him away from the East End, but I wasn't sure where. Anyway, first, we had to get him up into the hallway.

I went upstairs and told Carol and George we would be clearing up for a little while longer, and urged them again to stay where they were. Then Bender and Tony and me carried McVitie up the stairs and laid him in the hallway.

Tony went out and drove McVitie's car, from across the road to outside the house. But getting the body down the path and into the car without being seen was tricky. There was a never-ending stream of taxi drivers picking up bagels from a Jewish bakery opposite, and three men putting a bulky eiderdown into a car in the middle of the night would hardly go unnoticed. We had to wait for a break in that stream of taxis. It seemed to take forever. Finally, we got the break and ran the body to the back of the car. The boot was the obvious place to put it, but we could not close the lid. I decided to lay the body across the back seat. It was risky and I didn't like it. But we had no alternative.

We raced back into the flat and carried out the carpet. Thankfully, that *did* fit in the boot. Then we went back for a final check. The wooden fire surround was burning nicely; the room was spick and span.

McVitie had driven himself to his own death. Now, it was time to take the poor bastard away from the scene of the violent, bloody killing.

Bender and Tony were still looking at me to make decisions. But I didn't have a clue what to do with the body. What I did know was that *I* was not driving McVitie's car. No way. I'd done my bit, stayed to help Ronnie Bender when I could easily have left him to it. But that was *it*. I was finished with the whole business.

'Well, I'm not driving,' said Bender.

'You've got to, Ron,' I said. 'Tony's not.'

'Chris, I can't drive it,' he said. 'I can't.'

Looking back, I can understand why he didn't want to. He was a soldier, not long out of the Army. And he was a family man, too, with a wife and three kids. He had come out for a quick drink and got himself into something he could never have imagined in his wildest nightmares. Why would he want to risk driving a car with a dead body in it?

But, then, I was not going to move from *my* stance. I was definitely not getting in that car.

We stood in that room, where McVitie had been so cowardly cut to pieces, and argued about who would drive him away.

And then, finally, Tony said quietly, 'I'll do it.'

'No, you won't,' I said.

'Someone's got to,' he said.

'Tony,' I said, raising my voice. 'You're not getting in that car.'

'I'll do it,' was all he said.

I tried to talk him out of it, but his mind was made up. He struck me as terribly brave. It took a lot of courage to get behind that wheel. If he was stopped by police, what was he going to say, 'Yeah, that's a dead man. This is his car. I'm taking him for a drink?'

None of us had a clue where to take the body. For a moment, I did think of changing my mind about driving the car. I thought it might be best to take it up the road to Birmingham, well out of the way. At least that would protect Tony. But I dismissed the thought almost immediately. I'd done more than I could have been expected to do. I didn't want to risk anything more than I needed.

All sorts of permutations were whirling around in my brain, and the more I couldn't come up with a reasonable solution, the more I started thinking about the Krays. Where were the twins now? I asked myself. Where were these guys who prided themselves on running such a professional firm?

Professional? From what I'd experienced in the past couple of hours, it was more like the Keystone Kops. If they had wanted to kill McVitie they could have got him in a car, as we had, and shot him in the back of the head. They didn't have to take him to a three-ring circus, with a dozen people or so with front-row seats. And, having done that, what sort of people were they to run away, leaving the unfortunate Bender to carry the body sixty yards up the road and chuck it over a railway bridge? Their handling of the whole scenario was not so much a comedy of errors as a tragedy of errors!

If the murder had been planned, if the Krays had the merest clue what they were doing, there would have been a sensible directive, other than an arrogant 'Chuck it on the railway'. As it was, neither Ronnie Bender, nor Tony, had any idea, and it was left to me to come up with something.

'He's got to go over the water,' I said at last.

'We'll dump it on the Richardsons' manor,' I said. 'Go through the Blackwall tunnel and find your way to Camberwell. Me and Ronnie will be behind you all the way.'

Charlie Richardson and his brother Eddie had been gaoled in the notorious 'Torture Trial' a year before. I didn't know them from Adam, but I didn't care. I just wanted McVitie off our manor and onto someone else's. I wanted it to look as though Jack had had a row with some of Charlie's pals and copped for one.

I went back to the Regency to pick up my car, which was now not blocked in. The gun was still in my waistband, but I was not worried about being stopped. I often walked about London late at night; I'd never been bothered by anyone.

Still wearing socks over my hands. I drove the car back to the flat. A few minutes later, me and Bender watched Tony drive off down Evering Road, towards Clapton. Then we pulled away ourselves, following about a hundred yards behind, across Southwold Road, right into Upper Clapton Road, then into Lower Clapton Road, before turning right into Mare Street, towards Hackney. It was now about 2.45 a.m.

Since leaving Evering Road we'd seen hardly anybody. But now, as we followed Tony along Mare Street, a police car with two officers in it pulled out of Powerscroft Road, a little side street on the left. The car settled in behind Tony and in front of us. I froze. It was what I had been dreading. All we needed was for a bored copper to be a bit nosey and it would be all over. Holding the wheel with my left hand, I felt in my waistband with my right and took out the Webley. I'd told Tony I'd be behind him all the way, and that meant taking care of him. He was my kid brother, and he'd looked to me to protect him nearly all his life.

'If they stop him,' I said to Bender, 'I'm going to have to do something. I won't let them take him.'

Bender didn't say anything. There was nothing *to* say. All we could do was keep our distance, as though we had nothing to do with the Zodiac, and pray nothing would happen.

I slowed slightly, increasing the distance between us and the police car to about 200 yards or so, but keeping it in view. My heart started racing again. My throat felt so dry I couldn't swallow. My stomach knotted. Then I began to sweat. It was like the tenseness and slight fear of the unknown I'd always got before going into the ring for a fight. But this was worse. This was going to be a matter of life or death. I'd never been afraid to use a gun and I wasn't going to be afraid now. My right hand gripped the Webley. I stared ahead at the rear of the police car. The second it showed any sign of overtaking Tony and pulling him over, I would put my foot down and go into action. I didn't know whether I'd kill the coppers or just fire a few shots into them to let Tony get away. What I did know was that I would do something. There was no way I'd let them take Tony. And he knew it.

Fortunately, for everyone, it didn't come to that. The police saw nothing to concern them in Tony's driving, and turned off into Dalston Lane towards Stoke Newington.

I don't know what Tony was thinking, watching a police car in his rear-view mirror for those tense minutes. But I could almost feel the relief in my car as we passed Dalston Lane and increased speed to catch Tony up.

I'd told him to go through the Blackwall Tunnel, but for some reason he went along Cambridge Heath Road towards Mile End and the Rotherhithe Tunnel.

And it was somewhere between there and Commercial

Road that I lost him. Whether the police had made him panic and put his foot down, I don't know, but he was gone. And, although it was getting on for three, and the streets were deserted, I couldn't see him anywhere. I knew he wouldn't stop if he lost us, so all I could do was carry on in the hope of spotting him.

Suddenly I saw a sign to the Rotherhithe Tunnel. I was sure Tony would have taken the Blackwall, but I turned right at that sign anyway. We came out the other end and drove around for a few minutes. There was no sign of Tony. My stomach started to tighten again. South London was a big place; Tony could be anywhere. If he had gone on to the Blackwall Tunnel, he could be in Greenwich, further south, while we were in Bermondsey. For all I knew, more police, nosier ones this time, could have flagged him down, could be asking him to explain the contents of the eiderdown on the back seat.

Now panicking, I doubled back towards the river. And for some reason I can't explain, even today, I turned into Rupack Street, a little turning just before the tunnel on the left.

And there was Tony, walking towards us.

I stopped beside him. 'Where's the car?'

'I ran out of petrol,' Tony said.

'Where is it?' I asked.

He pointed towards a church. 'I've left it round there.'

Tony got in and told us to follow the road round a couple of hundred yards. And there, outside St Mary's Church, was the car.

The church was ancient, but the huge amount of confetti from the previous day's weddings told me it was well used. I felt sure the Zodiac's lifeless owner would be discovered sooner or later.

'Let's get out of here,' I said.

Now that we'd got rid of the body, I wanted nothing more to do with Bender. We'd said all we had to say to each other. I wanted to lose him, fast. I needed to speak to Tony on his own. He had witnessed a murder and I was up to my neck as an accessory. We had a lot to talk about.

'Where do you want me to drop you, Ron?' I said as we hit the tunnel.

'Poplar,' Bender said. 'I've got to see Charlie.'

I didn't know why Bender wanted to see him when Charlie had been nowhere near Evering Road that night. But I was in no mood to want to find out.

I let Bender out in Commercial Road, at the junction of Burdett Road, and drove on to our dad's flat, the Webley now safely out of sight behind the pedals. Sleep was out of the question. We were in deep, deep trouble and needed some questions answered before McVitie's body was found and the police started investigating his last movements.

My main concern was for the Mills brothers. I'd invited them for a night out on the town and put them in the middle of a horrific slaughter. I didn't know what they were feeling. I didn't even know where they were. But I would have to find out fast.

Of course, the ones we really needed to speak to, the men who had *all* the answers, were Ronnie and Reggie Kray. But they had vanished into that October night and were unlikely to be around for a while.

Sitting in our dad's flat, talking about the madness of it all, I asked Tony the question burning away in my brain: had he known what he was luring Jack McVitie into?

Somehow, don't ask me how, Tony avoided answering it. Somehow he changed the subject and I never got to know.

Later that morning, about seven o'clock, I drove back to

Birmingham. I remembered Ray Mills saying he had to be back there for Sunday evening, and I needed to straighten him out.

On the drive, I had plenty of time to think. I thought of Tony and why he had not given me a straight answer, and I thought about Ronnie and Reggie and why they had run away leaving Ronnie Bender in the shit, and I thought of my old man and what he would have thought if he'd known I'd left the flat with a gun down my trousers.

And, of course, I thought of Jack McVitie.

Poor Jack The Hat. Many thought he was a dog, a lairy, loud-mouthed troublemaker. But, to me, he was a puppy, a likeable guy who loved life. Yes, he was a hard man, a villain. But he was also a clown, the sort of bloke who would fall down and go to sleep where he was. He did not deserve to die the way he did, set upon by a crazed pack, and butchered like a defenceless animal.

As I reached the outskirts of Birmingham that Sunday morning, what I'd said to Ronnie Bender in that bloody basement came back to me. We were lifting McVitie's body onto the eiderdown and I suddenly noticed his shiny black shoes.

'Ron,' I said. 'Maybe I should take his shoes.'

Bender was puzzled. 'Why?'

'Because I think I'm going to be walking in them an awful long time,' I said.

CHAPTER TWELVE

I rang Ray Mills later that Sunday morning.

'It's never going to come out,' I said. 'We've put the body over the water. There was a gang fight in South London and Jack got it. End of story. Even if they find him there'll be no lead back to you. Just keep your mouth shut.'

Ray was as good as gold. 'There'll be no comeback from me, Chris. It never happened. I don't know what you are talking about.'

'What about Alan?' I asked.

'He's a hundred per cent,' Ray said.

'Make sure he is. We must shut down all the avenues, so there's no connection to any of us.'

I went to put down the phone. I paused. 'Ray,' I said quietly, 'I'm sorry about what happened. I had no idea.'

'I know,' Ray said. 'Just leave me out of it, OK?'

I phoned a few people, trying to find out where the twins were, but no one was saying much. All I got was that they were in the country, somewhere in Suffolk, with Ronnie Hart, and would not be around for a while.

For the next few days, I scoured the newspapers. Anything that smacked of gangland murder always hit the headlines and I felt sure Jack's body would have been found by now. But, strangely, nothing appeared. A sixth sense told me Jack's car, and its bloody contents, had been taken to a place where they would never be found. And, on the Wednesday following the killing, I learned I was right.

I got a message that Donaghue wanted to see me, so I came back and met him, in the Carpenters. He said everything was sorted: McVitie's body had been taken to a pig farm, just outside Ongar, in Essex, and would never be found. That made me feel a little easier. I didn't like what had happened to Jack, but I couldn't turn the clock back – for him or for me. Now, it was safest for all concerned that he had seemingly vanished off the face of the earth. If everyone who witnessed the dreadful slaughter kept their mouths shut, pretending, like the Mills brothers, that it had never happened, Jack McVitie, and his trilby, might be forgotten.

If I was feeling easier, the twins were not. When they heard that Jack's body had been dumped over the water, they hit the roof. They said they did not want a South London firm getting the blame for something it had not done. The truth is they were more concerned that they would lose face if people thought they had deliberately ordered the body to be left in a rival manor.

The twins were worried about me and Tony too – particularly me. They had seen me break down in the flat and saw that as a dangerous weakness. They got a message to Charlie to straighten me out, but it was unnecessary. I was up to my neck as an accessory after the fact of murder and I was not about to blab to anyone.

It cut no ice with Ron or Reg. When they surfaced in the East End, a week or so after the murder, they wanted to know where I was and what I'd been doing. I was living up the road in Birmingham, well away from it, and had no intention of going back to London. But the twins were paranoid about me and, suddenly, I started getting phone calls from various members of the Firm, telling me to drive down to London because Ron and Reg wanted to see me. It was always for nothing. All we would do is go out for a drink, in the Carpenters or some other pub, and they would spend the evening giving me frosty looks.

At first, I was unconcerned. But the more I was ordered to drive down, the more I began to worry, not only for myself, but Tony, too. We knew too much. We could be the difference between the twins being stuck up for murdering McVitie and his disappearance remaining a mystery. We were prime targets to go the same way as poor old Jack. I feared for my own life, but I feared for Tony's more. At least I was a hundred miles away. He was on the twins' doorstep every day.

Somehow, we all got through November and Christmas. Still nothing appeared in the papers, and, more important, there had been no whisper of any police interest in McVitie's disappearance. But then, one weekend, early in 1968, I was warned that everything was about to come on top. Not only did the police know of the murder, but they knew who was involved.

I was down from Birmingham and having a drink in the Regency. Jimmy Nash came up to me with a mutual pal, Mickey Bloom.

Jimmy looked me straight in the eye. 'Get yourself well lost, Chris,' he said. 'Go abroad or something.'

'Why?' I said. 'I haven't done anything.'

'Rumour has it that you were involved in the McVitie thing. It's fairly strong. The twins are going to fall for it. Get yourself out, Chris.'

'Thanks for telling me, Jim,' I said. 'But I've got nothing to worry about. I *wasn't* involved.'

I knew what Jimmy was saying was 100 per cent. He was not the type to give me such a strong warning unless it was justified. But I was not going to be panicked into running away, least of all abroad. Not only was there Tony to consider, but I had a lot going for me in Birmingham. I had spent a lot of time building up contacts in the car business, and certain projects looked promising. I'd recently gone into business with a friend, Tony Hart, who had a car wash in Walsall and we'd started to sell cars too. I could actually see myself going straight, away from the twins and all the madness they revelled in.

I decided to try to distance myself from them. I would still pop down to London from time to time, but I would make myself less available, not be at the twins' beck and call. I should have done this long before. From the moment I was summoned to meet them, and got to see how their operation worked, I was less than impressed. It was hardly a professional outfit. They had a firm of between twenty and thirty hard men, but the twins never paid them wages. The firm had to go and get their own, and they did this by nipping, a fiver here and a tenner there, off people who would be too frightened to ask for it back. People thought the twins were rolling in it, but they weren't; no one was. I never saw my future with the twins, but I had got sucked in and found it difficult to stay clear of them. Now, with the Old Bill on the case, I had to keep away as much as I could. Despite Jimmy's warning, I still felt safe. For a start, McVitie's body would never be found and, even if the twins were suspected of killing him, none of those who had seen the slaughter was likely to admit it.

What I did not know, during those early months of 1968, was that a team of Scotland Yard detectives, under Commander John Du Rose, had started an investigation into the Krays even before McVitie was murdered. A top-secret government directive had been sent to the Commissioner of Police, instructing him to: 'Get the Kray brothers – at all costs.' And the only way the police could do that was to persuade people close to the twins to grass them up.

It was to prove easier than any of the Old Bill could have imagined.

On Tuesday, 7 May, the twins invited me down to London for a night out at the Astor Club. Most of the Firm was there, taking up three tables, and we had a fun evening. Reg was relaxed in the company of one of my ex-girlfriends from Birmingham, June McDonald, and Ronnie seemed happy enough with a fresh-faced young boy. It was now more than six months since McVitie's murder and still nothing had appeared in the papers. If the twins were worried about me or anyone else opening our mouths, they did not show it that night.

Normally, I would have slept the night at the old man's flat, but I had business in Birmingham the next morning, so I drove back in the early hours. I'd learn later that, as I headed north, Commander Du Rose was giving a final briefing to sixty-six police officers – plainclothes and uniform – in a building on the Thames Embankment called Tintagel House. A ten-man team, led by Detective Chief Superintendent Leonard 'Nipper' Read, had spent many months fishing in the murky waters of the Kray empire to hook their prized catches. They had got a bite. Now it was time to reel them in.

In the early hours of that Wednesday, the twins went back to their flat on the ninth floor of Braithwaite House, a tower block in Bunhill Row, in the City of London. Ronnie went to bed alone; Reggie snuggled up with June McDonald. All three were woken at dawn by police smashing the front door with a sledgehammer, then faced guns pointing at them.

Later that morning the phone rang at my flat in Birmingham. It was Tony Hart. He sounded excited.

'Have you heard the news?'

'What news?' I asked.

'About the twins,' he said. 'They've been nicked.'

It did not take me long to find out what had happened. The evening newspapers and radio and television news bulletins were full of the dramatic dawn swoop by sixty armed police and the arrests of the twins and their firm. But there was no mention of murder, no mention of Jack McVitie or George Cornell. All the twins – and their brother, Charlie – were going to be charged with, it seemed, was conspiracy to defraud.

With everything seemingly sorted, I relaxed and got on with my life in Birmingham. Three months later, however, Tony phoned me, saying he and our brother Nicky had been arrested in the East End and questioned about McVitie's murder. Apparently, one of Nipper Read's team, Superintendent Frank Mooney, had been told, wrongly, that Nicky had been at Evering Road on the night of the party, and had driven the car carrying McVitie's body. Mooney released Tony and Nicky after twenty-four hours, telling them to give him a ring if they had anything to say.

I was not unduly concerned. The Mills brothers, and others at the party, had not been arrested, so there was little chance of me being linked to the killing in any way.

The next day, though, I was pulled in myself. I was staying at Hart's, a hotel in Walsall, and was woken early in the morning by police breaking down the bedroom door. They said that I had 'some knowledge' of a murder, and they were taking me to London.

I expected to be taken to Scotland Yard, and was surprised when we pulled into Tintagel House. Nipper Read came quickly to the point. He said he knew I was at a party in Evering Road on 28 October 1967, and had broken down on the stairs when I realized what was going to happen. He related everything that had happened that night and asked if I was prepared to talk. I was shell-shocked; someone had obviously made a statement. But I was not about to incriminate myself.

'I don't know what you're talking about,' I said. 'I live in Birmingham, not down here. I've had a drink with the Krays, but that's as far as it goes. I wasn't at any party. I don't remember going to *any* party with someone named McVitie.'

Read looked at me intently. 'Are you absolutely sure?'

'One hundred per cent,' I said. 'I wouldn't have anything to do with anything like that.'

Read nodded his head slowly. 'All right,' he said. 'But I'd like you to think the whole thing through. On the information we have, we wouldn't charge you. And we certainly wouldn't charge either of your brothers, Tony and Nicky.'

Then he handed me a business card. 'There's my phone number,' he said. 'Give me a ring if you want to talk to us again.'

I got a taxi to Tony's home in Blythe Street, in Hackney, thinking fast. It seemed clear they were trying to get me to open up against the twins, but why? Why, when they had already persuaded someone to tell them what had gone on that night? I could only assume that they felt whoever had grassed was involved in the killing and would not impress a jury, whereas someone like me would. Someone who had actually protested about what was happening would be an ideal witness.

I felt I had to let the twins know what had happened. I needed to warn them the Old Bill was on the McVitie case and was trying to get me to go hookey. I wanted to assure them that I had everything under control and not to worry. But there was another reason why I wanted to make contact: I wanted some assurances myself, wanted to be told, 'Don't worry, you haven't done anything. We'll make sure you stay out of it.'

I did not think it was a bright idea to try to see the twins who were on remand in Brixton, so, the next day, I went to Bunhill Row to see their mum, Violet, and old man, Charlie. I was not that familiar with either of them, but they knew my face.

Charlie was not in, but Reggie's regular girlfriend, Carol Taylor, was looking after Violet. By the look of her, Violet needed all the support she could get. As soon as she opened the door I saw in her face that the strain of the past three months was taking its toll. But she was a lovely, polite lady, Violet – just like my own mum – and she asked if I was OK.

'No, I'm not OK,' I said. 'Yesterday I was pulled in by the police and questioned about a murder I know nothing about.'

It was clear Violet was oblivious to what had happened that terrible night in Stoke Newington. She sat there, numb with shock, as I told her that it seemed the police were hell-bent on charging her sons with murdering Jack McVitie.

'You must tell them this, Chris,' she said.

I shook my head. 'I can't go to Brixton,' I said. 'That's the last place I should be seen.'

Violet looked at me, pleadingly. 'Chris, please. You can't leave them without this knowledge.'

'I can't go, Vi,' I insisted.

'Chris, you must help them. Go and let them know what's going on – *please*.'

I tried to explain why it was unwise for me to visit the twins, but Violet was desperate for anything that might help her boys.

'It's jealousy,' she said. 'People are jealous that everyone thinks the world of them. They need help now, Chris. *Please go.*'

'I can't, Vi. I really can't,' I repeated.

'Chris, you *must* go. You must help them. *Please*.'

I looked into her tired eyes, imploring me to help her boys, and suddenly it was not Violet Kray I saw, but my own mother, and I was back in time, back to that unhappy night before she went to Newcastle and died.

'Please, Chris, you must go and help my boys,' Violet was saying, and I felt I was listening to my own mum. It was that that pulled me, made me change my mind and go against all my instincts and streetwise intuition.

'All right, Violet,' I heard myself saying, almost with despair. 'I'll do it. I'll go and see them, and tell them all I know.'

As I spoke, I knew I was doing it more for my own mum than for her.

'Thanks, Chris,' Violet said. 'Carol and I are going this afternoon. You can come with us. If anyone asks, you're one of the family.'

So, around lunchtime, we all got in a taxi and went to Brixton for the two o'clock visit. Throughout the entire forty-minute journey across London, Violet was tense and fidgety. She was just a typical, lovely East End mum, naive and un-knowledgeable about the criminal way of life, and you could see that she was having to build up her strength and steel herself to walk through the prison gates.

Nobody seemed to check the visitors' book in the prison, so I scrawled, 'Mickey Mouse, Disneyland, America'. Fifteen minutes later, we walked through into the visiting room and I saw the twins' brother, Charlie, who was being visited by his wife, Dolly, and their son, Gary.

Charlie was astounded to see me. He looked up to the ceiling and shook his head, as if to say, 'I've got no choice. My name is Kray. But why are *you* here? You must be mad.'

I smiled briefly and sat down in a nearby cubicle with the cigarettes, sweets and fruit I'd bought for the twins.

They came in together. Reg, always the more lively of the two, bounced in like a fighter eager to burn off some energy, but Ronnie strolled in like Noël Coward, not a hair out of place, nonchalantly smoking a cigarette, which, as usual, he put out after five puffs or so, before lighting another one. He had an arrogant, dismissive air about him, as if he were saying, I'm awfully put out at being here. I really don't know what all these nasty people are doing, but they'll all go away in a moment. Oh, and sorry about the dismal surroundings, old bean – they're nothing to do with me.'

Reg was the more positive of the two, but I felt that Ron was still the guv'nor. He had an awesome inner strength that people, villains and Old Bill alike, found impossible to break. Reg was different; he could be broken fairly easily. The suicide of Frances, his wife, had affected him dreadfully and I don't think he ever fully recovered from it. On that visit, I got the impression that Ron saw the wide picture of the awful mess they were in, but I always had the impression he felt he could control the situation, that he could stamp his mark on it whenever he wanted, no matter that he was locked up.

I had fifteen minutes with Reg first. He was pleased to see me, and thanked me for taking the trouble. When I told him why I was there, he said I should talk to Ron; he would know what was best.

Ron was quite sure what to do.

'You've got to go to Ralph,' he said. 'You've got to protect yourself – otherwise they might fit you up. Ralph will sort it all out. The police ain't got nothing on us. Fuck 'em. Mugs.'

I knew that Ralph Haeems was the Krays' solicitor. He worked for a firm of lawyers, Samsons, run by Manny Freidy, in Fleet Street, and I went there with Carol after leaving Brixton.

It was the worst place I could have gone. I was digging my own grave.

I went to Samsons' office. Luckily, I was able to see Manny Freidy himself. He told me he knew of the police investigation into McVitie and assured me I had nothing to worry about. I told him about being questioned at Tintagel House and said I did not want to be bothered by the police again because I knew nothing about the murder they were investigating. Freidy drew up a statement to this effect and I happily signed it. Assuring me Nipper Read would get the statement, he ushered me out of his office, and I went back to the East End.

It was late August. I had two weeks of freedom left.

Back in Birmingham that night, I felt, deep down, that I'd made two bad mistakes. I had listened to a mother, which was stupid, because they are guided by emotion, not logic, and I had gone to see a solicitor, which gave the impression I had something to worry about. If I had said nothing, and kept out of the way, with my head down, that one visit to Tintagel House might have been my last. But by visiting the twins, then complaining about the police to their lawyer, I had placed myself firmly in the Kray corner.

I feared it might upset the police. And I was right.

Just before midnight, two weeks later, I left a club called the Rum Runner, in the centre of Birmingham, to go to the Elbow Room, in nearby Aston, when my gold American Galaxie 500 was ambushed by several cars. Assuming they were a firm of villains out for trouble, I jumped out of the car and grabbed a starting handle from the boot, ready for battle.

Suddenly, what seemed like a hundred armed men converged on me and one of them said they were police. At first I did not believe them, but then I looked down a hill and saw a Jaguar Mark 10 police car, in the middle of the road.

I was told to put my hands on the bonnet of my car while I was searched. Then they said they were taking me to a police station.

'Why?' I asked.

'For doing virgins out of season,' someone said, sarcastically.

I tumbled it then. I had a friend, whose father – a high-ranking Birmingham detective – and mother were on holiday. All afternoon I'd been enjoying a seventeen-year-old girl's body on their bed, and the police knew. Obviously, they had been following me.

I was taken to the Regional Crime Squad headquarters in Steelhouse Lane, in the town centre. I knew then it was serious. There was not just one police force involved, there were several. And they were not going to pussyfoot around.

'Come down here,' one of the detectives said, as we entered the CID room. 'We want to show you something.'

Five or six of them led me downstairs into a tiny office, crammed with drawers.

One detective opened one of the drawers and pulled out a card with someone's photograph and personal details on it.

'That's you,' he said.

I didn't know what he was talking about. I looked at the card, then at him. 'No, it's not.'

'Oh yes it is,' he said. 'We found you on the street tonight. You were dead. The victim of a gangland fight.'

It dawned on me what he meant. I was in the police 'morgue', where details of dead and missing persons were stored, and I was being given a warning. Co-operate with us or we can arrange for you to end up as a statistic in a drawer.

My bottle went. They were deadly serious. I knew they would do it. I knew they could do it that night.

About three hours later, six of Nipper Read's team drove up to take me back to Tintagel House. When we arrived, at about 6 a.m., I found Read in a foul mood.

'You lied to me,' he said. 'You told me you knew nothing about the McVitie murder.'

'I don't,' I said.

'You're lying now,' Read said. 'What do you take me for – a fool? When I pulled you in before, I gave you an out. I was trying to help you – if you helped me.'

I said I didn't know what he was talking about.

'You were there that night,' Read said, angrily. 'You didn't touch the man, but you saw what happened.'

'I didn't see what happened,' I said. 'I wasn't there.'

'You *were* there,' Read roared.

'I *wasn't*,' I insisted. And I meant it. I wasn't in that bloody flat to see McVitie hacked down.

Furious, Read told someone to take me to a room and leave me there to think things over. An hour or so later, I was brought before him again and he started bombarding me with questions, getting angrier and angrier, as I kept refusing to admit anything that might incriminate the Krays.

Throughout the morning he kept questioning me, then leaving me on my own. I was knackered, I hadn't had any sleep for more than twenty-four hours. But my brain was racing, like a computer, looking for all the angles.

I wanted to tell the truth, but I couldn't without incriminating myself. Or the Krays. I had not witnessed the killing, but I *had* cleaned up the flat and helped carry McVitie's body to his car. I *was* an accessory after the fact of murder.

There was nothing I could do except stick to my story that I had never gone to the flat. And the more I denied what Read knew to be the truth, the more frustrated and angry he got. He was desperate to put the twins away and was pinning his hopes on me.

Finally, around lunchtime, his patience ran out and he snapped.

'You want to do time for those kind of people,' he shouted. 'You must be crazy.'

And then he took a pistol from a drawer, then ran across the room and whacked me round the head with it.

'You want to be with those people? Right, you can *be* with them. And you're going away for an awful long time.'

Then he turned to a colleague. 'Take him over to Bow Street. We're going to charge him.'

Read was giving me another chance, one final opportunity to grab the lifeline he was offering me. But I didn't take it. I just sat in the chair, trying not to let the pain from the gun whipping show in my face, and said nothing. Hitting me like that made me distrust him. He thought it would make me crack, but it only made me stronger. I was a Greek and the Germans had found they could not break the Greeks' wartime resistance. I was also an Eastender, and the code I'd learned since those long ago days when I worshipped Ronnie Diamond was: Say nothing and the police won't be able to prove anything.

At around 1.30 p.m., I was taken to Bow Street Police Station in the back of a squad car, with four top detectives. There was an escort car in front, another behind and motorcycle outriders. We sped east along the Embankment, towards Covent Garden, the ringing of the police bells convincing me, if it had not sunk in already, that I was in trouble. Big trouble.

They locked me in a small concrete cell. Apart from the pale glow from a dirty overhead bulb, the only light was from a tiny window in the thick steel door. There was no bed, only a thick lump of wood, covered by a grubby well-worn blanket, like a hair shirt. There was a yellowed striped pillow, but the hundreds of heads that had lain on it had knocked the stuffing out and crushed it flat.

I was left alone in that cell for nine hours. It was the loneliest time of my life – lonelier than those hours I spent wracked by grief after the death of my mother.

And then, around 11 p.m., I heard someone call, 'Lambrianou, C. Bring him out.' The huge steel door of the cell creaked open. Two giant policemen in uniform were standing there, waiting to escort me. We walked to a room, where I was told to sit down on a kind of bench in front of three CID top brass. After a couple of minutes, one of them told me to stand up.

'Is your name Christopher Michael Lambrianou?'

'Yes,' I said.

'On the 28th of October 1967 you did knowingly take Jack McVitie from the Regency Club, in Stoke Newington, to a private house in Evering Road, where he met his death . . .'

I stared ahead, not taking in what was being said. It was as if they were talking to someone else.

'. . . you are being charged with the murder of Jack McVitie. Anything you say will be taken down and may be used in evidence against you. Have you anything to say?'

I shook my head. I showed no emotion; it still was not touching me. The police officer was talking to a lump of flesh, not me. I was up, out of it, looking down on the whole thing.

'Take him away.' And the two giants came into the room to take me back to the cell. It was only a short walk, about twenty paces or so, but it seemed to take forever. They slammed the huge steel door shut, deliberately harder this time, as if to make the point that a cell was going to be my home for a very long time.

Out of the darkness came a voice: 'Chris?' It was Ronnie Bender. He was in a cell further down the corridor.

'Yeah,' I said.

Then another voice: 'Chris. It's Tony. They pulled me in, too.'

My heart sank. What was going on here?

We could not see each other, but we could hear, so we had a three-way conversation about how, when and where we had been nicked. We could not see much out of the tiny square window in the steel door, but we assumed the police were listening, and probably recording everything we said. So, we kept the chat general, without incriminating ourselves or anyone else.

Finally, exhaustion overpowered me. I stretched my long, bulky frame on the insulting lump of wood that served as a bed, and pulled the grubby, hairy blanket over me and closed my eyes. I had not slept for forty-one hours.

CHAPTER THIRTEEN

Early the next morning, the raucous sounds of the drunks and whores and the others arrested while I slept were a welcome relief – a touch of normality amid the madness that had engulfed me.

Cells were needed for the new arrivals, so I was put in one with Tony Barry, while my brother shared another with Bender. It was a lucky break; I needed to talk to Barry. He was not at Evering Road on the night of the killing, but he knew what had happened and who was there. He was vulnerable, perhaps the weakest link in the chain.

'We're going to be all right. Tony,' I said. 'You didn't kill anybody. I didn't kill anybody. They can't do anything to us – nothing – if we keep our mouths shut.'

'I'm not going to grass on anyone,' he assured me.

The worst we felt could happen was that the twins would go down. It was unlikely, because of the lack of evidence, but if they did, we were sure they would get everyone else out of it. They were, after all, honourable men.

'Don't worry,' I told Barry. 'They'll do the right thing – they're totally professional.'

As I said it, part of me knew I was fooling both of us.

Later that morning, we went up in front of the Bow Street magistrate and stood together in the dock as the charges were read out: 'Christopher Lambrianou, Ronald Bender, Anthony

Barry, Anthony Lambrianou, you are charged that on so-and-so day at so-and-so address, etc., you did, with others, murder Jack McVitie . . .'

It sounded so ridiculous: four people – *with others* – did murder Jack McVitie. I found myself thinking of Caesar's Ides of March. I knew the four of us had not murdered Jack. Who were *the others*?

What I did not know was that, at Tintagel House, Nipper Read and his team were orchestrating a lavish and costly production, which they hoped would culminate in a hugely publicized show trial at the Old Bailey. That morning, at Bow Street, they had set the scene. They had brought four of the minor players in from the wings and fed the public's curiosity with a little piece of scenario. It made just a tiny item in the national press. But . . . who would be next on stage?

Us being high-security prisoners, bail was refused and we were all remanded in custody – me and Bender in Wandsworth, Tony Barry and my brother in Brixton. My top priority was to get my defence clear in my mind, and in Samsons', but Ralph Haeems's first visit to me in Wandsworth filled me with dread.

He said, 'Ron and Reg have instructed me to tell you to deny that there was any party at Evering Road.'

'But that's crazy,' I said. 'The police know there was a party. And they know I left before anything happened. I can get out of this.'

Haeems shook his head. 'You can't say there was a party, Chris. It will incriminate the twins.'

'Come on, Ralph,' I said. 'I'm in here charged with murder. I haven't done any murder.'

'You can't say it, Chris. You'll put the twins there. If you put them there, they're convicted.'

'Not necessarily so,' I said. 'They could have been at the party, too – and left, like me. What happened afterwards had nothing to do with them.'

We argued the point and, finally, Haeems said he would discuss it with the twins. But the following day he returned to Wandsworth, saying, 'Under no circumstances must you say there was a party.'

The first signs of panic set in. Haeems was my solicitor, but it was clear his first priority was the twins, not me. Read had warned me to employ another firm of solicitors but I'd ignored him. Now I started to worry. How was I going to get out of a murder charge if I wasn't allowed to tell the truth as far as it affected me?

I needed to speak to Ron and Reg themselves, and two weeks later I got the chance, because they joined Bender and me in the dock at Bow Street, with their brother Charlie, my brother Tony, Ian Barrie and Tony Barry. It was a complete surprise: the police picked up Bender and me from Wandsworth, then went on to Brixton for the others. None of us had a clue what was happening.

In the cells at Bow Street, I told the twins I had to admit there was a party, to get myself out. They still would not hear of it. 'It was a party that never happened,' they said. 'Don't even *think* it did.'

I could not believe they were serious. I knew for certain that at least twelve people knew there had been a party at Blonde Carol's flat that Saturday night in October. How many other people had that dozen told? I was shocked at the twins' stupidity. I genuinely believed they were going to put up some kind of defence – maybe say, yes, there was a party, but they had left before any trouble broke out. At least that would have been a viable defence. But they would have none of it.

Which left me between a rock and a hard place.

I was struggling to come to terms with my impossible position when two huge uniformed police officers called, 'Kray, Reginald. You're wanted outside.'

Less than ten minutes later, Reg came back to the cell. 'They've done me on McVitie,' he said.

Then Ron was called. He, too, was charged with murder. Then Charlie: he was charged with something I knew for certain he had not done – getting rid of McVitie's body. I did not know what to make of it. But there was another surprise for all of us when we went before the magistrate. In the corner of the dock was a squat, little man I'd never seen before. It was only when his name was read out that I realized it was Freddie Foreman. He was an extremely well-known villain from South London, and I was looking at him, wondering where he fitted into the picture, when the clerk of the court announced that he was also being charged with disposing of McVitie's body.

I stared ahead in disbelief. When was the madness going to stop?

As we filed back to the cells, remanded in custody until the full committal proceedings, a burly police officer gave me a meaty shoulder barge. I pushed him against a wall, ready for a row, but Reg stepped in and glared at him. 'If you so much as lean against him again,' he said, 'I'm going to break your jaw.' The copper said nothing and we never saw him again.

We were kept in the cells for several hours. Reg spent a lot of time going round to each of us in turn, massaging our necks and shoulders. 'Take it easy, relax,' he kept saying. 'You're all knotted with tension.'

Reg might have got it wrong with many things, but he was spot on with that. We *were* tense. Tense with fear at going down for something they had done – not us!

Around 3.30 p.m. we were taken back to our respective prisons. The tiny windows of the armoured police van had two layers of glass, which were heavily scratched, but I could read the evening paper bill posters on the news-stands as we sped back across the water: 'KRAYS IN COURT'.

So, now, it was no longer a tiny newspaper paragraph, involving four men no one had heard of. Nipper Read had brought his leading characters on stage. His production was ready for a dress rehearsal before the main event. Now, it was big news.

The proceedings began at Bow Street, and from the word go it was a drama everyone, it was clear, wanted to see. The Profumo Scandal, the Great Train Robbery and the Richardson 'Torture Trial' had whetted the public's appetite for sensation, and queues for the public gallery formed every day, long before we arrived. It was edge-of-the-seat stuff. No one knew what to expect. Anything was possible.

By now the twins had been charged with murdering Frank Mitchell, the so-called 'Mad Axeman', and Ronnie, separately, with killing George Cornell in The Blind Beggar. But, still, they were convinced the cases, like the McVitie one, would collapse through lack of evidence.

The burden of proof was on the prosecution, but the twins kept saying the police had no witnesses – and, in two cases, no bodies! – to back up their claims. I was not so confident. The razzmatazz the police had engineered throughout the earlier remand appearances was not for nothing. They would not be spending thousands of pounds of taxpayers' money on such a high-profile police presence if there was a chance the charges would not stick. On the contrary, Scotland Yard's flamboyant Hollywood-style approach, with a cavalcade of escorting cars and motorbikes, and the incessant clanging of bells, seemed as if they were saying to everyone, 'We've nicked the most dangerous men in the country. And they're going away for a very long time.'

As the committal hearing went on, the police began to play a psychological game. They allowed all sorts of disquieting rumours to come into the prisons to feed our paranoia about who was, and who was not, going the other way against the twins. First, we heard that certain supposedly solid friends and acquaintances of the twins were being spirited away from various gaols for 'days out' and questioned about their relationship with the Krays. Then we heard, via Haeems, that certain members of the Firm had gone hookey. First, 'Scotch' Jack Dickson, who had driven Ron and Ian Barrie to The Blind Beggar to kill Cornell. Then, Albert Donaghue. I could not believe it. I'd seen them long before I was nicked, and they had assured me everything was sound and under control. Now, it seemed, they had been working out their own little deals with the police.

I began to get depressed. The way it was going I could see no way out. Not being allowed to say I'd been at a party was like fighting for a boxing title with my hands tied behind my back: I had no hope of winning.

If I'd wanted to go hookey, too, I could not without dropping Tony in it. I wanted to discuss my position with him, but he was my co-defendant and I was not allowed to see him. Anyway, he was 100 per cent with the twins and they were not interested in helping me. It would have been a waste of time. Their feeling was that we all had to keep our mouths shut and take our chance at the Central Criminal Court.

It was while I was waiting for the trial to begin that the hopelessness of my position plunged me even deeper into despair and I tried to kill myself in Wandsworth.

Men charged with murder were supposed to be kept in the hospital wing under twenty-four-hour supervision, but, for some reason, me and Ronnie Bender were moved to the punishment cells below ground level. In the hospital, the lights were bright and there were windows, but the chokey block was dim, and you never saw daylight, or people, only the red light above that shone through the gloom all day and all night. It was like being in the belly of hell.

The first day I was sent down there, all the depression that had been weighing me down for months hit me. I kept thinking, 'I haven't killed anybody, but I'm down here. I'm never going to be allowed to tell the truth, defend myself. I cannot put myself, or, more important, my dad through such torture.' Suddenly, death, I felt, was a desirable alternative.

I looked up at a tiny square hole cut into the two-feet-thick wall. A window should have been there, but it had been smashed, probably by someone needing air in the stifling summer heat, and only the bars remained. I took off my belt, then stood on a hot-water pipe to reach the window. I tied one end of the belt round one of the bars, the other round my neck, and stood there, about a foot off the ground, contemplating jumping off the pipe and tightening the belt round my neck.

Precisely what happened next is a mystery. All I can remember is lying on the floor, semi-conscious, spinning round and round, towards a bright, white light, and fighting to grab on to things to try to stop myself reaching it. Finally, when I came to, I thought I was dead.

I got to my feet and stood in the middle of the cell and screamed, 'I'm in hell.' Then I grabbed a chair and smashed it against the steel cell door, shouting, 'Let me out. Let me out. I'm not supposed to be in prison – I'm dead.'

Within seconds, the cell door opened and masses of screws were standing there, staring at me, at my bulging eyes and the red marks round my neck.

'What's going on here?' one of them wanted to know.
I couldn't tell him.

'Get him over to the hospital – quick,' he said.

As I was escorted out of the cell, I felt a cold dampness on my legs and realized I'd pissed myself.

CHAPTER FOURTEEN

The first face I looked for, when we climbed up the steps from the Old Bailey cells into the legendary Number 1 Court, was my dad's. I desperately wanted him to see that I was OK, that I was still fighting, and not defeated. As I sat down in the corner of the dock, I glanced up at the public gallery. An area at the side had been roped off for the families of the accused and there, in the middle, with the twins' father, Charlie, was my old man. My heart went out to him; he was tense and grey with worry.

Then I heard the judge, Mr Justice Melford Stevenson, speaking and turned to face him. His look, as much as his tone of voice, left no one in any doubt that he was the guv'nor. It was as if he had spent all his legal career being trained for this one moment, and had been handpicked for the job of putting the Krays and their firm away. The contemptuous way he looked at all of us said, 'I'm a very heavy judge and you lot don't impress me at all.' I thought that the justice in his name was about to be very rough indeed.

After the jury was sworn in, Stevenson looked at them meaningfully and said it was important they took note of what he was about to say. They were not going to deal with one murder case, but two. The first was the shooting of George Cornell at The Blind Beggar pub in March 1966; the second would be the killing of Jack McVitie, in Evering Road, Stoke Newington, nineteen months later.

There was no dispute, he said, that the majority of defendants in the second case knew nothing about the first, but, nevertheless, both cases were going to be heard together in one trial. And the reason for that was because the prosecution believed both murders were linked by a statement Ronald Kray, accused of Cornell's murder, allegedly made to Reginald Kray, who was charged with killing McVitie. That statement, said the judge, was, 'I've done mine, Reg – now you do yours.'

Ronnie, I'm certain, never said those words. But the prosecution needed a link to have the cases tried together and, despite protests from the defending counsels, it was accepted. The twins were gutted. Like the police, they were sure they would each be acquitted for lack of evidence if the cases were tried separately.

I doubt that the prosecution would get away with such a dubious tactic today. But in the mid-1960s, a directive had come down from on high to nail the Kray Firm, once and for all, and, at that show trial, the judge and the prosecuting counsel could do what they damned well liked.

On only the second day, Stevenson tried something outrageous. And he might well have got away with it had I not set off a chain reaction among the rest of the men in the dock and spoiled his plans.

Kenneth Jones QC, for the Crown, started it off. He was concerned about the number of men in the dock, he said. How on earth was the jury to know who was who?

'I've already thought this out, Mr Jones,' said Stevenson. 'Maybe we ought to think about numbers.'

What a splendid idea Mr Jones thought that was.

After a short adjournment, we were brought up from the

cells and each handed a large piece of cardboard with a number on it, which we were told to hang round our necks with pieces of string.

I was not going to sit there, looking like some Nazi war criminal at the Nuremberg Trials, so I said, loudly: 'There's no way I'm wearing this.' And I ripped the label off and threw it over the dock. 'Tell Nipper Read he can put it on 'cos I'm not having it.'

Then Ronnie and Reggie took off *their* labels and threw them down. Tony and Ronnie Bender followed suit, then all the others, until there was a pile of labels on the courtroom floor.

Furious. Stevenson called another adjournment and we were warned that the trial would not go ahead unless we wore the labels. 'Great,' we said. 'Stop the trial.' Of course, they didn't. But it forced them to give in over the numbers, and, the next day, the papers were full of the fact that the first point in the Trial of the Century had been won by the Krays.

Only Ronnie Kray and Ian Barrie were accused in the Cornell case, but the rest of us were made to sit in the dock throughout the ten-day hearing. Which, to my way of thinking, was an outrageous liberty. Where was the justice in that? It was a travesty.

It was the East End's worst-kept secret that Ronnie Kray had walked into The Blind Beggar, in Whitechapel Road, at 8.30 p.m. on 9 March 1966, and blasted George Cornell to death with two gunshots to the head. But no one had been brave enough to come forward to say they had seen him do it, and Ronnie was confident no one would at the Old Bailey. We all hoped he was right, because an acquittal for him was bound to harm the prosecution case in the McVitie trial.

It looked promising until the fourth day of the Cornell hearing, when the prosecution called a surprise witness – a pretty, little, open-faced young woman in her early twenties, who had been serving behind the bar in the Beggar that fateful March evening. She had a soft, fascinating voice, and when she spoke and told the story of what had happened when Ronnie walked into the saloon bar, I knew Ronnie and Ian were goners.

The young lady had lied to the police when she was first questioned. She said she had not seen who had shot Cornell. Now, in the hushed Number 1 Court, she was asked why she had lied.

'Quite frankly, I was terrified,' she replied, so quietly that everyone leaned forward, straining to hear her. 'I knew who had done it. I knew his reputation and I feared for my life. It wasn't until he was under lock and key that I felt capable of coming forward and speaking.'

All I could think was, 'What a lovely voice.' It was like listening to a beautiful bird sing, and I sat there, transfixed, thinking how much I'd love to get her into bed, so that she could talk to me all night long. When she paused and asked for a glass of water, it was all I could do to stop myself jumping up and offering to fetch it for her. Even if she was about to damage us all beyond repair.

Kenneth Jones's significant, probing questions, and the young barmaid's damning answers continued and, with every one, I could see Ronnie's chances of an acquittal disappearing.

That softly spoken barmaid was genuine. She was word perfect. And she was credible.

She was an unexpected quality witness for the prosecution – a witness who reached people at a very deep level and made them feel that everything happened just the way she described it. And she had something else, too – a vulnerability that patently affected everyone in court, including me. It was almost painful having to watch her up there in the box, giving such an incriminating testimony.

It was quite apparent she had not been coached; she was too natural and sincere. There was no 'I hope they all go down forever' or 'Ronnie Kray made me a nervous wreck and ruined my life'.

Her evidence was understated from start to finish. Calmly and very deliberately, she described how Ronnie Kray and Ian Barrie walked into The Blind Beggar: how Barrie fired one shot into the air and Ronnie fired two, into George Cornell's head. She remembered what Cornell had said to Ronnie before he died. And she even knew what had been playing on the jukebox at the time.

It was credible, damning stuff. And we all knew it. I glanced at the others in the dock. They were all visibly shaken. You did not have to be a fortune-teller to know that our futures, like Ronnie's, were being destroyed in front of our eyes.

The barmaid was in the box half a day. When Kenneth Jones had finished with her and handed her over to the defence, he was smiling. I looked at Nipper Read. He was smiling, too.

The ace in their pack had come up trumps.

After that. 'Scotch' Jack Dickson and various policemen gave evidence. But, as Stevenson himself indicated, anything following the barmaid's testimony was 'knocking on an open door'. The point about Ronnie Kray's guilt had been made.

Stupidly, the nail was then driven into his coffin even harder by a witness called by Ronnie himself – 'Mad' Frankie Fraser. The idea was to prove that there was no friction between the Krays and the Richardsons, so why would Ronnie want to murder one of the South London gang? But it was the silliest move ever, definitely one of Ronnie's maddest moments. Frankie, who had been subpoenaed from prison, was a waste of time and did Ronnie more harm than good. Although he was all heart and had come along wanting to support us, the prosecution tore him to shreds.

All of us in the dock had agreed not to give any evidence ourselves; we knew we would be ripped to pieces. But the evidence against Ronnie was so overwhelming that his counsel told him his only chance of getting off was to go into the box himself. Reluctantly, Ronnie agreed.

Again, it was a mistake: he left himself wide open. On home ground, against his own kind, Ronnie was a force to be reckoned with. But, under the most extreme pressure, in the highest, most awesome, criminal court in the land, he was a babe in arms. And certainly no match for one of the most agile brains in the British legal profession.

From the moment Ronnie stepped into the box, Kenneth Jones set out to wind him up, to make him lose his cool. Ronnie did his best and threw all Jones's opening questions back at him, but the eloquent QC would tell him, 'I am not here, Mr Kray, to answer these questions. *You* are. Now, tell me, is it a fact that you are homosexual?'

For the first time, Ronnie felt an answer of sorts was required, and he quoted a remark he had been taught many years before by his older brother, Charlie: 'I find your presumption precisely incorrect and your sarcastic insinuation far too obnoxious to be appreciated.'

This caused a titter. But Jones was far from amused, and pressed on with further embarrassing questions that wound Ronnie up so much he lost his temper and called Jones 'a fat slob'.

It was a masterstroke of cross-examination and, of course, the blow-up made headlines.

From the dock, Ian Barrie watched and listened, impassively. He knew he was going down for a long time. I think we all did, and it was sad because Ian was a nice guy. He had been in the Royal Scots Guards. When the tank he was in caught fire he helped to get his mates out, only to be badly burned himself.

The Cornell trial ended on a Friday, and Stevenson said he would not sum up until after the McVitie hearing, which would begin on Monday. The jury went home to spend the weekend pondering the ghastly events at The Blind Beggar that wintry night in 1966. Me and the rest of the accused went back to Brixton and Wandsworth prisons, wondering what lay ahead for us in a case where there was not even a body, let alone any witnesses to murder.

To me, the McVitie case, unlike the Cornell trial, did not warrant much attention, because the vital ingredients were missing. But, amazingly, it became the main event. The mystery caught the newspapers' imaginations and hit the headlines even more spectacularly than Cornell.

As I sat in my usual place in the dock, I glanced up at my dad. He was looking down and our eyes met. I forced a reassuring half-smile, anxious again for him to know that my spirits were still up. I knew it was not easy for him. Over the weekend, Ronnie Kray had said that his own dad had told him that the press had tried to get hold of my dad for a comment. Old Charlie Kray had told them, 'Leave him alone. Isn't it enough that he has got two sons down there? Let him be. He doesn't know what day it is, or what's going on.' I really appreciate old Charlie doing that, having his own heartbreak to contend with.

In a way, it would have been better to have spared my dad the anguish of all those days in court, but, if he hadn't been there, I don't know how I would have coped. He was like an angel looking down on me, and he gave me the strength to sit there and take whatever they threw at me. I had to be able to handle it and he was my reason.

My hopes soared when the judge ordered the court to be cleared while my counsel, Peter Crowther, made an opening submission that there was not one scrap of evidence to show that I knew anything was going to happen to McVitie in Evering Road that October night; and that, even if the prosecution proved I did, there was evidence to prove I wanted no part of it and had, indeed, left the flat and gone home before the alleged murder.

Stevenson conceded that Crowther had a good point, but said he would wait to hear what the prosecution had to say. And what Jones said did, in effect, give Stevenson the key to open the prison cell and rob me of my liberty.

Jones said he accepted what Crowther was saying was true, but, despite the lack of evidence, the prosecution felt I must have known something was going to happen to McVitie, and they wanted to continue with the murder charge. My involvement was on a point of knowledge.

The closed court submissions went on for two days; two long, tension-packed days in which I went through an emotional wringer, one minute high with hope that good sense and justice were going to get me out, the next rock bottom with despair that I was fighting something too big, too powerful, which would not and could not let me win.

Me and my brilliant counsel were shocked when Stevenson ruled that the prosecution could proceed with the murder charge: it was beyond belief. But, then, the trial of the Kray twins and their firm was not about justice and matters of law, or truth; it was about putting us away at all costs. As I said, the judge and the prosecution had a mandate to do what the hell they liked – provided we all ended up behind bars.

Of course, I could have saved myself by going back on the statements I'd made. All I had to say was, 'OK, there *was* a party that Saturday night. I went along, in total innocence, and left when an argument started. I didn't see anything.'

If I'd said that, I would have walked out of the Old Bailey a free man. I would not have served a single day in prison.

But I didn't. I *couldn't*. The twins were saying there was no party and if I said there was, their defence went out of the window. My sense of loyalty would not let that happen. That's why Jones knew he had me cornered. He knew that if I denied the party, he would almost certainly get me convicted for murder.

It never crossed the twins' minds to tell the truth, to save me and the other innocents, if not themselves. They were too selfish, too arrogant, for that. They really did believe that no party, no body, no witnesses brave enough to speak out, would mean they would walk free from the Old Bailey, as they had on the 'demanding with menaces' charge four years before.

So, the submissions over, the McVitie trial began. I sat in my customary corner, filled with dread. I had been thrown into the arena, without a spear or a net. And I was fighting lions.

From the moment Kenneth Jones got up to outline the prosecution's case, there was, frankly, only one outcome. The defence was denying that anything at all happened at Blonde Carol's flat, but after hearing the number of witnesses Jones was going to call, it was evident to even the most biased observer that there *had* been a party – and that Jack McVitie was, unfortunately, the Kray twins' specially invited guest.

Blonde Carol herself put the boot in early on. 'Was there

a party?' she was asked. 'Of course there was,' she said. It was common in the East End for twenty or so people to go back to someone's house and carry on drinking and dancing after the pubs closed on a Saturday night. The night of 28 October was no different. A party was about to start in her flat when she was asked if the Kray twins could borrow it for one of their own. She and her own pals had moved to a different flat, leaving hers in the hands of the Krays and their mates.

Returning at 1 a.m., with her boyfriend, George Plummer, she had seen me on the landing.

Was there anything unusual about him?

Yes, he had a bucket in his hand.

Could she see in the bucket?

Yes, she could.

And what was in it?

Blood, she said.

I scribbled a note and handed it to one of Peter Crowther's assistants. Carol was telling the truth, I knew, but I needed to rubbish her evidence. She had been watching too many Dracula films, I said. And, of course, that made the headlines the next morning.

Carol tried to help me, saying I was a sincere, gentle person, who didn't belong in the dock. She couldn't believe I would be party to a murder, and never would.

Sadly for me, the damage had been done. She like others before her, had banged another nail in our coffins by confirming the Krays *had* organized a party.

The killer blow for the twins, however, came from an unexpected witness – Ronald Hart. If The Blind Beggar barmaid had been a surprise, the appearance of Hart for the prosecution was a mind-numbing shock for them. He was their cousin, and when they heard his name called, they looked at each other in disbelief. Never in a million years would they – or any of us – have thought that a blood relative would turn against his own. It was unthinkable.

The jury must have been in no doubt there had been a party. Now, they were to hear from someone, actually there, precisely what had happened.

Hart told a hushed, expectant court everything that took place in that basement flat, from McVitie's noisy arrival, to his attempt to escape through the window, and, finally, to the moment when Hart handed Reggie Kray the kitchen knife, with which he murdered McVitie.

For the prosecution, it was another trump card. For the Krays and the rest of us, the whole pack was falling down.

I should not have been surprised that Hart betrayed the twins to save his own skin. He was only in the Firm for the image and all the glamour that went with it. He loved boasting that he was related to the Krays.

But I never expected the Mills brothers to go over to the other side. They were genuine guys, from a solid area, Notting Hill, and they cherished their reputations as honourable, trustworthy people. For them to help the police was almost like the sun falling out of the sky.

But they did. Each of them went in the witness box and told the truth about that Saturday night. How they had come down from Birmingham and met Tony and me in the East End. How we all had gone to Stoke Newington for a drink in the Regency. How we had gone to Evering Road for a party.

And how they had seen their Saturday night out with a couple of pals end in a horrifying killing.

Like the barmaid's, their evidence was too detailed, too credible, to be anything other than the truth and, as I listened to it, the tightening, nauseating knot in my stomach told me it was all over for me.

I did not like the Mills brothers for not keeping their mouths shut, but I could understand why they didn't. They had come out for a quiet drink and had walked into a nightmare that had nothing to do with them. Why should they be expected to destroy their lives for that? And for a couple of arrogant, selfish egomaniacs, who would not deem even to say thank you?

If the jury had been in any doubt that I had gone to Evering Road for a party, they were not now. Like Ronnie in the Cornell case, my only hope was to go into the box myself and somehow convince them that everything they had heard was all a load of rubbish, and that now I was going to tell what *really* happened that Saturday night.

'I swear by Almighty God that the evidence I shall give shall be the truth, the whole truth and nothing but the truth.'

What a defamation of God's name! From the moment I handed the Bible back to the Clerk of the Court, I looked Kenneth Jones, unblinkingly, in the eye and let one lie after another fall, unashamedly, from my lips.

Had I met a man called Jack The Hat in the Regency?

No, I had not.

Did you know Jack The Hat?

No, I did not.

Were you in his company in a flat in Evering Road?

No, I wasn't.

Did you see Jack The Hat attacked in that flat?

No, I certainly did not.

And so on . . .

As the lies, the pointless, ludicrous lies, came pouring out, I looked at the dock, at everyone in it, and they were all staring back at me, some impassive, others willing me, with their eyes, to go on: 'Go on, my son, you tell 'em. You tell 'em they've got it all wrong.' I wanted to look good in their eyes, but, at the same time, I knew how foolish I must look, how stupid I must sound.

Then, suddenly, there was drama.

Did your brother, Tony, tell you that Jack The Hat was going to have harm done to him?

I went to answer, but Tony shouted from the dock, 'I'll answer that when I go in the box.'

The judge glared at him furiously. 'Mr Lambrianou, you will be quiet, or I will have you for contempt of court.'

There was a bit of a stir in the gallery and I looked at the old man. He was shaking his head, sadly.

I gave what was put down in the court records as 'evidence' for three hours. When I was told to leave the witness box and return to the dock, I glanced up again at my dad. He was holding his head in his hands.

He had watched, in shame, as I had made a public fool of myself. He had listened as I had disgraced the Lord's name with one blatant lie after another to protect two people who sent me into the war zone with my hands tied behind my back, my head filled only with ideas and principles I had learned in the university of crime.

And, like me, he knew I was going to have to pay a heavy, heavy price for that.

Early on in the McVitie trial, it was clear how biased Stevenson was. When the prosecution had the floor, he was alert, pulling faces and making gestures for the jury's benefit, and punctuating every salient, incriminating point so that it sank in. When it was the defence's turn, however, he would rock backwards and forwards and look around the court, often sighing and yawning theatrically, as if to say that what was being said on our behalf was irrelevant, unimportant and should be dismissed as a waste of everybody's time.

Once, during one of the defence counsel's long speeches, he did actually appear to be asleep, prompting Ronnie Bender to quip, not too quietly, 'Wake him up. The thirteenth member of the jury's nodded off.'

Judges come into their own when they sum up. And when that moment arrived, on Friday, 28 February, Mr Justice Melford Stevenson ensured his place in legal history with a résumé of Britain's longest trial that left the jury in no doubt that, for all, except Tony Barry, there was only one possible verdict: guilty.

Stevenson did not waste too much time on the Cornell murder, believing, rightly, that the refreshingly candid testimony of the frightened barmaid would carry more weight than anything he could say. But when it came to McVitie, he slaughtered us, stressing once again the vital importance of those words, attributed to Ronnie Kray, 'I've done mine, Reg – now you do yours' – the alleged utterance that had provided the link and made it possible to hear both cases together.

I was hanging on Stevenson's every word, waiting for him to come to me and my part in the tragic McVitie affair. And when he did, my hopes, which I thought had long since died, rose a fraction.

There was no evidence, the judge said, that Christopher Lambrianou took any part whatsoever in the killing of Jack McVitie; he did not appear to be part of the overall plan.

My optimism was short lived. For Stevenson went on to say that if Tony told me McVitie was going to get even a slap, that would constitute knowledge of a violent act that would be taking place. If I had that knowledge, I was as guilty as everyone else and should be found guilty of murder.

A chill ran through me. The judge had laid it on the line:

if the Krays had just spat on McVitie and he subsequently died, I was as guilty of murder as them. Forget the lack of evidence that I knew anything untoward was going to happen – just lump me in with them, *guilty by association*, and get that prison cell ready.

Listening to Stevenson taking my future away, I was too ashamed to look up at the gallery. I could not bear to see the pain and sorrow I knew was etched on Dad's ageing face. I felt like breaking down and sobbing my heart out, for him as much as myself, but I had to be strong for him. So I stared ahead, as though the judge's crushing words had not got to me. And when he interrupted his summing up for the weekend break, I got up and trotted down the stairs to the cells, forcing a bounce in my step I didn't feel. I was beaten. I knew that for certain now. But I could not let my dad see me broken and on the floor.

We were all pretending it was not as bad as it looked. Even after Stevenson concluded his summing up at lunchtime on Tuesday, and we waited for the jury's verdicts, we were cracking jokes and laughing at the little victories we'd won, trying to lift each other.

The twins, particularly, were unbowed. They knew they were going down, almost certainly for a life sentence, but they were young, and confident they could come again. 'Never mind,' Ronnie would say. 'I've seen this lovely yacht in a book and I'm going to sail it to the Caribbean.'

'When do you think this will be, Ron?' someone asked.

'About eight or nine years,' he replied, puffing away on another Player's cigarette.

He genuinely believed it. Reggie did, too. And, if I'm honest, so did I. Life sentences, with a recommendation that a prisoner serve a minimum number of years, were unheard of in 1969. Life, as most people knew, did not really mean *life*. It was, indeed, possible that we could all be out in less than ten years.

The all-male jury retired eight minutes before one o'clock. They returned six minutes after seven that evening – taking just six hours, fifty-four minutes to decide the fate of ten men in a thirty-nine-day trial, arguably the most complicated ever to be tried at the Old Bailey. Obviously, they had had very little difficulty reaching their verdicts.

For the past nine weeks, we had climbed the steps from the cells together. Now, we would go up one by one.

Ronnie Kray was the first to be called. He was back in less than five minutes.

How did you get on, Ron? 'Guilty,' he said. 'On both Cornell and McVitie.'

Reggie was next, and seemed to be back even more quickly. He was guilty of killing McVitie and of being an accessory to Cornell's murder.

Someone else, I think Ian Barrie, went next, and someone else after that. I sat in my cell, in a daze, my mind in turmoil with all sorts of emotions, and then I heard my name being called, and I was climbing the steps myself, about to face the full power and majesty of the law.

The Clerk of the Court faced the foreman of the jury. Have you reached a verdict in the case of Christopher Michael Lambrianou?'

'We have.'

'Will you give that verdict to the court.'

'Guilty.'

I looked up at the gallery and saw old Charlie Kray reach over and touch my dad's arm. Then I stared at the judge.

'You have heard the verdict of the jury of your peers.' he said. 'Take him down.'

Stevenson's face was stony, full of loathing, his tone contemptuous.

Before stepping down, I glanced again at my dad. It seemed as if he had got to his feet, then collapsed, because he was being held up by my brother Jimmy and Leon's wife, June, like some soldier who had been shot and wounded in the war. That was the last sight I saw, and I took the image down into the cells with me.

'How did you get on, Chris?' they all wanted to know.

'Guilty,' I said, quietly.

'Never mind, mate,' Ronnie said. 'You won't get that long. They won't keep you forever. You didn't kill anybody.'

Reggie came over, but didn't say anything, just squeezed my hand.

Tony was up and back before I had a chance to talk to him. He was guilty, too. He strolled back into the cell, smiling out of bravado.

The others in the Firm, except Tony Barry, who had been accused of being an accessory to McVitie's murder, were found guilty, too. But still Ronnie was strolling around, puffing on a cigarette, refusing to be anything less than positive.

'I can still get that yacht,' he was saying. 'I think I'll go to Egypt. Lots of beautiful boys in Egypt. And I'll have a nice house in the country with a couple of horses and a goat . . .'

Given that he was facing not one but two murder charges, and the wrath of a fearsome judge, hellbent on wreaking society's revenge, it was a mad, mad fantasy.

But, then, that's what the Kray world was all about – a frightening madness of murder and mayhem from which, for me, there seemed no escape.

CHAPTER FIFTEEN

That Wednesday morning of 5 March 1969, I wasn't thinking of myself. All that concerned me was my dear old dad. I'd come to terms with what was going to happen to me, prepared myself for the inevitable life sentence. But how on earth was he going to take it – not just the humiliation, but the implications of the sentence for *him*? He was seventy years old. How was he going to cope, realizing he would probably never see his eldest son again outside a prison visiting room?

They called Reggie first. He was back in less than five minutes. He had got life, he said. With a recommendation that he serve at least thirty years. We were all shocked. Ronnie got the same, then Ian Barrie came back, visibly shaken at getting life with a twenty years' recommendation. When Tony walked back down, saying he had to serve a minimum of fifteen years, I thought, 'If he gets out then, Dad will be eighty-five.'

And then I heard my name being called and I walked towards the steps that led up to the court. Capital punishment had been abolished just four years before, but I felt I was walking from the condemned cell to the hangman. As I reached the top of the stairs, I looked up at the public gallery and saw my father sitting next to the Kray brothers' father,

Charlie. Our eyes met. All I could think was, How could I keep his spirits up when he heard the sentence?

And then I heard Melford Stevenson's sonorous tone. 'Christopher Lambrianou, there is only one sentence I can pass on you. I sentence you to life imprisonment with a recommendation that you serve fifteen years.' I glanced up at the gallery. 'Send him down.'

A couple of police guards stepped towards me. I moved away. I pointed up at the gallery. 'I'll see you later, Dad,' I called out. He just looked back at me, blankly. Then I was grabbed and forced to turn and go back down the steps. The sentence had not hit me. It was just words, and I'd heard so many over the past thirty-nine days that something in me had switched off and I was on automatic pilot. I would deal with that another time. All that was filling my mind now was the image of my dad's lovely old face and the pain I'd seen in his eyes.

The others asked what I'd got and I told them. They were all sympathetic, especially Ronnie. 'Never mind,' he said, as positive as ever. 'It'll soon pass. We can do this time.' He was even thinking ahead to his own release. 'I can just see myself in a few years. Retired and doing what I want. A lovely house in the country. Holidays on my yacht. A nice couple of boys.'

Reggie was quiet and sombre beneath that famous Number 1 Court: he did not see his sentence as just 'a few years'.

Eventually we were herded out of the back of the court into the van, all of us cramped into our single cubicles, looking out through the tiny, scratched windows, with haunted eyes, at a world we would not be seeing for a long time. The motorbike outriders set off towards south-west London and Wandsworth Prison. Once away from the Old Bailey, the police bells started clanging again, like a hundred town criers, all ringing out the comforting message to London's multitudes: 'These people once ruled the underworld. We have them for you. There's Ronnie Kray . . . there's Reggie Kray . . . there's the Lambrianou brothers . . . We have them under lock and key. You can all sleep safely now. We've brought down the empire . . .'

The police were shitting themselves at what they had got, what prize prey they had caught. But that did not stop them making the most of it on the way to the slaughter.

Inside the van, all was quiet, too quiet. I thought that was wrong. It symbolized defeat and I didn't feel defeated. I don't think any of us did. The system had destroyed my life, but it was not going to crush my spirit. I wanted my spirit to be free.

So, softly, I began to sing. I began to sing one of those old wartime songs I always seemed to hear coming from the East End pubs as an eleven-year-old, a song I'd learned on chara-banc rides to the Essex seaside: 'It's a long way to Tipperary, it's a long way to go . . .'

It was a warm, moving song, evoking thoughts of cama-raderie and pulling together in the face of adversity, against the odds, and it struck a chord. One of the Firm started singing with me. Then someone else joined in, softly at first, as if embarrassed, but then the others joined in, too, until the van was alive with song. We went into another one, 'She'll be coming round the mountain . . .', and it was as if we were a carefree bunch of office workers celebrating some happy event on a coach outing. There was a lot of laughter, too, a bizarre humour amid the madness that had taken over all our lives. It was as if we were saying, 'Yes, it has happened. But we're not accepting it. We're not going to lie down on the floor and let you gloat over us in your victory. We're different. We're somebody.'

For the first time I felt part of the Kray Firm. We were

Mum, who never gave less than her best, and Dad, faithful to the end.

Taken in the late 1960s, I'm on the right, with my brother Nicky next to me.
Behind Nicky is Tony Bender, and my brother Tony is on the far left.

Above Reg (left), Charlie and Ron Kray outside their house on Vallance Road on the day they were acquitted of demanding money with menaces, in April 1965. *Below* Inside The Blind Beggar, the spot between the chair and barstools where George Cornell was killed. Hearing about the murder, I knew the Krays were out of control.

The seedy Regency Club where we bumped into Jack (The Hat) McVitie that fateful night.

The house on Evering Road, where Jack was murdered.

Jack (The Hat) McVitie.

The Kray Firm arrives at Bow Street police station to be charged.
Artist's impression of the accused in the dock. (*Daily Mirror*, 5 March 1969).

A VIEW FROM THE BENCH

Ronald Kray, 35

John, 'Ian' Barrie, 31

Ronald Bender, 30

Reginald Kray, 35

Charles Kray,

Mr Justice Melford Stevenson who told us, 'You lot don't impress me at all'.

Superintendent Nipper Read and Inspector Frank Cater.

THIS WAS THE JUDGE'S EYE-VIEW AT THE OLD BAILEY, THESE WERE THE FACES IN THE DOCK FOR 39 DAYS

Christopher Lambrianou, 29

Anthony Lambrianou, 26

Anthony Barry, 40

Frederick Foreman, 36

Cornelius Whitehead, 30

OLD BAILEY IMPRESSION BY OLIVER WILLIAMS

A typical prison cell when I began my sentence.

With Charlie Richardson. I met him in Leicester prison, early in my sentence, and my dark existence began to brighten.

The day I left prison.

Happy memories. With
(front left to right) David,
Becky, Laura and Christopher.
I love being a dad.

Above left With my lovely wife Helen, who I married in 2006. *Above right*
With Freddie Foreman and my brother Jimmy at the *Legend* preview.

At the *Legend* premiere with (left to right) Maureen Flanagan, Holly,
Tom Hardy (who played the twins), myself and Christopher.

bonded together, brothers in arms, in a unified 'up yours' to the system and it was a unity that seemed to impress the prison officers. When we reached Wandsworth Prison, they all shook our hands, and the driver even asked us for our autographs.

A welcoming party of police top brass was waiting to greet us.

Once inside the gates of the prison, there is a crescent-shaped drive, with a green lawn in the middle. All round the crescent were what seemed like a dozen newly washed white Jaguars. On the green, waiting for us to walk past, were the policemen responsible for our arrest, all looking pleased with themselves, all thrilled to be able to gloat, rub our noses in our defeat, their triumph. There were many prisoners looking out of the cell windows and the police were pleased about that, too. They wanted them to see us, the villains' heroes, walking into captivity; wanted them to see for themselves that 'You can't beat the police', and to pass the message on.

Nipper and his men wanted us to step forlornly from the van and creep to the gaol, pathetically. But we didn't. We were all broken by the verdicts, but none of us wanted them to see it. So we stepped out sprightly like men – *real* men – and filed past them, our heads held high, looking each one in the eye, conveying the message: 'You may have us down, but we're not out.'

I had already decided how I was going to do my time. If I was to survive, not go out of my mind, it had to be one way – and one way only. Prisons were full of predators, and I had to make sure I was a bigger predator than any of them. Like in the Army, I would have to make my mark early, let everyone, screws and cons alike, know that I was not taking crap from anyone. There was no point, no incentive, in being a good boy. There wasn't a carrot dangling in front of me, not even the flicker of a gleam of a light at the end of a pitch-black tunnel. There was no reward for good behaviour. Staring me in the face was a certain fifteen years behind bars. And that was just a minimum. Who knew what would happen to me in 1984?

As I began that first day of my sentence, however, I knew I had an extra burden that would almost certainly make life worse for me. I had a brother, who was consumed with his image as a gangster, a fully paid-up member of the Kray Firm. It worried me greatly because I knew he would want to live up to that image, and that it would rebound on me. He had always been a reckless, unreasonable individual who would do things regardless of the consequences, knowing I'd always be there to clean up the mess, pick up the pieces. Prison would be no exception.

I got my chance to make my mark – at least with the screws – shortly after I was locked in my cell on Category Double A. There was a light knock on the spyhole. A voice said, 'Are you all right in there, Chris?' It was Terry Kenning, 'Scouse' Terry, who had nearly lost an arm in an axe attack after double-crossing the twins. He was hard, but honest.

'Are you all right for snout?' he asked.

'No,' I said.

'Press your bell,' he said. 'Go to the toilet and you'll find some behind the seat.'

A few minutes later, I rang my bell. A screw came. 'Yes?'

'I want to use the toilet,' I said.

'You've got a pot in there. You'll have to use that.'

'Don't come that with me, you slag,' I shouted. 'Get the fucking door open. If I have to do it in this pot, it's coming over you first thing in the morning. Now, just behave yourself and open the door.'

His bottle went immediately: he opened the door and let me through to the toilets. Behind one of the cisterns, there was a copy of that morning's *Daily Express*, with virtually all the front page devoted to the Kray trial. Inside were three cigarette papers, enough tobacco for one long smoke, and some matches, each of which had been split into four thin strands with a needle. I stuffed the newspaper down the front of my prison underpants, which had been worn by a couple of hundred men before me, and went back to my cell.

I sat on my metal bed, on a two-inch mattress that had been flattened by a million men before me, and made up a long, thick cigarette. I lit up, then laid back, in a shirt and socks that, maybe, another three hundred men had worn before me, and inhaled slowly and deeply. I had not had a cigarette for weeks and the tobacco hit me hard. Thankfully. I was out of my mind for a little while.

The next morning, I heard that Ronnie, Reggie, Charlie and Freddie Foreman were not there. They had gone on to Brixton to await trial on the Frank Mitchell murder, leaving me and Tony and Ian Barrie and Ronnie Bender the celebrities of London's toughest prison.

A chance to make my mark with other prisoners came a few days later, after an incident in the workshop, involving my pal Connie Whitehead. A rumour had been going round that Connie had grassed the twins, and a misguided geezer, named Tony Lang, decided to put himself in favour with them and other prisoners by having a pop at Connie.

We were all sitting down, working quietly, when Lang got up and smashed Connie on the chin. The force of the blow, and Connie's hard jaw, broke Lang's hand, but Connie just sat there and took it. Then he got up and walked out of the workshop.

I was full of admiration for Connie for that. I knew what he could do; I knew that he could have destroyed Lang in a few seconds, if he had wanted to. But he had turned the other cheek.

The incident bothered me. Connie was in a weak position. Because he was no longer under the Krays' protection it had been easy to attack him. Lang had taken a liberty. I felt I owed Connie. That October night in Stoke Newington, he was the one who had begged me not to go back to Blonde Carol's flat. He was the one who had tried to save my life. I thought hard about it the rest of the day and during the night, and when I woke, I decided I would avenge Connie. It would repay him, in some way, and let the other prisoners know he was not an easy touch.

I made it my business to see Lang as we slopped out.

'Hi, Chris,' he said, cheerily. 'How ya going?'

'I'm not going well at all,' I replied.

'Oh, why's that?'

'You're a fucking rat, that's why,' I said.

And I laid him out.

Swarms of cons and screws were on us in seconds. As he got up, Lang said, 'What was all that about, Chris?'

'You know what it's about,' I said. 'You knew Connie was weak. And you took a liberty. You would never live with him. Get out of my sight.'

I didn't speak to Lang again; there was nothing to say. I had made my point, done what I thought was right, on behalf of a good man who had tried to do right by me.

Unfortunately, it rebounded on me, Tony, Bender and Barrie. Instead of being allowed into the workshop and the exercise yard, we were locked in our cells for twenty-four hours a day, except when we were allowed to go to the toilet. We spent most of the time sewing mailbags.

We were checked every twenty minutes, even at night when we were trying to sleep. A dull red light was on in the cell twenty-four hours a day, so that the screws could see what we were doing every time they peered through the Judas hole. It was sheer hell, trying to sleep under that red light: I'd keep waking up, feeling as though I had sand in my eyes, and then I'd drop off again, only to be woken by the Judas hole being pulled back. After a while, I became very ragged, never quite sure if it was night or day.

And then, suddenly, the authorities began to get paranoid. We were told they believed highly dangerous, sophisticated prisoners with vast amounts of money on the outside and Mafia connections were plotting to spring us from Wandsworth and the twins from Brixton, using tanks and machine-guns and even helicopters. We started to be moved around, so that if anyone *did* want to help us escape they would not know where to look. The mistake the authorities made was giving us too much importance. They elevated us to a celebrity status, which meant that wherever we went it was always a big deal: transfers to this or that part of the prison always had to be documented in a red book, so that everybody knew where we were at any given time. The screws were terrified of losing us. I said to one that he would rather lose his wife than me, and he agreed. He said he'd be sacked on the spot and, whereas he could always find another wife, he would never ever get a job within the prison system again.

Paranoia about us got so bad that we were moved from one cell to another every two days or so. It got to a point where none of us knew which cell we'd be sleeping in. The reason was obvious: they did not want us getting too comfortable anywhere, or getting to know people who might be able to send messages out for us.

The shifting went on for five or six days and then it happened: the 'Gestapo' came for me.

It was a rare night when I'd managed to get to sleep, despite the red light and the twenty-minute check-ups.

Suddenly, I was brought up out of dreamland by a loud banging on the door. It opened and through half-closed, sleepy eyes, I saw four tall, heavily built men in hats and long, black raincoats, with the collars turned up.

There was no daylight coming in the window, so I assumed it was night-time. But what time? It transpired that it was four in the morning. My mind began to race; I felt a nervousness, an anxiety. I had no idea why four sinister-looking men, like the German secret police, were in my cell. Was I going to get a kicking? Were they going to kill me?

'What's going on?' I demanded to know.

'Get your stuff packed,' one said. 'You're going.'

'Where?' I asked.

'We can't tell you that.'

'Fuck off. I'm not leaving here till I know where I'm going.'

'*Get your stuff packed.* We're moving.'

'I want some breakfast. I want a wash first.'

'You can have all that when we get where we're going. Just get moving, all right?'

It didn't take me long to get my things together; I didn't have a wardrobe to choose from. I just stuck my bits and pieces – letters, tobacco, etc. – in a pillowcase and got dressed. Carrying the pillowcase over my shoulder, I walked out the door.

And what I saw outside shook me rigid.

Standing in two lines were no fewer than forty more prison officers, all waiting, it turned out, to escort not only me, but Tony and Ronnie and Ian on a mystery tour. 'Where

did they find that many screws at four in the morning?'
I thought. And how much were they costing in overtime!

The four of us were handcuffed and led out of the building. And there, standing on the lawn, beside the drive,
waiting for us, were the welcoming committee – Read, his
deputy Frank Cater, Du Rose and all the team. There were
no smiles on their faces this time, however. And no van for
us, either. We were split up and each told to get in a different
squad car, which would form part of a convoy, with other
police cars separating us from each other. There were ten cars
in all, I seem to remember. And a helicopter overhead. Where
they thought we might go, should we suddenly slip off our
handcuffs and overpower the massive police presence, no one
was saying. Nor were they saying where we were going. I did
ask the three escorts in my car, but they said they had no idea;
they would know once they were out of London. Apparently,
each police driver had been given an envelope which they
were to open once they reached a certain point. Inside would
be their destination and a route map showing how to get
there. This information could easily be given over the police
radio, or walkie-talkies, of course, but the paranoia about an
ambush to help us escape was so high, Nipper and his top
men did not want to risk anything being picked up on the
airwaves.

After the stifling drabness of Wandsworth, it was a relief
to be out in the open, if only in a car hemmed in on all sides
by policemen. Entering prison is like walking into a garden
where no rain has fallen, no sun has shone, and the flowers
are dying through lack of care; where there are no trees, no
green of any kind, just grey, a very miserable, tedious grey.
That morning, heading north through London, seeing people
in cars and taxis and buses going about their business, was a
wonderfully exhilarating experience. I had been plucked from

my dull, drab existence where time stood still, and allowed to glimpse the world I'd left behind, a world bursting with colour and movement and life, and I was mesmerized by it.

At some point, the envelope must have been opened, revealing our secret destination, because we were heading, very purposefully, at very high speed – maybe 90 m.p.h. – up the M1 into Bedfordshire.

Finally, my curiosity got the better of me, and I started making conversation with my escorts to try to find out where we were going, and what the activity was all about. I did not get very far, because the car leading the high-speed police convoy hit a traffic cone, which flew in the air, hitting the following car. The car screeched to a halt, causing all the following cars to concertina into each other.

'Get me out of this car,' I screamed. 'We're all going to die if we just sit here. Cars tear up here at 100 miles an hour. They're going to plough into the back of us.'

George, the screw beside me, was so terrified he shit himself, literally. The smell was so strong I had to move my head away, towards Eric, on the other side.

'I don't want to die,' George was saying. 'I've got a wife and family.'

'Well, I'm telling you. Get us out of this car and onto the central reservation, otherwise we're gone. I used this road all the time. I know. The cars – they're not going to stop.'

Suddenly I looked out of the side windows and saw the grass banks on either side of the motorway alive with armed police. They appeared to come from nowhere. I couldn't see what was happening further up the motorway, so maybe they had run out of the cars. Then, a policeman came running by and said the motorway had been sealed off a mile or so back, and minutes later police Land Rovers and Jaguars were pulling up alongside us and big, heavy men piled out, wielding shooters, looking menacing. It was motorway madness. For a while, the police had not even known it was their own crash; no one seemed to know what had happened, or what they were supposed to do. There could have been bloody carnage, and the police would have been to blame.

Finally, they sorted out the mess and put us all in fresh cars and off we went, again at high speed, and we didn't stop until we pulled into Nottingham gaol for lunch. The journey had been chaotic, but it was worth it, because I had the tastiest meal I'd had in months: roast lamb and two veg, followed by a succulent jam pudding with custard. 'If they eat like this,' I thought, 'why can't we stop here?' But then, the food was probably from the officers' mess, not the prison itself.

Still no one was saying where we were going. But when we hit Catterick, in North Yorkshire, a couple of hours later and then kept on the A1 at Scotch Corner, the penny dropped. I knew the area fairly well from my visits to my grandparents in Consett, County Durham, and felt certain the only place we could be going was the city of Durham itself. And the legendary hard gaol there.

I started playing up then and feeding the police paranoia.

'I know where we're going. Do you want to know?'

'I don't know where we're going.'

'I do,' I said. 'And I'll tell you how to get there an' all.'

I was really ribbing them; they genuinely believed I had some prior information.

'Where are we going, then?' one of them asked.

'Durham,' I said. 'Mind if we pop into my Aunt Teresa's on the way? I'm sure she'll make us a nice cup of tea!'

That did it. They were so stupidly paranoid about the far-reaching power of the Krays, they thought I'd known all along, and that I'd been fooling them.

We sped on and I saw the first sign to Durham, and, yet

again, I felt the familiar ache in my heart: with every yard, every mile, my freedom was ebbing away. I looked out at the spectacular mountainous countryside hurtling past, praying for some hold up, some roadworks or something, so that I could soak up the startling splendour of it all. My life, like the prison flowers, had died a little every day, and now, the wild, craggy, untameable beauty of those rolling hills and deep, dark green valleys took my breath away. I wanted to stop and get out of the car and run and run and not stop running, away from all the hype and garbage and misery that was the Kray madness; or fly away from it, free and out of reach of those who had dragged me into murder and those who were making me pay for it.

But, of course, there was no way out. I was handcuffed on both sides and locked behind doors that could be opened only by the driver. So, I could just look and marvel, sadly, at that scenic wonder as the convoy hurtled on towards the forbidding fortress that was Durham gaol, and the forgotten flowers that were dying behind its drab, grey walls.

CHAPTER SIXTEEN

From the security, you would have thought they had four crazed, psychopathic terrorists who had kidnapped the Royal Family: that we had a hidden army waiting for the right moment to pounce and whisk the four of us off to freedom.

We were driven up to the prison entrance and got out of the car to find ourselves surrounded by prison staff with dogs. We were taken, one by one, through two huge gates, each of which was closed behind us, before our handcuffs were removed. Then we were escorted into the prison itself, through three steel doors, to an L-shaped wing, split into two levels. The top one was smaller, like a cage, and enclosed in wire.

This was part of E Wing. Only ten high-risk prisoners at a time were held there. And they were not just top-security, Category A – they were Double A, meaning that they never left the wing, and no other prisoners were allowed into it. There was never an excuse to leave our part of the wing, because it had everything you needed. Even if a prisoner needed his teeth looked at, a dentist came to the wing.

You had to be nuts even to think escape was possible: we were watched twenty-four hours a day – even when we were in the toilet – by cameras, operated from a bunker from which the gates could be opened and closed electronically. And every window was surrounded by razor-sharp barbed wire. Anyone foolish enough to try to climb out and jump the thirty feet to the ground would have cut himself to pieces before the guards hauled him back. Even if he, miraculously, got out of the window and jumped, he would probably break a leg or two before the dogs pounced.

If I thought the security was over the top and unnecessary, the governor and his staff certainly did not. They were still recovering from a riot six months before, and the last thing they needed was the Kray Firm stirring up trouble. Everyone was on edge. They did not know us, only what they had read in the papers and heard on radio and television. But they expected the worst.

The ten of us had two screws responsible for each of us. There was never any physical contact between us and them. They just sat on the landings, drinking tea and reading books. There was seldom any familiarity. Occasionally a screw would call me by my first name, but I never felt comfortable with that; I suspected an ulterior motive and I could not afford to drop my guard.

Above our level was the cage known as the Monsters' Hideaway – the closely guarded refuge of sex offenders, such as the Moors Murderer, Ian Brady, who were locked away for their own protection under Rule 43. There were six of them up there and, not surprisingly, the evil Brady was the most hated. Many attempts had been made to kill him, not only by physical attacks, but by poisoning his food in the kitchens, and, at night, prisoners in the main part of the wing would scream at him for hours. 'Brady, you're going to die in prison . . . You're going to die of cancer . . . Your skin is going to fall off, you evil cunt . . .' The hate-filled threats would go on and on, long into the early hours, night after night.

I grew to hate Brady, too. I did not see him very often, because the screws kept all the nonces well away from us, but when I did set eyes on him he came across as an extremely arrogant bastard, trying to be the prison hard man. I felt there should be a stoop, or a hanging of the head in shame. But not once did I see one sign of remorse or compassion in Brady. He did not seem to see anything wrong in what he had done. By the way he strutted around, his head held high and his shoulders straight, in a military sort of way, I sensed he might even be proud of it.

Like most of the other cons, I could not wait to get my hands on him, and, late one afternoon after I'd been in the gaol a few weeks, I got my chance. I'd been to the toilet and, by a fluke, the screws had locked everybody else up and forgotten about me. I came out of the toilet, unnoticed, and wandered up onto an overhead landing which led to the Monsters' Hideaway. There was a shower area there and I decided to have one. When I finished, I wandered out onto a walkway and saw Brady was being escorted back to his cell by a couple of screws after making an application for something in the chief prison officer's office. I nipped back into a recess and waited. When Brady was level with me, I leaped out and gave him a thumping right-hander to the jaw. He went down like the proverbial sack of potatoes, and lay on the ground, screaming in terror. I went to grab him, but the screws grabbed me instead and dragged me off to my own cell. I never got punished for that attack, possibly because it was the prison's fault that I was left to wander around without supervision.

In contrast, John Straffen, another infamous murderer, who strangled two little girls in the 1950s, inspired no anger or hate in me at all. He was a simple individual and had been transferred to Durham from Broadmoor because he was not mad enough. He was given certain privileges, courtesy of the Cadbury's Trust, and used as a dogsbody around the wing. They allowed him into our section to make the tea, but I never let him make one for me. I found what he had done wicked and repulsive and I didn't want anything to do with him. Certain other prisoners had some sympathy for him, which I found hard to understand. The man was a nasty nonce, who took two children's lives. To me, his simplicity was no excuse. I never thought about hitting him, though. He was a creepy, insignificant little man, too pathetic to punch.

At the start of the summer a rumour started buzzing that Ronnie Kray was going to join us. He was being kept in Brixton while the Frank Mitchell murder trial was going on, but, guilty or not, he would start his thirty-year sentence in earnest in Durham. The immediate reaction was, 'Oh, God, is he going to have his medication?' It wasn't that nobody wanted him there – it was just that he was a real handful if he was not sedated and began feeling that self-destructive paranoia.

The rumours turned out to be true. On Wednesday, 28 May 1966, having been found not guilty of the Frank Mitchell murder, Ronnie walked into E Wing.

And he was as good as gold: cool, calm and as positive as ever. He was still talking about what he was going to do when he got out. 'Chris, I'm going to have this wonderful yacht with some sweet young boys on it. You must come and join me for a world cruise . . .'

'Yes, Ron, I'd love to,' I'd say. 'I will . . .'

There was something about Ronnie I really, really liked. He was hard, but he was honest. And he was loyal. Which is why, with my appeal coming up, I decided to go to his cell to talk to him about what I wanted to tell the court.

Ronnie was standing at an easel, palette in one hand, painting a cornfield. An opera was playing on the record player. Ronnie loved painting as much as he loved Puccini.

He would have been in his element if someone had stopped by and said, 'Here you are, Ron, I've got this painter's smock and hat for you!'

Ron stood back from his painting.

'What do you think of it, Chris?' he asked, in his quiet voice.

Quite frankly it was a mess. But I did not want to offend him. He was doing something he was enjoying, and, anyhow, who was I to criticize?

'It's brilliant, Ron,' I lied. 'Marvellous.'

'I'm gonna send it to Reg,' he said, proudly. 'Do you think Reg will like it?'

'Yes,' I said. 'I'm sure he will.' Then I looked at the bright yellow sun Ron had painted above the yellow cornfield. 'Tell you what, Ron. The sun's too bright. Why don't you paint it black?'

'Do you think so?' Ron said.

'Have a look at it. You've got too much yellow. You should paint the sun black. It'll make the picture different.'

So Ronnie painted the sun black. When he eventually finished the painting the next day, he did not send it to Reg – he sent it to someone else, who was so impressed, he, in turn, sent it to a national newspaper, which published it, saying the black sun gave the painting a religious significance.

Having passed on my artistic tip for the day, I told Ronnie I wanted to clear the air with him over something that was bothering me – what I needed to say at my forthcoming appeal to give me a chance of getting out of my life sentence.

'You know I didn't kill anybody, Ron,' I said. 'You know I, like Tony and Bender, stood and took it for you. To be quite honest, I want to go on the appeal and say, "Yes, there *was* a party, and, yes, something happened there. But I left and did not see anyone murder anybody." That will be new evidence.'

Seeing Ronnie start to shake his head, I went on quickly, 'We've been through months of hell, but I've stood beside you and Reg, shoulder to shoulder. Now that there's no hope you will get out on appeal, at least give me a chance to try to. Let me tell the truth so that I can try and fight. Give me some help, Ron. Please. Back us up, Tony, Bender and myself.'

Ronnie let me finish. Then he said, 'You can't say there was a party, because that knocks our appeal sideways.' And that was that.

I felt terribly let down. I honestly felt that, at that late stage, when all was lost for him and Reg, he might say, 'Yes, Chris, you did it for us. One way or another, I'm going to do a lot of bird. So, say what you like. Try to save yourself. We will give you some help.'

When he didn't, when he dismissed out of hand all that I'd said, not given a monkey's, I just said, 'Ron, thanks a lot.'

Then I walked out of his cell and back to mine.

I was totally disillusioned and lost a lot of respect for both the twins. To me, they would have been heroes if they had turned round and said, 'We can say we were at the party. That's not a big deal. There's no evidence. They haven't even got a body.' But I don't think Ron realized it was as simple as that. To him, admitting they were at the party was as good as admitting murder.

I would never have stood up and told the truth if I'd thought for a minute they could have got out. But, at that late stage, the doors were firmly bolted on them and I felt I could do them no harm whatsoever. They could have helped us, though. That they didn't says a lot about them. We did everything for them, but they never did one thing for any of us. That's the bottom line.

I told Ron that I had no alternative but to tell the truth at the appeal, and take my chances. He did not like it. After that, things were decidedly cool between us. We didn't argue, and we certainly didn't come to blows, but the feeling was quite uncomfortable, to say the least.

I talked to Tony very seriously about the appeal. I wanted him to say there was a party but he would not. He said he was staying with the twins all the way.

'You can't,' I said. 'This is our lives. We've done everything for them. We've even gone down with a sinking ship and got fifteen years, at least, in front of us. Now, we've got to try to save ourselves.'

But there was no shifting him. 'I've got it. I'm doing it – that's it,' was all he said.

In July, me, Tony and Bender were driven to London and locked up in the top-security wing of Brixton gaol, pending our appeal. We were treated like celebrities, by screws and cons alike, but that cut no ice with me. My mind was focused only on the appeal. The dreadful prospect of spending the next fifteen years of my life in gaol, for something I did not do, was tearing me apart and I just wanted to learn whether the truth, at last, was going to save me.

My wife, Carol, was having a tough time, too. Since my sentence, she had visited me and written, but she was suffering the most agonizing emotional battle with herself, over her future, and our eighteen-month-old daughter Angela's and, one day shortly before the appeal, she knew what she had to do.

She was due to visit me with my sister-in-law – also Carol – and Angela, and was waiting for a bus outside Hackney Town Hall. When the bus arrived, my sister-in-law got on, but Carol hesitated.

'I can't do it, Carol,' she said.

'What do you mean?' my sister-in-law asked.

'If I go today, I will never stop going,' Carol said. 'I can't do that to him. I can't do that to me. But, most of all, I can't do that to Angela. I can't visualize fifteen years. I want to make a new life. And if I say that, I've got to mean it.'

With that, my sister-in-law told me, Carol handed Angela to her and said, 'Give Chris my love. Wish him all the best. But tell him I just can't do it.'

The news broke me up. But I could understand it. I really could. Carol was a young woman not yet out of her twenties. Fifteen years was a lifetime.

As my sister-in-law told me the devastating news, Angela was amusing herself on the floor of the Brixton visiting room. Unseen by us, she went up to one of the screws and pulled a long chain, holding a bunch of keys, from his pocket. He obviously noticed, but said nothing. Angela toddled back and handed the keys to me. I had to smile.

I handed them back to the screw, a symbolic act that locked the door on my marriage and dreams of a happy family life.

All the appeals began at the High Court on Tuesday, 15 July, but none of us, me, the twins, or any of their firm, were there during the next six days of legal argument. There was no new evidence; our hopes rested on points of law only. In the end, it was as futile as I'd thought, deep down, it would be. Through my lawyer, I *did* tell the truth. I did say that there *was* a party that October night in Evering Road, and that I did *not* see what happened after I left. But, of course, it was no use. I needed something significant to swing the Appeal Court's verdict my way. I needed Ron and Reg to admit that they were at the house. But they were still denying there was any party.

And that left me stranded, slowly sinking in the foul-smelling swamp that was my life.

The following Tuesday, the Lord Chief Justice, Lord Widgery, announced that all the appeals had been turned down and, within a day or two, me and Tony and Bender were whipped out of Brixton and taken at high speed up the Ml to the Submarine.

CHAPTER SEVENTEEN

They called Leicester gaol's security wing the Submarine because it was a tunnel-like building, about fifty yards long and twenty yards wide, and the prisoners entombed in it never saw daylight.

It made even Durham's incredible high security look tame by comparison.

At one end, the screws sat behind a massive bullet-proof screen, observing the twelve Category Double A prisoners, every minute of the day, on television monitors. Hidden cameras watched our every movement – even in the shower. We rarely saw a screw on the wing. They just sat behind that huge screen, out of sight, watching us move around. We could not go anywhere, do anything, speak to anyone, without being seen.

For men doing our length of time, the food was a disgrace: it was like swill. It was left in big universal cans outside the wing and, by the time we got to eat it – half an hour or so after the other prisoners – it smelled and tasted awful. I wondered how I was going to survive in the Submarine, being observed every minute of the day, like a rat in a cage, and being fed like one.

And then I met Charlie Richardson.

And my dark, depressing existence began to brighten with what he began to teach me.

I'd heard all the stories about the rivalry between the Kray twins and the Richardson brothers, who operated a scrap-metal business in Peckham, South London. But it was none of my concern and, anyway, it was vital we got along, not let old bitterness, or supposed hatred, handicap our fight against the system. We had to put up a unified front, be as one. If I was dragged away in the middle of the night for an unjustified beating, for example, I might need Charlie – the so-called enemy – to say, 'I saw what happened,' and put the record straight.

Charlie himself was keen to make friends not enemies. Shortly after I arrived, he would come up to me when I least expected it, and say, quietly, 'All right, mate? How ya going?'

At first, I didn't react too warmly. I was still early into my sentence; I was wary of being sucked into the wrong group of people. But then Charlie would give me books to read and I began to get to know him, and found him very interesting. He would devour a book as someone else might devour a meal. I had a love of books, but I had never read anything of any substance. My reading was limited to gangster books and Westerns – and the Spurs' programme.

When Charlie recommended a book, saying he was sure I'd enjoy it, he was usually right. The more books I read, the more I enjoyed them, and the more friendly we became. I found Charlie a warm man, with more than a touch of compassion and caring for others. He was good for me.

And then, one morning, another con, called Nobby Clark, came up to me and said, 'Do you want me to kill Charlie Richardson for you?'

I was horrified. Nobby, who was serving life for murdering a con in Walton gaol in Liverpool, was a total lunatic, a wild man, who would kill someone as soon as look at them.

'Why on earth would I want you to do that, Nobby?' I said.

'He's no good, Chris,' Nobby said. 'Not a good man at all.'

There was a lot of rubbish about Charlie being put around at the time and Nobby had been listening to it, believing it.

'Charlie's all right,' I told Nobby. 'He's a nice man. There's no need to worry.'

'I don't think you should be taken in by him,' Nobby insisted. 'He's on the opposite side, isn't he? If he's having a go at you or anything, I'll go and do the business.'

I did not know what to do for the best. I certainly wasn't going to end my friendship with Charlie. But I did not want to fuel Nobby's silly imaginings, risk him putting a knife in Charlie's back.

In the end, I decided I had to introduce them to each other. Although regarded by everyone as a nutter, Nobby was a literate man who wrote beautiful poetry. He had himself tried to educate me by giving me *The Complete Works of Shakespeare*.

So I said to Nobby, 'Forget about killing Charlie. Come and talk to him. Or, I'll bring Charlie to you. He's nice. He likes books. He likes Shakespeare.'

I brought Charlie to Nobby's cell and introduced them, saying they both had a common interest. Thankfully, they hit it off and got on brilliantly. After that, I'm pleased to say, I heard no more talk from Nobby about murdering Charlie.

Visits by my dad were always emotionally draining, painful times. He was seventy-one, and travelling more than a hundred miles to see me and Tony left him exhausted before he even got through the prison reception area. I felt for him so much and was always on a short fuse, wondering if anyone, or anything, was going to upset or hurt him more than he was already.

On one visit to Leicester that fuse snapped after just fifteen minutes. And it had disastrous consequences for me.

Dad had had a tough time with the screws on the gate, for one reason or another, so he was a little on edge. The atmosphere in the visiting room didn't help. It was like the condemned cell, with a very dim light over the table and two screws sitting in the shadows, watching, listening.

It seemed we'd barely sat down before one of the screws came over and said the visit was over.

'What do you mean, it's over?' I demanded to know.

'The visit is only a quarter of an hour,' he said.

I forced myself to stay calm, despite my fury.

'My dad's seventy-one,' I said quietly. 'He's come all the way from London and he's got to go back. Do you think it's right he should do that for fifteen minutes?'

'Sorry, Chris,' the screw said. 'That's the rules and regulations. In this wing, you're only allowed . . .'

He did not get time to finish. I went berserk. I started yelling at the screws and refused to leave the room. Seconds later a bell sounded and a mass of screws poured in and came for me. I struggled with them, trying to fight them off. There was a dinner trolley a few feet away. I turned it over, sending the filth and slop that passed for food all over the floor. The next moment, the screws had me over and I was rolling around in the food, punching and kicking wildly. Finally, about eight of them carried me out, still struggling, and took me to a cell beside the bullet-proof screen, where the TV monitors were. Inside the cell was an iron cage, about nine feet square. They chucked me in there, locked it, then closed the outer cell door and went out.

I was boiling with fury, outraged at the injustice of it all. I prowled around that cage like an angry lion, backwards and forwards, round and round, bouncing off the bars, one minute, then grabbing them the next, screaming: 'BAS-TARDS! Let me out, you bastards!'

An hour or so later, a screw opened the cell and came with my dinner on a tray. There was a gap under the bottom of the cage and he kicked the tray through.

I went over and picked it up. 'Is this for me?' I asked.

'Yes,' he said.

'YOU HAVE IT, YOU BASTARD,' I shouted. And I threw the tray against the cage, sending some of the prison swill over him. The screw was summoned.

'No problem to me,' he said. 'You're the one who's not going to eat.' And out he went.

The next day I was told I would be sent before the visiting committee of magistrates, accused of using foul and abusive language, making threatening gestures and being disruptive. A charge sheet was pushed under the bottom of the cage and I was asked if I was going to come out quietly.

I was still furious and thought, 'You treat me like an animal, then I'll behave like one.'

'No,' I snarled. 'No, I'm not.'

In that case, I was told, the magistrates would come to me.

And they did. All three of them. It must have been quite frightening for them, crammed into the cell, with a clerk and a prison officer, talking to what must have seemed like some crazed sub-human creature in that tiny cage.

I was found guilty, of course. They always found you guilty. The governor of Wandsworth, Beastie, once told me, 'If my officers told me you were riding along the landing on a motorbike, I would want to know where you got the petrol!' So it was not a surprise that I was given fourteen days' bread and water and stopped two weeks' pay (about two shillings and sixpence).

Before they left, one of the magistrates gave me the benefit of her advice. 'Mr Lambrianou,' she said, patronizingly, 'you are doing a very, very long time in prison and I hope you are aware of the fact that behaviour like this will get you absolutely nowhere.'

'Thank you for those words of wisdom,' I thought. I wondered how she would have taken it if *her* father was facing a two-hundred-mile round trip for a fifteen-minute visit!

I got through those two weeks' bread and water, thanks to a tip given to me by a con named Billy Gentry, who had been involved in a number of hunger strikes. He told me that warm water fooled the stomach into thinking you had had a hot meal and fought off the hunger pangs. Not only did it work, it cleaned my system out, too.

But I'd be less than honest if I didn't admit that being caged up on my own all that time was tough. It was. Those two weeks were when my sentence began to bite.

On the night of my fourteenth and last day, I went to sleep on my metal bed, a relatively happy man. Although I'd lost a stone in weight, I'd calmed down and managed to come through the experience unscathed. I was looking forward to being back on the wing. After the cage, it would seem a luxury. And I'd be back with the boys, and able to tell them what it had all been about; why I'd done what I did.

My sound, peaceful sleep was shattered at four in the morning. Four big men in dark raincoats, collars turned up, were standing there. The early morning 'Gestapo'.

'Get your clothes on, Lambrianou,' one of them ordered. 'We're going.' I sensed the anger and hatred in the sombre tone.

'Where?' I asked, sleepily.

'Don't know,' he said, predictably. 'We won't know until we're there.'

I got dressed and followed them out. I did not know and they did not know that they were moving the wrong man.

It wasn't me they wanted out of the gaol . . . it was Tony.

Someone in their wisdom had decided that, at just twenty-six and without a violent history, Tony should not be with dangerous criminals in a top-security wing. In the early days, the prison system was not always sure who it was dealing with when moving the twins, and with me and Tony it was the same: one Lambrianou was pretty much the same as the other one. So, later that morning, I arrived at Hull Prison.

I did not know about the cock-up, of course. However, after just twenty-four hours, I did know that the move was the best thing that could have happened to me. The gaol was like a holiday camp for degenerates. I was drunk on hooch every night for the first three weeks, and gambled on roulette and cards every weekend. The only vice I went without was sex. If the prison had had female screws, I would never have wanted to leave. As it was, freedom, and a lovely blue sky above me, was the greatest lure of all and one day a London kid named Terry Cutts told me he knew how we could get it.

Until Hull, the high security that followed me made escape merely a fantasy, but Terry was a do-it-yourself expert, who had come up with an ingenious idea I felt could work.

Several prisoners had been allowed to have as many as ten birds in their cells and Terry persuaded the authorities to allow him to start an aviary, too, with two large cages. He managed to get together a hacksaw, chisel, knife, rope and other escape tools, and the idea was to cut through the cell bars under cover of the cages. It started off well. Whenever a nosey screw came round, we'd throw him a sex magazine and say, 'Have a sit down and read this while we make you a cup of tea.' Then, when he had gone, forgetting to have a good look round, we went back to work behind the cages. Unfortunately, two weeks later, when we'd weakened enough bars to climb through, a screw decided to go behind the cages. He rapped the bars with his riot stick and they all fell out! His face was a picture – and so were ours!

At the time, I was gutted. There was no wire fence around the prison, just a wall. We would have got over it, no problem. But, later, I was relieved the escape plot had failed. In fact, I had a nightmare that I was on the run, and woke up terrified. I was already doing fifteen years' minimum and an escape bid on my record would have guaranteed me even more.

Whether it was the conspiracy to escape, or the realization that it was Tony, not me, that should be in Hull, I don't know, but a few days later I was on the move again. Not the heavy 'Gestapo' this time – just a couple of well-mannered screws, who did not want to be up and about at five in the morning, either.

'Morning Chris, how are you?' said one, pleasantly.

'Bit early, isn't it?' I said.

'Yeah. But you know how it is,' he said. 'We've got to take you somewhere else.'

'But where?'

'Honest, mate, we don't know. We won't until we get on the road.'

Once we headed north, however, I knew where I was going. My five-month 'holiday' was over. I was going back to that dark, depressing fortress in the north-east: Durham.

I was filled with dread, not so much for myself, but for my dad. Hull had been bad enough for him to visit, but Durham was 400 miles or so from London; an 800-mile round trip at his age would be an ordeal. The prospect of life back on E Wing after the carefree atmosphere of Hull was daunting, but my mood brightened when I heard that my old mate Charlie Richardson had been moved there from Leicester. Also on the wing were the Great Train Robber, Bruce Reynolds; Paul Seabourne, who had got Bruce's pal, Ronnie Biggs, over the wall at Wandsworth; and the notorious Black Panther, Donald Neilson. 'That little lot should make life interesting,' I thought. And I was right.

In no time at all, Neilson, who had arrived at the gaol at a mere seven stone, ballooned up to a gross eighteen stone. Nobody could understand why, but then somebody noticed that there was not as much milk as usual in the huge universal can the screws left for everyone's use. It turned out that Neilson was drinking it by the gallon and I pulled him on it. I told him he was taking a liberty. It was insignificant really, but it always was the small issues that niggled. Certain prisoners would harbour grudges at the least little thing.

I must confess I was in awe of Charlie and Bruce. They had been to places I'd only heard about, mixed with intelligent, cultured people and knew how to communicate. I, on the other hand, had an inquisitive but untutored mind and had no idea how to communicate. I felt inferior, awkward and embarrassed in their company, but instead of being myself and admitting my limitations, I tried to bluff them that I was as worldly and experienced as they were. It was stupid and immature and, of course, they saw through me immediately. However, I was bright enough to know I was in a position to learn from them, and I took notice of the books they devoured. Reynolds, at that time, was interested in poets, such as Browning and Keats, and the Brontë sisters; while Charlie was fascinated by the letters of Charles Dickens.

I began going to the library, too, and Charlie encouraged me, as he had at Leicester. I took his advice on many books, but my communication problem bothered me, and I was anxious to find some literature that might teach me to write letters. I was drawn to the letters of Chaim Weizmann, the father of Zionism, and grabbed it from the shelf eagerly. Sadly, it taught me little: I found Weizmann a self-centred, bitter man, who seemed to be whingeing all the time, and I found his letters most depressing. However, I quickly turned to the letters of Bruce's favourite poets and they inspired me no end.

After six months or so I was reading the autobiographies of world statesmen and famous generals and, believe it or not, books on Buddhism and yoga. I found I was fascinated. The more I read, the more I wanted to read. I was drawing on a well of spirituality inside me, so far untapped. Those wonderful meaningful books helped me start to believe in something outside myself.

Then, two psychologists, Stanley Cohen and Laurie Taylor, from Durham University, came onto the wing twice a week to research a book, *Psychological Survival*. They would wander around the landings talking to cons about their feelings, then started weekly classes in psychology. Bruce and Charlie went, so, of course, I did too. I thought it would give me something in common with them, at least one topic I could communicate on.

There had been no let up in the desire to poison Ian Brady, so uncooked food was delivered to our wing and we were allowed to cook it ourselves. It was then that I discovered, surprisingly, that Charlie was somewhat impressed with Bruce Reynolds himself.

Charlie quickly saw an advantage in being the cook, even though he didn't know a chilli from a chive.

No sooner had he been given the job than he came over to me and said, 'Could you help me out, mate?'

I did not want to look a prat, so I agreed. Then I quickly went to the library for some cookery books to give me the recipes for some exotic dishes.

All went well for a couple of weeks. The rest of the wing were more than satisfied with what they thought Charlie was preparing them. They had no idea I was the cook, not Charlie.

Late one morning, Charlie came up to me.

'What are we going to do for the chaps today, Chris?'

'I thought I'd do a nice beef curry,' I said. 'You go and chop the onions – I'll do the sauce.'

In a restaurant in the 1960s, I'd had a wonderful curry that was a light brown, reddish colour and I wanted to create the same for Bruce and co.

When I'd prepared everything, I told Charlie I was going to add a little colouring to make it look like the curry I'd had years before.

'All right, mate,' he said. 'You know what you're doing.'

I added only a little bit of red, but the curry turned almost scarlet.

Charlie looked at me horrified. 'You can't give that to Reynolds,' he said. 'He'll hit the roof.'

I knew Bruce had spent a lot of time in Acapulco and other exotic cities, and was very critical, but it cut no ice with me.

'Sod him,' I said. 'So what if he does hit the roof? The bottom line is, we've done our best. Anyway, it'll still taste the same.'

'But look at the fucking colour of it,' said Charlie.

I did. And it looked as if someone had died. It was like blood.

'All right,' I said. 'I've heard that if you mix green with red, it goes back to brown.'

'You sure?' Charlie asked, apprehensively.

I didn't answer, just walloped in some green colouring and stirred, hoping for the best.

It turned the most beautiful green – blue-bottle green.

I looked at Charlie, looking in the saucepan. I thought he was going to cry.

'Fucking hell, Chris,' he said. 'We can't let Reynolds see that.'

He was only bothered about Reynolds, no one else. He was worried about losing face if Bruce complained.

'What are we going to do, for fuck's sake?' Charlie was more worried than I'd ever seen him.

'I don't know,' I said. 'I honestly don't.'

'Oh dear,' said Charlie.

We played about with the mixture for over an hour, but everything we did made the colour even more grotesque. We got it back to a very rich brown using yeast extract, but it did not do much for the taste.

Finally, it was time to present our lunchtime offering. Every meal I'd cooked before had gone down well and Charlie had been happy to take the credit.

He walked in, proudly carrying the trays.

'Here comes the *maître d'*,' Bruce joked. Then he stared at his plate. 'What is it, Charlie?'

'Beef curry,' Charlie replied.

'Hope it's all right.' Reynolds did not look convinced.

'It's beautiful,' said Charlie. 'We had a little taste downstairs.'

We had, too. And Charlie was right. It tasted all right.

But Bruce was shaking his head. 'I don't like the colour. It doesn't look right to me, Charlie.'

'Taste it, Bruce,' Charlie said brightly. 'It's lovely.'

Bruce took a spoonful. He grimaced. 'Nah, Charlie old

son,' he said, pushing his plate away. 'You've really let yourself down this time.'

Poor Charlie. He blushed with embarrassment and stood there, not knowing what to do or say. Bruce was only winding him up really, because he knew Charlie wanted to be the business. But Charlie was seething and, later, when he got me downstairs, he pulled me to one side and whispered, 'Chris, mate, we must never ever make a mistake like that again. Don't ever let Reynolds say that again.'

Although he could not cook himself Charlie acted as though he *was* the *maître d'* of a top London hotel!

His desire to do the best he could, to be a winner, stretched even onto the tennis court. In their book, *Psychological Survival*, Cohen and Taylor talk about how, to prisoners, tennis becomes a predatory game of honour, where winning becomes all important, the difference almost between life and death. And they were right.

Charlie and I teamed up for doubles and we would psyche each other up before every game. 'Come on, Chris,' he would urge, 'we've got to give everything. We've got to beat them today.' It was like that with everyone, really, but I sensed there was an extra edge to his will to win when we played Bruce Reynolds and Paul Seabourne.

Paul was a genuine guy with a pleasant nature, who became a bank robber after coming out of the merchant navy. He was an 'old-school', honourable thief with the British-bulldog spirit and he went down in prison folklore in 1964 when he helped Ronnie Biggs escape from Wandsworth in a pantechnicon, supposedly for no financial reward.

Like Charlie and me, Paul and Bruce took tennis seriously. The court was like a battlefield when we played, with the four of us doing our best to knock the shit out of the balls and playing each shot as if our lives depended on it. With each team wanting desperately to win, there was a lot of psychological winding up going on, which, of course made the battles more intense.

One day it boiled over and me and Bruce found ourselves before the governor, accused of fighting.

It all started when I was serving to Paul in a critical game that was going to win me and Charlie the match. I took my time, deliberately stoking Paul up.

'You watching this one, mate,' I said, mockingly. 'It's going to go right past your ear.'

'Yeah, yeah, I believe that,' Paul countered.

Bosh! I served a beauty that I felt brushed the line.

Paul did not move. He called out, 'Bruce. Was that in?'

'What are you asking him for?' I shouted. 'The four-eyed cunt's got glasses, but can't see nothing.'

With that Bruce came up to the net and glared at me. 'Who are you talking to like that?'

He lifted his racket, as if to warn me that I'd get a clout for insulting him. That incensed me and I ran to the net. Bruce went to whack me, but I knocked his racket aside with mine, then hit him over the head with it. We ended up having a bundle. And the next day we ended up in front of the governor, Steinhausen.

He asked us if we had anything to say, but we didn't. It was just a game of tennis that got a bit heated, we said. There was nothing more to it than that. Steinhausen asked us to apologize to each other and we did.

'That's the way it should be,' Steinhausen said. 'Worse has happened at Wimbledon. Both go away with a caution.'

Charlie was surprised that I'd got away with a caution. 'Didn't Reynolds drop you in it?' he asked.

'No,' I replied. 'Bruce wouldn't do that.'

Later that day, the four of us went back on the court to complete our unfinished business. It was still tooth-and-nail, no one giving an inch, but the needle wasn't there, thankfully. As usual, winning was all important, but I can't remember who did.

The screws often said that no man could survive more than three months in the environment we had to endure. But, as 1970 drew to a close, and I approached my thirty-second birthday, I had been there more than a year. I, along with Charlie, Bruce and Paul and the others, had conquered Durham's claustrophobic, stifling E Wing and were relatively happy there. We had become compatible, learned to know, just by looking, how each was feeling, and when we wanted space to be on our own. The visits were the worst times. There were no good visits. With relatives having to travel 400 miles, not knowing what to expect, the short time we had together was always tense, often traumatic, and, afterwards back on the wing, most of us wanted to be left alone.

The dread of the early morning 'Gestapo' was always there, but it had lessened now that I'd been there so long. And then, just when I had begun to relax, thinking they were going to leave me alone, I heard that E Wing was to be closed because it was inhumane and counterproductive to the prison system.

For my dad's sake, I prayed I would be moved nearer London. My prayers were not answered. I was sent to Albany, on the Isle of Wight.

For him, it would mean getting a train, a ferry, then a taxi to see me.

For me, it would mean the worst months of my sentence.

CHAPTER EIGHTEEN

Albany was not ready for people like me.

It had opened in 1969 as *the* brand new prison of the modern system and was like a leisure centre. There were five full-sized football pitches, a fully equipped gym that was the pride of the prison service, beautiful dining rooms and kitchen, spacious woodwork rooms and carpentry shops, and exquisitely designed churches. There was even a cinema. The gaol was intended for short-term Category C and D prisoners. And it was perfect for them.

However, the notorious Parkhurst riot of 1969 forced Albany to become a dispersal prison, taking Category A prisoners, and it caused a lot of friction because the screws did not want them there. In addition, most of the long-termers had been involved in bad situations and the screws were not trained to deal with them. Ideally, a small number of Category A prisoners should have been transferred, giving the screws a chance to get used to them. But, suddenly, top-security men from Parkhurst and other tough gaols converged on them over a short period. And the screws did not have a clue how to cope.

They were not ready for me. And I was not ready for them. I had got myself into a routine at Durham and did not want to leave the place, or the people. For the first time in my sentence, I was devastated, and filled with trepidation at what lay ahead. My main fear was that my reputation, 'one of the Kray Firm', would go before me and cause me problems, not only with the screws, but with cons out to make a point and a name for themselves. But I had another fear, deep down more worrying: that at Albany I would not be given time to read and that I'd regress, not progress. I was aware of the changes in me and I wanted them to continue. I was desperately anxious to improve myself, to learn to communicate, and not to resort to violence when I couldn't. To me, Albany was a place where I'd heard they sent old lags. And I didn't want to be one.

I was driven to Portsmouth in a white van, with five screws for company, on a dark, grey, rainswept November day. I was lonely and frightened, and when the ferry pulled away from the harbour at Portsmouth, taking me on a new journey to uncharted territory, I felt a terrible helplessness and hopelessness, as if part of me was dying.

I felt it was impossible now. I did not care any more. I had got to the point where no one could do any more to me. The sentence, the fifteen lost years of my life, I could deal with. But this – forget it.

In one gaol I'd been in, there was a sign on one of the walls: 'ABANDON HOPE ALL YE THAT ENTER HERE'. As the huge electronic gates of Britain's newest prison swung silently open, and the white van moved through it, those words came back to me. And I'd made up my mind before it stopped that, as on that journey to join the Army, in Wrexham, I would not be staying. My spell in Albany was going to be brief, no matter what.

About forty screws, intimidating and threatening in peaked caps and overcoats with collars turned up, were waiting to go off duty but seemed like another welcoming committee. As soon as I saw them I knew what was in store for me.

'Lambrianou,' said the chief prison officer, 'we are the governors. You are nothing here. Absolutely nothing. You have no power here whatsoever.'

I was not going to let them know what they were doing to me. I raised my head and looked him, and all the others, in the eye, defiantly.

The officer pointed to a small waiting room. 'In that room. Wait in there.'

'What about reception?' I asked.

'You will wait in there.'

'It's going to be like that, is it?' I said.

I went in the room and sat down. Then I got up and paced up and down, thinking a thousand thoughts: Who was on the wings? Would I know anyone? What was the food like? When would I get hold of some snout . . .?

They left me in that room for over an hour, then, around 8.30, they took me to A Wing. I was relieved to see Bobby Welch and Charlie Kray, and a couple of other guys I knew. It lifted my spirits slightly, made me feel less alone.

I had brought my toiletries from Durham, but they had not been sent onto the wing. I went downstairs to the PO's office and asked for them.

'You'll have them tomorrow,' said a screw behind the desk.

'I want them now,' I said, courteously.

'You heard me. You can have them tomorrow.'

I leaned forward, sticking my face into his. 'I want them now,' I said. 'And if I don't get them now, this office is going up.'

I was trying to communicate. But he wasn't hearing. The impotence I felt was excruciating. Threatening violence was, I believed, the only way to get my point over. There wasn't time to drop a note to the governor. And he had gone home anyway.

A screw came up behind and tried to reason with me. 'I know you're feeling uptight, but there's nothing we can do because your bag is in reception and it's locked. You've had a lot of pressure today.' He was holding a plastic cup; in his other hand was a tablet. 'Take this. It'll help you sleep.'

I pushed his hand away angrily. 'Keep away from me. I don't want that gear.'

'Please take it,' the screw said. 'If you go in the cell, not having your things, it's really going to wind you up. This will calm you down.'

He was right. I was ragged from the journey and in need of sleep, not trouble.

'All right,' I said.

I took the tablet and, in less than a minute, had passed out. The next thing I knew it was the next morning and I was in bed in my cell.

I thought I'd be staying where I was, but the screws explained it was only a reception wing, and I had to move to another part of the prison. Charlie Kray might have been behind it. He was doing only ten years, for a crime I knew he didn't commit, and he would not have wanted someone with my attitude, doing a life sentence, causing trouble that might reflect on him and set him back a few years. I don't know if this is true, but I've always believed Charlie felt I'd be an embarrassment to him.

I didn't mind being moved in the least, because one of the guys I met on C Wing was Freddie Sansom, a smashing bloke, whose nephew Kenny later played soccer for Crystal Palace and Arsenal and England. The first thing Freddie said was, 'Here you are, Slim. There's two ounces of tobacco, there's your grub, and there's your sweets – all sorted.'

The second thing he said was, 'Come down to the canteen – I want to show you something.' I stood by, intrigued, as Freddie asked the serving screw to put ten two-pound bags of sugar on the counter.

When they were all lined up, Freddie pointed at them. 'See those, Slim,' he said.

I nodded, mystified.

'That's what you're carrying round your waist. You've got to lose it.'

I stared at the twenty pounds of sugar, then down at my oversized belly. Freddie was right. I was eighteen stone, far too heavy, even for my six foot two inches. I decided, there and then, to go on a 1,000-calorie-a-day diet. It was not difficult: the food was atrocious and I did not want to eat anyway.

At that time, new parole laws had been introduced to encourage prisoners to tell the authorities what was going on, in return for an earlier release. Someone grassed me up for suggesting a sit-down strike in protest at the bad food, and I ended up doing three weeks' solitary. The governor, Gilbert Footer, was so concerned that I was a disruptive influence that he came to the segregated block where I was locked up twenty-three hours a day, and put a proposal to me: he would let me out if I assured him I would cause no more trouble. I said I could not do that, because I didn't know what I would have to cope with in the prison. I laid it on the line that I could not foresee anything but trouble because he and his staff were not equipped to deal with Category A prisoners.

The three weeks' solitary did nothing to calm me down. And when I went into the dining room for breakfast one day and heard everyone still moaning about the food, I felt I had to do something about it.

I stood in line, waiting to be served, and was charming to all the screws serving up the grub: 'Hello, there, how are you?' and all that.

It worked a treat. 'Do you want some more, mate?' said one of them. 'Yeah. Love some. Thanks, chum.' The next one, serving the bacon, was equally generous. 'Hungry today, eh? Have an extra couple of rashers.' I went down the line, accepting extra bits of this and that, until my plate was filled with a mountain of sloshy eggs, vile, yellowy baked beans, bacon, sausages. Then a screw asked me if I wanted some porridge. 'Love some,' I said, gleefully. 'Load it on there!'

I stood back, holding the tray out so the screws could see it.

'See that,' I said. 'It's SHIT!'

And I threw the tray in the air.

Seconds later, somebody in the queue behind me threw his in the air. Then someone else did the same. Soon, the dining room was filled with the sound of trays and plates hitting the floor and the screws just stood there, watching, open-mouthed, not knowing what to do. I walked through the debris and went over to the workshop, followed by the others who had chucked their food in the air.

Five minutes later ten screws came in. 'You're wanted down the wing,' one said.

'If you want me down the wing,' I said, 'you'll have to carry me.' And I lay down on the floor.

'You'll have to carry us an' all,' said the others.

The screws came to me and picked me up. I didn't resist, kept my arms and legs perfectly still, and let them carry me the hundred yards or so to the wing.

I was in my Gandhi period. I'd been reading how the great Indian leader had used non-violent disobedience to make his point, and I thought it was brilliant. The screws did not know what to make of it, and that gave me the incentive to wind them up.

'I'm not in prison,' I said, as they carried me to the chokey block. 'I'm having a day off.'

'You can't,' they said.

'But I'm not here,' I said. 'I'm not your prisoner any more.'

They looked at me as if I was off my rocker, a total lunatic.

'This is non-violent, non-co-operation,' I said, patronizingly. 'I'm following the path of peace. I'm not co-operating with you at all.'

They carried me upstairs to the chokey block and, for the second time in my life, I was charged with starting a mutiny. A little later, another five cons were charged with the same offence.

I went in front of Governor Footer, who seemed at a loss what to do with me. Finally, he released me from the chokey, with a caution, saying he needed to look into the matter further. I could not make out why he was being so lenient, but when I got back to the wing, I discovered that 400 cons had followed my 'Gandhi' protest and were sitting in the compound, refusing to move until we were freed.

After winning a small battle like that, we got more confident and the prison authorities got more frightened. When they learned we were planning more silent protests they decided to put me and three others – Freddie, a friend of his named Ali and another pal, Alan Tayne, back in the chokey block on Rule 43, Good Order and Discipline.

It was a mistake. It gave me a wonderful chance to get into my diet, lose those ten bags of sugar. Dieting and exercise became an obsession. The more weight I lost, the more I wanted to lose, and the leaner I got, the more aggressive I became. I was angry at the injustice of it all. All my choices had been taken away. I did not have a say in anything.

Nobody ever discussed my life with me. It was as though it didn't matter. Well, it still mattered to me.

I wanted to fight, to buck the system. But I was locked up in the chokey, unable to rage against anyone other than myself. So, the battle against my weight became a fight with myself. It became all important; it was as though I had to get as much weight off as possible, to win, to survive psychologically.

I got dramatically thinner. It worried the screws and they sent me to the doctor. He was shocked, said I was losing far too much. But I could not stop. It was as if I had anorexia. The thinner I got, the thinner I wanted to be. Before my diet I'd been eighteen stone. Now I was just eleven. After seven weeks, I was taken off Rule 43 and sent back to the wing. But it did nothing to lessen my resolve about my weight, and I started running around the compounds and the enclosed fields that surrounded the prison. I ran and ran and, of course, being lean and fit, I could run for a long time. Soon, the authorities started to worry, to get paranoid. What had happened to me? they wondered. What was I about? Was I in training for some spectacular, daring escape?

Finally, they sent me to see the prison psychiatrist. What, he wanted to know, did I think of my time in Albany?

I told him the truth. 'I hate it,' I said. 'I am serving an unjust sentence. I can't justify it in my own mind, let alone justify it to someone else.'

We talked it through and, finally, we got to the root of the problem. The notorious trial, and all the hype that went with it, meant that my reputation went before me wherever I went, and people expected me to live up to it. No matter where I went, I could never be myself. In people's minds, I was one of the Firm.

I had lost Chris Lambrianou and become more of a Kray than the twins' brother, Charlie!

I continued to provoke other prisoners into bucking the system, too, and eventually I was summoned to Governor Footer's office.

He came quickly to the point. 'Lambrianou. What do you want?'

I had no idea what he was talking about and said so.

'I mean precisely what I say,' he replied. 'What do you want, to get back into line and stop disrupting other prisoners?'

The penny dropped. He was offering me a deal, just like Nipper Read had offered me a deal to squeal on the Kray twins and save myself.

If I'd been sensible, I would have said, 'Actually, Gilbert, I'd like to go to a mainland prison, preferably near London, for my father's sake. I'd also like to be treated with some kind of respect and, perhaps, get some education, and go on to the Open University.'

But I wasn't sensible. I was hard-nosed, arrogant, and not about to let my mates down.

'Whatever I get, I want everyone else to have as well,' I said.

'That's not possible,' Footer replied curtly.

'But it is,' I replied, equally brusquely. 'If you give it to me, you've got to give it to them.'

I was not interested in battling for myself. I was still in my Gandhi period and knew the great man would have campaigned for benefits for the people, not just himself. It was not as if I was asking for much – just an element of freedom, improvement in the food, permission to use the TV, snooker and table-tennis rooms when we liked, and not to have such a heavy presence of screws around us all the time.

But Footer told me his deal was for me only, because of the

length of time I was serving. He could not possibly offer it to everyone. So, I turned it down and went back on the wing, leaving him surprised, and maybe a little disappointed.

I told the others we needed another protest to get what we wanted. We barricaded ourselves in our cells, but that didn't cut any ice with the screws. They sensed we were looking for trouble and left us in there. After a while, I needed to go to the toilet. When I came back, I found Freddie, Ali and Alan being held down on the floor by six or seven screws. I did not know what had gone on. But I didn't ask questions. My non-violent approach went out the window and I waded into the screws, punching and kicking whoever I could. One of them managed to get free and raise the alarm and, before I knew it, two screws had grabbed my arms, another had my legs, and I was being carried to the chokey block. There were about twenty cells there and, over the next few minutes, they started filling up with other cons involved in the battle.

I feared there would be trouble and, around eight o'clock, it started. Freddie asked to be let out to go to the toilet. The screws ignored him.

'Let me out, let me out,' Freddie screamed. Getting no response, he yelled, louder, 'LET ME OUT, YOU BASTARDS,' then started banging on his cell door with a cup or something. We all took it up, thumping our cell doors with whatever we could lay our hands on.

When the screws continued to ignore Freddie, I went to town in my cell, firstly smashing the windows with a chair, then breaking the chair itself.

It wasn't long before cons on the wings heard the racket and started banging their fists on their own cell doors in support. It was a chilling sound, like the drums of Hades, and it went on and on throughout the night. The island was put on red alert and off-duty prison staff were called in to patrol the wings with riot batons. To hear that deafening cacophony was a frightening experience, even to me who was part of it. When it went on and on, I actually wished I could turn the noise off. We had unleashed a powerfully evil force and it scared the hell out of me.

Around four in the morning, everything quietened down. No one was sleeping though. At 6.30, I heard a door open, then a commotion, with lots of yelling and screaming. I heard a screw shout, 'YOU BASTARD, TAKE THAT. GET HIM!' – followed by the sound of someone getting a beating. I learned later that it was Freddie. As soon as the screws opened his door, he ran out and threw his piss pot at the nearest one.

I heard another door open. A young kid was in there and he went out quietly to the toilet, then came back. He did not get a kicking. A third door opened and I heard another scream up, then a fourth. I was thinking, 'How am I going to handle this? I don't have to leave my cell at all. I can say, "I don't want to go to the toilet." Or I could walk out calmly, then come back to the cell without any confrontation.' Either would have been the clever approach to take. But I wasn't clever. After what had happened in the previous twelve hours or so, I was ready for aggro. I wanted it. I could not wait for it.

I picked up my pot. It was full to overflowing with piss and shit. A screw unlocked my door and enquired, 'Toilet?'

I looked past him and could see another six or seven screws behind him. 'Yes,' I said. I ran out the door and chucked the pot towards them, trying to cover as many as I could. Then I ran among them punching and kicking wildly. What I didn't know was that there were another five screws hiding in a recess, and they grabbed me from behind, sending me crashing to the floor, amid the piss and shit, and started kicking me about the head and chest and groin.

In the middle of it all, I could see a load of other screws down the corridor, all with riot sticks. There must have been seventy of them. All looking for aggro.

The only chance I had was to try to get back to my cell and reduce the odds. Only one or two could come through the door at the same time and I'd be able to get in a few punches, and the odd nut in the face. I did not have to battle hard to get in the cell. One massively built screw gave me an almighty kick and I crashed in. I staggered to my feet, covered in shit, and screamed like a madman, 'Come on, you bastards, COME ON! Kill me, bastards. Come on, KILL ME. Come here and I'll kill YOU.' I was totally gone. I was a powerfully strong, super-fit eleven stone and I meant it when I said, 'You'll have to kill me.'

They didn't fancy it. They wanted me back in the cell and locked in, alone. But they couldn't get the door shut. It opened inwards and every time they tried to pull it I was able to punch or nut one of them. Finally they managed to smash me to the ground and pull the door to, but before they could shut it, I grabbed one of the screw's arm and held on to it. The door slammed, breaking some fingers. He screamed like a stuck pig.

I staggered slowly to the bed and eased myself onto it, numb from all the pain. I felt like a boxer who had been on the receiving end of a fifteen-round hammering. But it was not just my face and upper body that was hurting. I was in agony all over. I lay on the bed, the nauseous smell of excreta and urine filling my nostrils, and passed out.

Some time later that morning, I was woken by a voice from the next cell: it was Ray Powell. 'Chris . . . Chris . . . Are you all right?'

I came round slowly. I tried to move; I couldn't. I forced a feeble laugh. 'I don't know, mate. I can't get up.'

'Try,' said Ray.

I did. But my whole body was racked with pain, as if it had seized up.

'I can't,' I said.

'Chris. Just try. Try to get to the window.'

I rolled off the bed and crawled slowly towards the window. I hauled myself up and put my head through the little square and looked towards Ray, who was looking at me through his own window. His face was a mess.

'Christ, Ray,' I said. 'They gave you a right chewing up. The bastards.'

'I hope I don't look like you,' he said.

'Don't worry about it,' I said. 'They'll have to move us now.'

I told Ray I didn't want to talk any more, to him or to anyone. I was so tired, so battered and bruised. I just wanted to get back onto the bed and sleep.

Throughout the rest of the day and the following night, I refused all food that was brought to the cell. All I wanted, I said, were the cowards who had beaten me, smashed me with their sticks. Of course, they didn't come.

Governor Footer was supposed to visit every day, but we did not see him until ten o'clock the next morning, forty-eight hours after we had started the protest.

My cell door opened. A screw said loudly, 'Lambrianou. Stand to attention. It's the governor.'

I could hardly move my body lying down, let alone stand up. I said nothing, just lay there. Footer walked in.

'Oh, my God,' he said. 'What's happened to you?'

'It don't matter what's happened to me,' I said. 'Just send

those bastards in again. Let's finish it off. I don't give a shit. I'm past hurting. Past caring.'

'No,' he said, sharply, 'It's over. It stops here. You haven't seen yourself. You're in a hell of a mess. You're going to the hospital in Parkhurst, and we're going to put right what is wrong. You won't be touched again. And you won't be touching anyone else. Do you hear me? It's *over*!'

He turned and walked out. He looked at the chief prison officer. 'Don't lock the door,' he ordered, angrily. 'You leave that man's door open.'

As the governor walked away down the corridor, the chief said, 'It's all right, Mr Lambrianou. Mr Footer's got it all under control.'

'Under control?' I said, sarcastically. '*You* gave the brief for them to come in and do this. *You* gave the brief.'

He did not have the bottle to look me in the eye.

Shortly afterwards, Footer came back, 'Parkhurst are sending a van immediately. They're getting the dogs and the Category A book and you'll be moved in a matter of minutes. They're sending a stretcher and an ambulance.'

'I'm not going to be carried out on a stretcher,' I thought. 'I'm going to get to my feet, somehow, and walk.'

As I inched myself off the bed, I felt there was not one bone or joint in my whole body that didn't ache, wasn't bruised. Somehow I got myself into my old overcoat they had brought from the wing, and shuffled slowly out the door, handcuffed on both sides. One eye was completely closed and I could only see out of a slit in the other one. But it was enough for me to see that the long, L-shaped corridor, leading to the dining halls and the main gate, was lined with dozens of screws on either side, giant screws with hatred in their eyes. I forced my bruised, aching limbs to carry me along the line and I glared at the screws with a defiant look that said, 'You haven't done me. You haven't broken me.'

CHAPTER NINETEEN

Dad broke down when he saw me.

'Chrissie, whatever happened?' he asked, through his tears. 'Why have they done this to you?'

'It was just one of those things, Dad,' I said, desperate to ease his pain. 'It happened.'

He sat beside my hospital bed, his eyes filled with sadness as the extent of my injuries sank in.

The doctors had saved my eyes, but my nose and one of my fingers were broken; I had lost five teeth; my face was cut and seven ribs were fractured. I was black and blue from head to toe, and my swollen testicles were as big as tennis balls.

When Dad got over the shock, he became angry and demanded to see the governor of Parkhurst. Gilbert Footer came over to see my father, too.

'You treated my son like an animal,' Dad said. 'He is not an animal. This is 1970, but you are still beating human beings, thinking that will make them do what you tell them. In my country, we don't beat animals, much less people. We know it doesn't get us anywhere.'

Footer was understanding. 'I know, Mr Lambrianou,' he said, sympathetically. 'And I am terribly sorry, I really am. We are trying to put everything right.'

He was in serious trouble from his superiors in London. The story of the riot had hit the national press and he was under pressure, not only to explain why I'd been given such a severe beating, but to do something about the cause of the prisoners' protest.

I was a major problem to Albany. Something needed to be done about me. But what? Certain hospital staff in Parkhurst started marking my card with what the authorities were up to, so I wasn't totally surprised when, a few weeks later, the prison's chief medical officer came to see me. He was kind, charming and smoothly seductive. After a few minutes' general chit-chat about my condition, he started enthusing about the lives patients have in Broadmoor, the hospital for the criminally insane, in Berkshire.

'They get to wear their own clothes and have money of their own,' he said. 'And there's women there. Patients can walk round the grounds with them. There are even dances.'

The alarm bells began to ring. 'They're trying to nut me off,' I thought. 'They want me declared insane to justify their action, to be able to say, "We had to do what we did because he was a dangerous, uncontrollable madman."' I wasn't having it.

'Why do I want to go to Broadmoor?' I asked. 'I can deal with prison.'

'Yes, I know you can,' the medical man said. 'But you're in for an awfully long time, Chris. You've got a recommendation. You are going to have to do fifteen years. And even then you might not get out.'

I knew that. And I knew it was going to be tough. The 1980s seemed light years away. But that didn't mean they were going to put me in with the loonies just to get them off the hook.

'I can deal with it,' I said, simply. 'I can deal with anything.'

But I knew I had to keep my wits about me, and watch

what I did. If they could provoke me into more violence, they would be able to label me a nutter.

It didn't take them long to try.

A screw handed me a shoebox that had been brought over from Albany. 'Thought you'd like your mail,' he said.

That evening, I settled down to read the letters. I got a shock. They were not for me. They were love letters from a woman to a man. And they sickened me. They were for Ian Brady from Myra Hindley.

I demanded to see the screw who had given them to me. 'Take that filth away from me,' I said.

'He's just been transferred here,' the screw whispered, motioning to another room down the corridor. 'He's three doors down.'

'What interest is that to me?' I asked.

'Just thought I'd let you know,' he said.

He claimed he had given me Brady's mail by mistake. But I was convinced he was trying to wind me up to go into Brady's room and beat him up, giving the prison ammunition to pack me off to Broadmoor.

After six weeks, I had recovered enough to be moved to a main prison, but no one was saying where. There had been no more talk of Broadmoor, but no mention of an alternative prison either. I was fairly sure it would be Hull; at least, I hoped so. One place where I wouldn't be going, I was sure, was Albany. They would not send me back to the place where I'd been beaten and kicked so badly. It would be asking for trouble.

But I was wrong. On the day I was due to leave, Parkhurst's chief prison officer came to me to tell me my escort was ready.

'Where am I going?' I asked.

'Back to Albany,' he said.

You could have blown me away. I could not believe it. I genuinely thought they would not be so insensitive. Or stupid.

And then, when the shock and disappointment had gone, I got angry. 'Right,' I thought, 'I haven't won. I am still here, still on Hell Island. Let's go and start it all again. They *want* it. They can *have* it. Only this time they'll have it worse.'

The escort van pulled up by the chokey block in Albany. As I got out, I saw one of the screws who had been one of the pack that had done me.

'All right, Chris?' he smiled, trying to be friendly.

I couldn't believe his nerve. 'All right?' I moved towards him. 'I want you. You bastard.'

The screw turned and ran across the yard and through a gate into the chokey block. Within seconds, I was surrounded by Alsatians, all yelping at my legs and going crazy at the screws. I wasn't bothered by them. I was like a wild animal myself, wanting only to get hold of my attacker. I ignored them and ran after the screw, but he got through another gate and locked it.

It was only later, when I was thinking about how much I wanted to belt him, that it dawned on me that he had run through a mass of cons playing football in the yard.

When I'd been in Albany, just seven weeks before, football had not been allowed. The only time cons went into the yard was to walk round in a wide circle, as a punishment.

'What was going on?' I wondered.

Then I came across Ali and I knew.

'We won the war, Chris,' he said, with a grin. 'We got everything we wanted.'

'You're kidding me,' I said.

'Straight up, Chris. We play football down here. We've got

tea and coffee in our cells. We have whatever snout we want. We can wander from cell to cell. We can even play cards in the chokey block.'

I thought he was winding me up.

'They're not giving us any grief at all, Chris,' he said. 'It's wonderful.'

Indeed it was. It was what I'd fought for. I was thrilled for us all. And a little proud.

I was having a cup of tea, watching a game of cards in a cell, when a screw came up to me and told me the governor wanted to see me in his office. He greeted me fairly warmly and asked how I was.

'Much better,' I said. 'And I must say I like the changes you've made since I've been away.'

Footer nodded, but said nothing.

'I'm pleased to be back, Governor,' I said. 'I'm happy to stay here now.'

'Oh, you're not staying,' he said. 'You've only come across to collect your things. We're moving you. You're going up to Hull.'

I arrived back in Hull sadder, but wiser. The system had allowed me my stand, conceded my small victory, but it always won in the end, because it could do anything it chose with me. It could simply move me around and give the problem to someone else.

I had not belonged in Albany. And I did not belong in Hull. I had a lot of London friends there, such as the Great Train Robbers Jimmy Hussey and Roy James, and Charlie Richardson's younger brother Eddie, and I commanded a lot of respect as one of them, one of the heavy Firm. But something in me had changed. I had stopped listening to people when I got my life sentence, and now I became deeply introspective and kept my own counsel. I became paranoid about letting people make decisions for me. I resolved never to place my life in anybody's hands again.

But that did not mean I was no longer a rebel. Back in March 1969 I'd decided there was only one way I'd serve my sentence, and that had not changed. So, in the summer of 1972, when someone said we should protest at being banged up while the Munich Olympics were on television, I agreed, and started organizing it.

At banging-up time a screw came into the TV room. 'OK, chaps,' he said, cordially. 'Time to go behind the door. Goodnight all.'

'Bollocks,' one of us called back.

'We're staying where we are,' someone else shouted.

The screw blushed bright red. He couldn't believe it.

Hull's governor had the same option as Gilbert Footer at Albany. He could come in very heavy, with the riot gear and all that, and cause a lot of problems. But he was an ex-soldier and prison officer; he had risen through the ranks and he was very clever.

He just said, 'Let the buggers stay out. They're doing long enough and they aren't going anywhere.'

He told the police and Army what was happening and they made the prison perimeters secure. Then he and his staff settled down to play the waiting game. He did not see his authority being threatened. And he certainly did not want to risk his gaol being smashed up by taking a confrontational attitude. He seemed to understand that all we wanted was to watch the Olympics.

So, for a week, the place was even more of a holiday camp than ever. Normally we were banged up in our cells at 8.30 p.m., but now we were wandering about the place at midnight. Many did watch the Olympics, but the rest played roulette and cards, or just strolled around the landings, drinking hooch or coffee, chatting among themselves. There was no violence, no screaming or shouting, no abuse. And no roll of the drums! We were happy just doing what we wanted, not what the regime wanted us to do.

If the governor was flustered, he never showed it. He would wander by during the day, and say, 'Hello, lads. How're you doing? How did so-and-so get on in the Olympics today?' He knew that, in the end, he would win; that if he played the waiting game, and allowed us to make our point, enjoy our little victory, we would come back into line.

That's exactly what happened. When the Olympics were over, he said, 'Right, lads. You've had your day, had your fun. Now, go back to your cells. Or I'm going to have to review the situation.'

We went quietly. We had wanted something and we had got it.

Despite the lack of violence, the governor had to take action against me and the other ringleaders of the protest. He fined everyone else a week's pay and knocked off three days' remission. But he had a problem with me because I was a lifer.

'You know I have to do something with you, Lambrianou?' he said.

'Yes,' I said.

'You will go to the chokey block and do a week behind the door.'

'Wonderful,' I thought. After all the late nights drinking and gambling, I needed some peace and quiet to do some reading – and have a good night's sleep!

One of the most memorable moments of my time at Hull was not a drinking binge or a hefty gambling win – it was a soccer match. At the time, Leeds were winning most trophies under Don Revie, and, being a Yorkshire gaol, me and the other Londoners came in for a lot of stick.

One day, we challenged the Leeds fans to a game. And from the way we all went into it, you would have thought it was the FA Cup and League Championship rolled into one! We called our rivals 'Sundays', because we always had Yorkshire pudding on Sunday and they, naturally, called us Cockneys. They had a couple of professionals, but we had twenty of the heaviest criminals around, and what we lacked in skill we made up in strength.

With Leeds currently top of the First Division, we desperately wanted to win, to restore some London pride to the prison, and we took the field with homemade coshes down our trousers to frighten the opposition. It was only a joke, to wind them up, but it proved to them that we were taking the game very seriously. Everyone in the prison knew it was a needle match and the touchlines were packed with screws and cons alike. The screws wanted the Yorkshire lads to win, naturally. And I'm sure they were secretly hoping the game would boil over into a physical battle with us all knocking lumps out of each other. It didn't happen. The game was hard, but fair. And, I'm pleased to say, the Cockneys triumphed, 1–0. Thinking about it, I'm reminded of the Michael Caine/Sylvester Stallone film, *Escape to Victory*. But that afternoon in Hull was different in one respect: the match was so important, we would have preferred to finish it, rather than escape!

One of our forwards that day was my old mate Freddie Sansom, who had been transferred from Albany. Sadly, he was to die tragically only a month or so afterwards, while playing in another match. I was watching from the line and saw Freddie fall to the ground after going up to head the ball. When he didn't get up I ran over and held him in my arms, but he had had a brain haemorrhage and was dead. I, like all the other Londoners, was devastated, totally inconsolable, and I couldn't wait to be on my own. It hit me so hard. Freddie was only thirty-five, and a dear mate. He had more bottle than anyone I'd ever met in my life. His widow, Elsie, was a lovely woman who knew we were good mates, and wrote to me a couple of times, trying to ease my pain.

A couple of months later I was reminded of Freddie when a nice-looking kid in his early twenties, named Kenny Richardson, knocked on my cell door, wanting a chat.

'Come in, son,' I said. 'What's the problem?'

'Chris, do you mind if I come and eat my dinner with you?' He looked terrified.

'What's the matter with you?' I asked.

He pulled out one of the biggest knives I'd seen in my prison experience. It was like a sword. 'If they come anywhere near me, I'm going to do them.'

'Kenny, calm down, mate,' I said. 'What're you going on about? Who's they? And what are they going to do?'

'There's a little firm upstairs who're going round raping guys. Gang-banging them.' He looked at his knife. 'If they try it with me, they're going to get it. I'm doing ten years. I've nothing to lose.'

Kenny was inside for killing a guy, and by the look of him he meant what he said. I didn't want to get involved, but I knew how I would feel in the same position. Homosexuality had always appalled me after that petrifying experience in the bushes in Ibstock, as a six-year-old. I remembered my horror one day, in Albany, when Freddie Sansom tried to fix me up with a young gay.

'Come with me, Slim,' he had said. We went to my cell and, inside, was an effeminate kid of about twenty-two, with long hair, cleaning it out. When I asked what was going on, Freddie said, 'You're doing a long time, mate. You're going to need someone to look after you. It's the right thing.'

'Right thing!' I was furious. It was as if Freddie had found me a bird. I turned to the queer. 'I don't want to be offensive, mate, but I don't want to know. I can do my own cleaning. I can wash my own windows. I can do my own fetching and carrying. And, as far as the other thing's concerned, I've got the five-fingered widow, thanks. Now, please, get out of my cell.'

I wasn't angry with Freddie. He knew I was doing a long stretch – with the possibility of *never* getting out – and was acting with the best of intentions. Later, he tried to explain why he had done it.

'You've got to find yourself some kind of life in prison,' he said. 'It's not about settling down, but just keeping your head above water – and sex is one of your emotional needs.'

I would not have any of it. 'I'm like you, Fred,' I said. 'You've got children, you understand. How could I stand in front of my daughter, as her dad, if I'm messing around with another man?'

The whole idea repulsed me. No matter if I was in prison the rest of my days, I could not succumb to homosexuality. So, now, in Hull, I could not ignore Kenny Richardson.

It was difficult, however, because the only thing we had in common was that he came from the north-east, where my mum and her family had lived; hardly a solid base for an easy relationship. In the end, I agreed to take him under my wing, but only as a 'gofer', fetching my dinner and making the tea. I didn't want other cons thinking he was a friend of mine and jumping to the wrong conclusions.

Me and Kenny and Ronnie Bender worked in the spray

shop and it was there that I was responsible for something that left me feeling, uncharacteristically, bad.

A civilian instructor came to work with us and he was such an affable, easy-to-talk-to type of bloke that I said to the others, 'I bet we can get into him, bend him.'

The guy was not searched at the gate, so he was able to bring in tobacco and drink. It worked well for a time, but one of the other cons grassed on him, in return for early parole, and the instructor was sacked, then taken to court and fined. I felt bad and thought of telling the authorities he had only done it because I'd terrorized him. But Charlie Richardson's brother, Eddie, talked me out of it, because it might rebound on me.

I wanted to get hold of the grass, but he was moved to a local gaol and, a few months later, I was transferred myself – to Gartree.

For me, it was the thin end of the wedge. There had been a riot at Gartree, with Tony as one of the ringleaders, and the Home Office, in its wisdom, decided to remove one Lambrianou and replace him with another. While Tony enjoyed the luxury of Wormwood Scrubs, I caught the backlash of the 1972 Gartree riot.

They were not pleased to see me at all and, for the first three months, I was banged up twenty-three hours a day. The only time I was allowed to mix with the other prisoners was during an hour's exercise when I played football, worked out in the gym or simply walked round and round the yard. If I did have to go anywhere else, such as the hospital or visiting hall, two prison officers and their dogs came with me. Cameras followed us all the way, of course.

I did not mind three months on my own. Being thrown into a different prison and having to get to know lots of different people all over again can be quite an ordeal and, anyway, there were a lot of heavy books I wanted to read.

While better than being in the main prison, solitary confinement did rebound on me. Never knowing if I was going to be woken in the middle of the night had destroyed my sleep pattern and now, doing nothing all day except read, I found it difficult to turn off at all. I'd be so weary, I'd drop off during the day, then lie awake all night. I could just about bear it in solitary, but when I was released and went onto the wing, I had to do something about it.

I asked to see the prison doctor, a skeletal, Ebenezer Scrooge-like character, more like an accountant than a doctor, who was so religious he had no fewer than a dozen statues of Jesus and the Virgin Mary in his office, which he assured me would cast away all evil spirits.

When I told him I could not sleep, he said he'd give me some medication and, at 8 p.m. that night, I joined the queue for medicine.

'Here you are, Lambrianou, Mandrax liquid,' said one of the medical screws.

I told them I needed more than one measure, so they gave me a second, and I collapsed on the floor quite drunk.

Sometimes the Mandrax liquid had not been made up and I was given tablets. One was enough to take you off to another planet, but I was conning the screws out of four at a time and taking them all at once.

My medication was later changed to sodium amytal, which provided the most amazing experience. It was like having a hundred pints of beer or ten bottles of wine. I remember walking along the corridor after taking some, feeling as though my body was vibrating as I put one foot in front of the other. Both these drugs and another I was given – Tuinal – were later banned.

It was so easy to con poor Ebenezer.

'Hullo, doctor,' I'd say. 'I'm sure I've got an ulcer.'

'What makes you think that?' he'd want to know. I'd quote the symptoms I'd read in a medical book and he would authorize me to have boiled fish and a pint of milk.

Getting the basic plastic prison shoes replaced with leather ones was just as easy. I secretly rubbed my feet with a bit of leather until they were virtually red raw, then hobbled into the doctor's office. 'How are you getting on, Lambrianou?' he enquired, cheerily.

'I'm reasonably OK, doctor,' I replied. 'But these shoes are making my feet sore – and I'm getting athlete's foot – I really need a different pair.'

He prescribed some cream – and ordered me to be given a pair of black patent-leather ones. It was these little victories over the system that kept me going. Now, of course, prisoners are serving their time in Nike trainers and Admiral tracksuits.

There was a long period of stability at Gartree. The screws had had enough of confrontations. The 1972 riot had worn them out. Now all they wanted was to get on with their lives. Sometimes, though, it must have been hard, because there were certain prisoners who were on the lookout for trouble morning, noon and night.

One of them was a six-foot-four, massively built, fearsome-looking West Indian in his early thirties named Les Hilton. He was inside for beating someone up in a row over prostitution in Yorkshire. He liked baiting most screws, but none more than Ron Bell, an equally big, gorilla-like rugby player, considered the toughest screw in the gaol.

We were queuing for our food one day when Bell glared at Les. 'Come on, Hilton,' he said. 'Move it along.'

Hilton did not move an inch. He glared back at Bell. Then

he growled, 'Let me tell ya something, Dingabell. Come the revolution, when the blacks take over, the first house I'm coming to is yours. I'm going to rape your daughter; I'm going to rape your wife. I'm going to give 'em both the most severe seeing to. And I'm going to tie you up and make you watch. And, then, my friend I'm going to do you, too!'

I feared the worst. I thought no human being, particularly one in a position of power, could take that. I watched Bell's face getting redder and redder and waited for him to explode. But he swallowed it and said nothing.

His tough image took a bad knock that day, but it was a totally different encounter with Ronnie Bender that made Bell a laughing stock throughout the whole prison.

Ronnie, who we called the Captain, was a kind, generous bloke, who went out of his way to lift everyone's spirits. One day, we were in the breakfast queue when Bell walked by. Ronnie suddenly started sniffing the air, loudly and theatrically.

'Who's got that aftershave?' he enquired. 'It's amazing. Absolutely wonderful.'

Most of us in the queue knew there was going to be a crack at the end of it. But we didn't know what.

'It's me,' Bell said, proudly, in his thick northern accent. 'It's my aftershave.'

Bender, who is about six foot two inches, left the queue and walked up to the big, bluff Yorkshireman. He took Bell's face in his hands, then held it still, while he gave him a full-blooded kiss on the lips.

Horrified, Bell struggled to get away. 'Get off, Bender,' he hissed, his face screwed up in distaste. 'Get off me!'

Then Ronnie released him and walked, nonchalantly, back to the queue. The rest of the screws were doubled up with laughter, but Bell did not see the funny side and slunk off to the staff canteen. Later, I heard the other screws wound him up further by blowing kisses and saying, 'Bender's after you.'

Whenever Bell saw Ronnie after that, he would turn and go off in the opposite direction. He knew how to cope with violence and aggression, but had no idea how to deal with what Ronnie did to him. Ronnie destroyed his macho, tough-guy image with a kiss.

That should have taught me a lesson in making one's point, but it didn't. A problem developed on the wing over a Home Office directive about furniture in the cells and immediately I got busy, organizing a two-day hunger-cum-sit-out strike. We liked the cells the way they were. We had been allowed to put up paintings and posters on the wall and all sorts of sentimental photos and the like on our notice boards. All of us had tried to make our cells as homely as possible and, at the same time, reflect our individual personalities. But now the authorities wanted us to have the same, dull, boring basic furniture. We won the day: the cells stayed as they were. But several of us, including Ronnie Bender, had to go before the governor charged with disobedience. Ronnie and I were given three days' bread and water in the chokey. When I came back on the wing, the chief prison officer summoned me to his office.

'I'd better warn you, Lambrianou,' he said, 'there are problems on the wing. The IRA have been running you and Bender down. It could be very serious.'

I went to my cell, put my bedding in, then went to a nearby cell and confronted four IRA terrorists.

'I understand you've got a problem with me,' I said.

They all looked puzzled. 'We haven't got a problem with you, Chris,' they said. 'We've a lot of respect for you.'

'I've heard you have been slagging off me and Ronnie Bender,' I said.

'We've got a problem with him,' they admitted.

'If you've got a problem with him, then you've got one with me,' I said.

I asked what it was all about and they told me they had heard that Bender had been talking about them to the screws. It didn't help that he was an ex-Army paratrooper.

'Something's not right here,' I told them. 'Ronnie is his own man. He won't have been bad-mouthing you to any screw.'

The terrorists asked how I had heard they were upset. I told them. Then I took them down to the chief prison officer.

'Would you mind repeating in front of these guys what you told me?' I said.

'What's that?' the PO replied.

I repeated what he had told me, but he denied it. 'I didn't say anything of the kind.'

'Come on, Bert,' I said. 'You know you did. Has Bender given you any information?'

'No.'

'What is it? What do you want? To see us give them a hiding? Is that what you want?'

His eyes gave him away. Of course, that's what it was all about. There were a group of them – all ex-military staff – who wanted to have the IRA over. And they wanted to stoke Ron and me up to do it.

There was no way we were going to do it. The terrorists were not hard men and they would have been easy to have over. But they had always been polite and kept themselves to themselves. They did not give us any grief and I didn't see any reason why we should give them any. Certainly I would not be used for that purpose.

Afterwards, however, the screws started giving me hassle: little privileges I'd been allowed to get away with suddenly stopped, and my cell would be thoroughly searched with no warning. When I questioned it, I was told that every prisoner got 'spun' every so often. But it didn't wash. I was being punished for not allowing Bender and myself to be used as a tool by ex-military personnel with vengeance in their hearts.

There was an Eastender on the wing named Tony Turner; 'Tubsy' Turner most people called him. I'd fallen out with him over something petty and we were not on speaking terms. But when a screw came up to me, ashen-faced, and asked me to help with a very serious matter concerning Tony, I agreed.

'What's the problem?' I asked.

'His wife drove away from Harrods this morning, after doing some shopping, and had a brain haemorrhage. She's dead. She was only twenty-eight or twenty-nine.'

The screw was carrying a medical box, containing syringes. He was planning to give Tony a shot to sedate him after breaking the news.

'Let me handle it,' I said. 'Come up in five minutes or so, but let me talk to Tony first.'

I walked along the wing. Tony, who was a cleaner, was sweeping the corridor.

'Hello, Tony,' I said. 'How you going, mate?'

He was surprised, but pleased, I had spoken to him.

'Hi, Chris,' he replied. 'I'm all right. How are you?'

'Tony,' I said. 'I've got to have a word with you about something.' I motioned towards his cell. 'Let's go in there.'

I told him to sit on his bed, I sat down and put an arm round him, 'It's killing me to tell you this, Tony, and I don't know how I've got the strength to do it, but . . . your wife died this morning.'

He turned his head and looked into my eyes. 'You're telling

me that . . .' But he didn't finish. He just let out the most deafening, piercing, primeval scream.

Tears streaming down my face, I put both my arms round him and pulled him towards me, hugging him tightly, until that initial shock gave way to pain, and he just cried and cried.

I had to talk to him, but I didn't know what to say. All I could think of was my own miserable marriage, so I started letting out some of my own pain and hurt.

'Tony,' I said, quietly. 'I just wish I'd had some of the happy times, like you had. You've been a good husband and you and your wife cared for each other, but I've been a right bastard. I never respected Carol, and treated her like dirt, always putting myself first.'

We sat in that cell, two big men, locked in an unlikely embrace, crying our eyes out, and I was crying for myself, and Carol, as much as for Tony. We sat there for two hours, and then I said, 'Come on, mate. We've really got to go now. I've got to get you over to the hospital, so you can get away and have some time on your own.'

In a top-security gaol, there is a long, complicated procedure before doors are opened, but on that walk over to the hospital, all the doors opened almost before we reached them.

When we reached the hospital, I sat with him another hour, then said, 'Are you OK, Tony? Would you like to be on your own now?'

'Yes,' he said. 'Yes, I would.'

'I'll be around if you need me,' I said, and left Tony in the care of a doctor.

Tony stayed in the hospital for four days. I visited him every day. He needed a friend and had come to lean on me. We had had our differences and he had disappointed me. But I could not desert him.

The day Tony Turner buried his wife, I buried mine; not literally, of course, but I got rid of all the anger and bitterness that had been eating away inside me since the day Carol refused to get on the bus and walked out of my life forever. It was a dark, dark day for Tony, but it was bright for me, as I stepped out into the light for the first time in six years, no longer feeling grief and pain at all the wasted, selfish years, but looking towards the future, whatever that might hold.

When Tony came back on the wing, they gave him a job on the hot-plate, and allowed me to work with him, as a reward for helping him over his grief. To be given the privilege of a soft job outside of a heavily guarded workshop was a miracle – a real blessing – and I accepted it, hungrily.

When Tony was transferred to Chelmsford he was worried about leaving me, and asked if I could go, too. But, of course, that was impossible. I was good to do what I did, but I was still a hard-nosed, violent, Kray Firm man and not good enough to go to a non-dispersal prison.

I was a guest of Her Majesty – but that did not stop me taking a holiday!

For a week every March, I would say, 'That's it – I'm not a prisoner any more. I'm not working on the hot-plate. I'm going to have a break.' And I would go to the sick bay and feign an illness that prevented me doing anything other than lying in bed.

My 'holiday' destination was always Cheltenham race-course for the annual end to the hurdling season. I would lie in bed, studying form, and have a bet with whoever was the prison bookmaker at the time, using tobacco as currency. I would listen to the races on the radio, shouting encouragement to my horses, as though I was there.

I always enjoyed my 'holiday'. I was confined to my cell,

officially sick, and an orderly would bring meals to my bed-side. The screws almost certainly knew I was not really unwell, but they always turned a blind eye, because one week off in a year, when I was serving so long, was no big deal.

During Cheltenham Festival Week, in 1975, Stuart Brown, a prisoner in an adjoining cell, came in to see me. It was a short visit, and we didn't speak much. But what Stuart did that afternoon had a startling effect on my life.

Stuart was a small, gritty Scot, who resembled the actor Charles Bronson. He was not the type of guy who would ask if he could do anything for you – he would just do it, and you would accept that he was doing it for the right reasons. On this particular day, he must have seen something in me that, despite my 'holiday', worried him, because he suddenly left the cell and returned with a poster, which he stuck on the wall in front of me.

The poster was of an American footballer. He was sitting on a bench, his head down, holding his helmet in his hand. It was a picture of dejection, symbolizing defeat. Above the footballer were the words: 'I QUIT.' Beneath the picture there was a smaller, but more powerful and poignant line: 'I DIDN'T – Jesus Christ.'

Stuart, who was serving seven years for grievous bodily harm, did not say one word to me about Christ, or religion generally. He just put up the poster and left it there, hoping that the message would sink in, the more I looked at it. He was spot on: it hit me like a ton of bricks.

The more I looked at the poster, the more I felt I *had* quit; emotionally anyway. My earliest release date, 1984, still seemed light years away and there was always the terrible dread that I would be kept far longer, perhaps forever. I had to admit that the fight had gone out of me. I had sunk into a depression, accepting the worst, whatever that might be. And then I found myself thinking of poor 'Tubsy' Turner, how my bad feelings to him had changed in his hour of need, and how I had gained something worthwhile from helping him; had actually been rewarded by the prison system. Over the next few weeks, I found myself staring at the defeated footballer, thinking that, perhaps, my life could improve if I took a more positive line with people and generally eased up a little, thinking more of others and less about myself.

I was right. The more I gave of myself, the more I seemed to get back. Cons and screws alike started seeing a different side to me, a less aggressive, more understanding and likeable side. And I started seeing a different side, too – one that I liked and felt comfortable with.

And then, just as I felt myself adapting to the changes in me, I was told that my brother, Tony, was being transferred to Gartree from Wormwood Scrubs.

And I knew it would mean only one thing . . . Trouble.

CHAPTER TWENTY

Tony had not changed. He was still self-centred, still mean, still pig-headed. And he was still living up to the image of one of the Kray Firm.

At first, I was overjoyed to see him, pleased that, with us under one roof, the old man would have to make only one journey to see us. But the more I saw Tony strutting around the gaol, the more it hit home to me how different we were; how, deep down, I didn't like him at all. With Tony, it was always me, me, me – never us. If I went to him saying I needed something, he would say he did not have it, even though I knew he had. He was very confrontational and we would have rows that ended up fuelling my bitterness towards him for putting us where we were.

'We're doing this bird because of you,' I'd rant. 'You got us into this. And we'll be paying for it for a very long time yet.'

And then we'd be off, often coming to blows.

It was not just his love of the Krays that angered me, I felt that he knew something was going to happen to Jack McVitie that night in October, and had said nothing to warn me, to give me the chance to get not only myself, but both of us, out of it. He roped me in to look good in the twins' eyes. That's the bottom line. I was his brother, his flesh and blood, who had cared for him all his life. But it wasn't me he cared about, it was them. Ron and Reg.

Unlike him, I did not want to live up to the Kray image; I never had, I'll admit being linked with them had proved useful in prison: there was a lot of protection, like a ring of fear, round me, which saved me a lot of aggro. But the link also brought its problems, with other cons wanting to make a name for themselves by having 'one of the Firm' over.

Now, in 1975, with nearly eight years of my sentence behind me, I had done a lot of soul-searching, read a lot of enlightening literature, and had, in my mind, shaken off the Kray image, thrown away the rotten carcass that had burdened me for so long. I had been a Kray man in so many eyes that I had believed it myself, but now I was finding the real me. I had grown my hair fashionably long and had become a bit of a hippie, preferring a puff on a joint to a punch up. Many took the change in me the wrong way – and one of them, who should have known better, was Ronnie Bender.

One morning, I walked into Ronnie's cell, while he was chatting to Tony.

'Chris doesn't know who he is, Tone,' Bender said.

What he meant was that I had changed. What he could not understand was why. I had not lost my identity; I was finding it.

While they were trapped in a time warp, still acting, thinking, speaking as they did in the 1960s, I was emerging from the evil mists that had all but destroyed me, into a bright new dawn where all was quiet and tranquil.

They thought I was off my rocker. But I was becoming saner by the minute; it was the madness I was leaving behind.

It was only a matter of time before Tony and I had a major blow up. What was surprising was that it took as long as it did.

For five months, we managed to live different lives. Although we were on the same Category A Wing, his cell was on another landing fifty yards away and we didn't have to see each other if we didn't want to. He had his friends and I had mine, and often we would go weeks without speaking. If we did meet accidentally, we would simply glare at each other, then walk on, saying nothing. We had nothing to talk about. If I'd wanted to, I could have gone out of my way to patch things up. But I hated Tony so much at times that I simply could not bear to have anything to do with him. He was so devious I felt I couldn't trust him. I didn't feel right around him. He was always liable to do the wrong thing for the wrong reason.

One day that summer I decided to go to Tony's cell. I needed a cigarette and felt sure he would have some tobacco. He said he didn't. But I could see it on a table.

'Come on, Tony,' I said. 'There's some there.'

'That's all I've got,' he said. 'It's got to last me all day.'

That was a lie. Tony always had tobacco.

'How can you do that?' I said. 'How can you be so mean?'

'You're always wanting something,' he said. 'Why don't you go and get it, like I get it?'

I couldn't believe it. I had an arrangement with a screw who smuggled in dope for me, and I willingly gave Tony half, despite our differences.

'Are you turning me down for a cigarette?' I said. 'After all I've given you?'

'You stay out of my face. Get away from me.'

My anger, frustration, all the familiar bitterness, rose up inside me. 'Who are you talking to? How dare you talk to me like that. You prat!'

'Get out of my cell.'

'Do you want a row?'

And then it was off. He rushed at me and caught me with a right-hander. I staggered back against the cell wall, then came back and got in one of my own. We were banging each other about a bit when a mass of screws appeared. They stood back, however, not wanting to get involved, because they knew that we could turn on them.

'Come on boys,' one said. 'This isn't on – you're brothers.'

We took no notice. We were more interested in knocking lumps out of each other.

'*Come on*,' the screw said, 'or your dad will be visiting different gaols again.'

That did it. We were still snarling at each other, still angry, but we calmed down, and I allowed myself to be taken back to my cell. I sat for over an hour, seething, and it took all my self-control not to revert to my bad ways and smash the cell up in frustration. I had a brother. But I didn't like him. He did not have an ounce of generosity of spirit in him. The meanness ran right through his life.

We appeared in front of the governor, on good order and discipline charges, and were asked to try and get along together. We said we would, not necessarily for ourselves, but for our father. It was not easy.

Dad was the one person who dominated my thoughts. I would sit in my cell, staring at the poster Stuart Brown had put on my wall, and I'd think, 'Christ wasn't the only one who didn't quit – my dear old dad didn't either.' He could have been forgiven for washing his hands of us, but he was still travelling hundreds of miles to see his boys, still thinking of us, not himself; still listening to our pain, not telling us his, even though, at times, he must have been in total despair. For nearly eight years now, he had been coming to see us, arriving tired and broken, but always forcing himself to walk into the visiting room in good spirits, determined to lift ours.

I would stare at the poster. And I would think of my dad,

the one person who had never deserted me; who, despite everything, loved me too much ever to let me see the tears of his pain and anguish and humiliation. He was the epitome of Christ to me; he was all I had that was worth anything.

I would think of the Kray twins, of the life I had allowed them to steal from me. I had stood up and denied things I knew to be true, and where had it got me?

About seven months later, Stuart was released. Before he left, he came to me and told me to help myself to some books he was leaving in his cell. Then he shook my hand and said, 'I have a feeling you won't forget me.'

It was a Sunday evening. Outside, the sun had been shining all day, from a clear blue July sky, and it was still warm. I was lying on my bed in my cell, listening to the radio. Suddenly I heard the distinctive voice of Bob Dylan singing 'Knockin' on Heaven's Door' on a record, on the landing below. I tried to listen to what was being said on the radio, but the words kept invading my mind, making it hard to concentrate.

Finally, the record stopped and I picked up the thread of the broadcast. But then, seconds later, it started again and I found I was not hearing the radio, only the song. Dylan's poignant lament obviously meant something to whoever was playing it because the record was playing over and over and over again. And the more it played, the more I wanted to hear it. I switched off the radio and lay on my bed, my eyes closed, thinking how much the words meant to me, too. 'Take these guns . . . I can't use them any more . . .' Dylan was talking to me, I was sure of that. All the violence in my life was gone, he was telling me; there was no justification for it any more.

Over and over, the record played, and I lay there, stretched out on my metal bed in the prison within a prison that was my home, thinking of all the wasted years of my life. 'Look over there,' a voice told me. 'You have your father, the epitome of Christ in your eyes, and you have let him down, shamed him in his dying years, when all he wanted was what was good and right and decent for you. Look over there. You have no wife to support you, no child to love you, no home, no friends . . . You have nothing. You *are* nothing.' As Dylan sung about it getting too dark to see, the voice continued.

'Look behind you. Nothing. Look in front of you. Nothing. Just the grey nothingness of the prison world and the empty years of a wasted, selfish life.'

Suddenly I was aware of my heart pounding, and then it was as if a thick, black cloud descended on my cell, enveloping me; an evil, clammy darkness, so real, so physical I could almost touch it.

I felt blood surging through my veins, a boiling, molten scarlet blood, and I turned and twisted on my bed, fighting the anger, the frightening evil fury, raging inside me.

And then the voices started again in my head.

'You are never getting out. You have fought the system to the very end. They don't like you. You gave your life away to the Krays. You are never getting out. This is forever . . .'

And then: 'Think how you feel now. This emptiness, this nothingness, this loneliness. This is how you're going to feel forever. It's never going to change.'

Frightened by the force inside me, I jumped off the bed and went to the mirror. Looking back at me was a scowling, snarling, sneering beast, shocking in its ugliness, and it was screaming, 'Kill yourself. You're never getting out. End it. End it all, Chris.'

Somewhere, deep inside my twisted soul, I heard another voice, faint, but insistent, pleading with me to drag myself out of the madness, to do something positive to break the evil spell, before it pulled me over the line and past the point of no return.

I remembered the books Stuart Brown had given me when he left. I went to a box under my bed and opened it, looking for Krishnamurti's *Kingdom of Happiness*. I couldn't find it. I started chucking hardbacks and paperbacks over my cell, looking for something else, something appropriate, something to calm me down.

And then my hand fell on a Gideon Bible. I didn't know it was there. It wasn't mine. And I couldn't remember Stuart giving it to me.

'What do I want that for?' I asked myself. 'I'll never read that.'

I threw it down and looked for something else. I picked up a light thriller. That wasn't what I wanted, either. I went through dozens of other books, and then, for some reason I could not understand, I found myself picking up the Bible again.

People had talked to me about this New Testament Jesus bloke, who walked up hillsides, telling cripples to get up and walk, but it had cut no ice with me. If it had been real it would have been happening all over the place, to everybody, and we would have had a nice world, without wars and all the problems. It was rubbish, I thought.

But I decided to give it a go, anyway.

I can never start things halfway through, so I started reading the first page of Genesis, about how the world was created. I gave up after a couple of minutes. 'It's rubbish to me,' I told myself. 'What do I want to know about that?'

But I couldn't let the book go; I didn't know what it was, but there was something there. A power. I put the Bible under my pillow, thinking that if indeed there were any good thoughts in the book, they would come through to me. I lay

in the darkness, exhausted, but unable to sleep. I kept thinking of the Bible, saying over and over to myself, 'If there
is anybody there, let me know. I don't believe, but if there is
someone there, please let me know . . .' I didn't feel comfortable with the Bible under the pillow; I wanted it nearer.
I took it and clutched it against my heart and closed my
eyes, fighting to control the rage burning inside me. Finally,
mercifully, I dropped off to sleep. It was around three in the
morning. I had been fighting the devil for nine hours.

At 6.30, the screws opened my door. I had to go to the
washroom, but I dreaded it. I feared the word would have got
round that I'd had a nervous breakdown, finally cracked.

I didn't want to let go of the Bible, but I knew I couldn't
walk into the washroom holding it. The other cons would
think I'd finally flipped my lid. I was thinking that I would
have some terrible battles on my hands, simply to survive,
when I heard a voice inside me, 'You don't need to do that.
Just take me with you.'

I picked up the Bible and stuffed it down my trousers. If
it dropped on the floor, I'd say it was for protection, in case
anyone came at me with a knife. I went into the washroom,
fearing the reaction. I need not have worried. 'Hello, Chris.
How you doing – all right?' a couple of guys said, cheerily.

'Yeah, lovely,' I replied. 'Nice to see ya.' Then other cons
came in and greeted me as normal, as though nothing had
happened.

Later that morning, I went to the workshop, the Bible still
down my trousers. I had this overpowering desire not to let
go of it, to have it close to me all day long. I didn't dare
let anyone know about it, or what was happening to me. I
didn't really know myself.

I started reading the Bible secretly in my cell and then
I started thinking about Christ more and more. One day I

woke up and found myself thinking, 'If Christ does, indeed, come again, he won't come in the way we think. Who knows, he may be in the next cell. If he is, how am I going to treat him?'

I started seeing Christ in every prisoner I met, and talked to them in the way I would talk to Christ. I started to lighten up and let people into my life, into the deeper part of me, and I found them responding to that. Alone in my cell in the evening, I would get down on my hands and knees and pray, thanking the Lord for the day, and then I found myself being grateful for little things – not the big ones, like opening the prison gates and walking out a free man. I didn't want that any more. I just wanted to be at peace in the day and, maybe, make what life I had a little better.

I was not a religious fanatic. And I was not off my trolley. I felt I was the sanest I'd been in my whole life.

They knew something was going on in my head, however, because, a few months later, in November 1977, I was moved to Maidstone, in Kent.

And that's where I had the most wonderfully exhilarating and enlightening experience that would change my life.

CHAPTER TWENTY-ONE

They transferred Tony to Maidstone as well. We were pleased about going to a relatively softer gaol, and being taken off Category A for the first time in nine years, but the move worried me. The gaol would be full of kids fresh off the street, serving shorter sentences, who would not know my kind of people. I wondered what effect they would have on me, and me on them. Would the whole Kray thing start all over again? In short, would I have problems? And, given the beginnings of my new outlook on life, would I be able to survive?

Fortunately, I saw a familiar face soon after arriving – Bruce Reynolds. I hadn't seen him since Durham, and I felt I needed to apologize again for that insult on the tennis court. I went up to him and offered my hand.

'Bruce,' I said, 'I want you to know that I didn't mean it when I called you a cunt. I *really* didn't mean it. You have never been that. It was something I said in the heat of the moment. I'm sorry.'

Looking me straight in the eye, Reynolds said, 'I've waited seven years for you to say that to me, Chris. It pleases me so much that you have.'

I was surprised Reynolds had harboured a grudge all that time. What I'd called him was said in the middle of a life-or-death game, when we'd all been psyched up, and I'd forgotten about it. I was glad I'd cleared the air. Obviously my calmer, more understanding, outlook on life was working. I think Reynolds recognized the change in me.

I continued to secretly read the Bible and was doing my best to see good in people, but the violent beast was still in me if things did not go my way. I had got used to taking drugs to help me sleep, for instance, and at Maidstone it was made clear I was not going to get them.

When I asked a medical screw for some Mandrax, saying my notes were being sent on from Gartree, he told me to come back the next day and speak to Dr Smitherman.

I saw red. Dr Smitherman was a psychiatrist at Albany during the riot. He and I had never got along. I picked up a chair. 'Come back tomorrow!' I yelled. And I started smashing the chair against the orderly's office wall.

'Come out of there,' I roared. 'Give me my drugs. I want 'em. You can't stop me. I've been having 'em for years.'

I was like a wild animal and I must have terrified the orderly. But it did no good. 'We can't give you drugs just like that,' he said. 'We need paperwork. Only Dr Smitherman can do it.'

But, the next day, Dr Smitherman would not do it. He refused to give me any drugs at all.

He told me, 'You are out of the stressful conditions of Category A and in a very loose environment. It's time to come off those drugs. They're not good for you. And you don't need them.'

'I *do* need them,' I said. 'I've been on them years. I need them desperately.'

'You probably think you do,' he said, 'but you don't. And I'm not going to let you have them. You'll be all right.'

I went into one, accusing him of getting his revenge on me for all the trouble I'd caused at Albany. But he said he wasn't. It was simply that *no one* at Maidstone was given any drugs.

There was nothing I could do. Breaking down all the walls in his office was not going to get me anywhere. I had to accept it. But coming off the drugs that had helped me survive for nine years would prove a nightmare from which I thought I would never wake and which, I was convinced, would plunge me back, even deeper, into the dark depths of madness from which I thought I'd escaped.

It was like cold turkey: my body needed to be cleansed of all the toxins that had been poisoning it for nine years. The 'liquid cosh' that had kept me more or less manageable had to be dried out.

It was a terrifying experience. For me. And for everyone else. During the day, nobody could control me. I was a walking storm of anger, raging at everyone, convinced cons and screws alike were plotting against me. At night, I hallucinated for hours on end, tossing and turning and yelling out to imaginary enemies and, when I woke in the morning, my sheets would be soaked in sweat.

My fear was heightened when I thought back to Vic Batty, who was in the hospital at Gartree when I took Tony Turner there. I'd heard him wrecking his cell because he wanted his drugs. He was going to be given drugs all the time he was on Category A, but only when the doctors said he could have them. Finally, Vic could take no more and killed himself by setting his cell on fire. He was only thirty-two.

I didn't feel like killing myself. At the same time, I was going out of my mind, not knowing what to do to keep the demons at bay. I would walk around the prison in a long, grey overcoat, a grotesque and ugly figure with shoulder-length hair, a long beard, my face contorted into weird expressions. I was like a wild man from another country, or an alien unable to communicate on even the most basic level. A million and one things were turning over in my head, but I could not string two sensible thoughts together. Everyone was convinced I was off my head and shouldn't be there. They were right. I was caught on the brink of insanity, wandering around in a mystifying no-man's-land, not knowing what was real any more.

There was nobody I could talk to, nobody to counsel me and talk me through what was happening to me. Even my brother was no use. All he would say was, 'I can't talk to you any more. You're not the same man. Do *you* know who you are?'

I'd say, 'Tony, leave me alone. I know what I'm doing. I'm my own man. I've got it under control. I *do* know who I am.'

I didn't know. I didn't have a clue. But I had to convince *him* I did.

I was angry, and would fly into a rage at the slightest provocation. Once I picked up a huge canister of tea and whacked Jimmy Humphries, the Soho Porn King, for taking one liberty too many. But the 'other' me hated the violence, and I would retreat behind my cell door and read my Bible, praying that someone would tell me what was happening to me.

I would get down on my knees, my face in my hands, and say, 'Jesus, if you are really there, come and help me. I have done too long. I can't do any more. I didn't kill anybody. I don't want to be this person. Help me change. Help me get out.'

The Bible had brought me through a crisis in my life and I clung to it. But I could not see how it could change me. I had still got to fight, whether I wanted to or not.

I didn't want the violence. I wanted to be free, to mix with people on the street, to integrate with them, show them I could be a polite, charming, warm man, a 'decent citizen'. But I was locked in a human zoo where I needed to be an animal to survive.

It was a weird existence. One minute, it seemed, I was raging like a wounded lion, lashing out all my bitterness and hate on anyone who said a wrong word; the next, I was a gentle lamb, praying softly in my cell.

And then, in the middle of it all, Charlie Richardson arrived at Maidstone.

He took one look at my long hair and beard and asked, 'What's the matter with you, Chris?'

I told him about coming off the drugs. 'I'm going off my head, Charlie,' I said.

'You're not,' he said. 'You're having a breakthrough. You're seeing the reality of life, that's all.'

'But what's happening to me?'

'Don't worry about it. Take it easy. It's all under control. Don't lose it now.'

Charlie always seemed to have an answer for everything and it was a joy to see him. At last, I had someone I felt I could communicate with. He was equally pleased to see me: he, too, was apprehensive about Maidstone, didn't know what problems he might face. There were plenty of people looking on, waiting for it to go off between Charlie and me – a Richardson and a manic 'rival' Kray man. But we disappointed them. We greeted each other warmly, like the old pals we were.

For the next six months, he shared the next cell and we spent a lot of time together. If you were interesting to Charlie, if he felt he could learn something from you, he would give you all the time in the world.

'Don't rush, Chris,' he'd say. 'Come and have a blow, or a cup of tea.' He was kind and generous, with a knack of making you feel relaxed, the sort of man you wanted to share your problems with, because he could probably solve them.

The other side of Charlie is that he was angry and bitter

about being gaoled for twenty-five years, merely on charges of grievous bodily harm, which, he claimed, were never proved conclusively. He always said he was a businessman, not a gangster. I feel there is a lot of truth in that.

I have Charlie to thank for helping to stabilize me during a critical and frightening time of my life. He resumed where he had left off in Durham, recommending this or that book, chatting to me endlessly about his philosophies, discussing what was going on in the world – educating me, basically. He also taught me to believe in myself, told me I was somebody very special, and, in some respects, helped steer me towards Christ.

One evening, about 6.30, Charlie invited me to his cell for a cup of tea and a chat. But I was tired and felt an overpowering need to be on my own.

'Not right now, Charlie,' I said. 'I'm tired. I want to go and have a lie down.'

I lay on my bed and started thinking about all the terrible problems in the world. There were around twenty wars raging, claiming thousands of victims every day. What a mess the world was in, I thought. The thought made me look at my own life. That was a mess, too; it had been a mess for years, and I had caused suffering and pain, too.

I had this vivid image of my life as a garden, and the people in it, the people who had been close to me, cared for me, were flowers and bushes and trees. God had given me this beautiful garden and I had been rampaging through it, ripping up the flower beds and pulling down the bushes and trees, trampling over everything that was good and precious, damaging everything I could touch and see, in a mindless, selfish orgy of destruction.

In my mind's eye, I could see a long trail of people who had tried to do their best for me, all damaged in some way.

And then I saw a doll-like baby in a playpen, amid a load of scaffolding, and its head was tilted back, as if on a hinge. The head was open at the top, and workmen and women were tipping bucketfuls of rubbish into it, as though the baby was a dustbin. That picture had been filling my mind for months; it was what I thought about myself.

I began to cry: thick tears of remorse for the world I had destroyed and lost, for all those loved ones I had left in pain. And then, through my tears, I saw three people in the corner of the cell. They looked Middle-Eastern and were wearing dark raincoats. The one in the middle, the only one I clearly remember, had long, jet-black hair and a neatly trimmed beard; under his raincoat, he was wearing a European suit with a white shirt and a tie. And he had the most wonderful, warm welcoming eyes I'd ever seen. He had such a clarity of vision I knew he was a man of purpose.

Through my tears, I said to him, 'How do I put it right? I have run through my life, wrecking everything. I've made a terrible, terrible mess. I'm so sorry.'

The bearded man said simply, 'Follow us.' Then he and the other two men vanished as quickly as they had come.

The following day I asked the prison chaplain what the vision meant. But he was very cynical and dismissive, and insinuated that it could not have happened.

I asked what I should do, who I should follow, and he just said, 'Pray about it.'

He didn't tell me how to pray. He certainly didn't give me any encouragement. He didn't tell me anything at all. He just left me feeling deflated, confused and a bit silly.

Within a few weeks, I became dissatisfied with praying secretly in my cell and began wanting to go to church to acknowledge what I was feeling. But I didn't have the bottle.

I could imagine what the other cons would say if they saw me trotting in there: that Lambrianou, he's a grass . . . he's a wrong 'un . . . he's weak . . . he's a poof . . . he's a religious nut . . . he's finally flipped his lid . . .' I would have got it from all sides. They would have destroyed me.

I thought about it. But I could not summon up the courage. It bothered me, because I'd never considered myself weak, or lacking in front, but there was nothing I could do about it. I just couldn't face the ridicule.

And then they changed my cell and I saw Bullet Proof Jack.

And I knew I could get off my knees and make that walk, no matter how frightened I was.

Bullet Proof Jack was an Irish Catholic; he had got his nickname by surviving a hail of bullets. He was a tall, powerfully built man and I saw him, one Sunday morning, walking briskly, suited and booted and head held proudly high, to church.

'He's got some guts,' I thought. 'I wish I could do that.'

A few days later I asked why he went to church. 'Because I believe,' he said curtly, and walked away, saying nothing more.

His reaction shook me. I'd expected the sales pitch: 'I've met Jesus. He's really wonderful. He's changed my life. I look at people differently now. I've got hope. I've been born again.'

But he didn't give me any of that rubbish, didn't try to explain or convert me. He just said, 'I believe', and left me looking at his back.

After that I started thinking more and more about going to church. It was as if Jesus was talking to me through Bullet Proof Jack, saying, 'If you believe, too, get on the bandwagon. Don't just mess about with me. If you want to play the game, come and play. I will take what you have to offer – even if it's only behind the door, on your hands and knees. I'll take that for starters. But you will want more of me, and I will want more of you. If I am going to change you. If you want to be something, if you want to be free.'

I knew I could not deny the positive influence that had helped me through my crisis. But I was too terrified to take that first, all-important step until I talked to Jack again, several months later, and he told me about the sign that had made him a believer.

When Jack was lying, near to death in hospital after the shooting, the one person he wanted to see was his father. But his father had 'disowned' him years before, and refused to come.

Jack had prayed, 'If you are really there, God, you will bring my father to this hospital. If you do, I shall see it as a sign.'

A few days later, his father did, indeed, go to the hospital. He merely looked at his son, and said, 'He's all right, he'll live,' then walked out.

It was enough for Jack, however. He saw the visit as a sign and it changed his whole life and religious outlook. From that moment, he started believing in God and going to church.

That was good enough for me, and the following Sunday I got suited and booted and took that daunting walk. I felt good, and a little proud of myself, but when I got inside the church my courage failed me and, instead of sitting in a pew like everyone else, I stood at the back, where there was a wonderful collection of books.

A handful of cons came and I could tell that they were thinking, 'Hello, the lunatic is here . . . is he going to have someone over? Is he here to sort out God?'

One of them asked why I was there. 'Only for the books,'

I replied, quickly. 'They've got some great books on philosophy. I'm really into that.'

'Oh, really,' he said, impressed, and went into the body of the church.

There were only about six cons in the congregation and I'm sure they were there only to improve their chances of parole. I wasn't bothered by that. I was not there to judge anyone. And I was the humblest one of all.

As the service began, I sat down, unobserved, in the back row, feeling very self-conscious. Jesus was very real to me and I started talking to him in my head. 'Well, at least I'm here, Jesus. But if you expect me to start singing those silly hymns and get down on my knees, you've another thing coming.'

But there were so few people there, I could not get out of it. There was no place to hide. Anyway, deep down, I didn't want to hide.

I saw the vicar looking at me. His face said it all: 'You're the last person who should be in my church. You're one of that Kray Firm. How could you possibly understand God?'

I went back to the wing with mixed emotions. I was elated at having climbed my personal mountain and been true to my own feelings. But I was *deflated*, too, at the cynicism of the dog-collar brigade.

I had gone through the most exhilarating experience that had changed my whole thinking and made me want to get closer to God.

And all they thought was, 'He's trying to con us and work his ticket.'

The governor, Peter Timms, was a Christian, who had spoken about his beliefs on TV and radio, but he was sceptical about me, too. If I had remained non-violent, there was an outside chance I could have convinced him that I was sincere, but I didn't. I reacted physically to a young bully, and what followed killed whatever rapport I might have had with Timms.

The bully, named Lyons, had been taking liberties with me because he knew I would not risk retaliating and being sent back into the dispersal system.

One day I came back to my cell to find him searching through my drawers, and I wasn't in the mood to mess around.

'Get out of my cell,' I said. 'I don't want you in here.'

'I wasn't doing anything,' he said.

'Just get out.'

'Who do you think you're telling to get out?'

'I'm telling *you* to get out,' I shouted.

And I let him have a right-hander, splitting his face, beneath an eye, very badly. I was carted off, yet again, to the chokey, amid rumours that I'd used a six-inch nail to damage Lyons.

The solitary confinement did little to ease my distrust of people and general paranoia. I had tried to speak to cons and screws alike about my religious experience, but no one had been able to offer me any guidance. It was as though everyone thought I was off my rocker. I came back onto Medway Wing and bumped into someone I really didn't want to see – Don Barrett, who had stayed behind his cell door during the Albany riot. I was feeling vulnerable, though, and when he offered me an ounce of tobacco I accepted it.

When I got to my cell, however, my mind went back to the riot and I was disgusted with myself for taking the tobacco. I felt Barrett was insulting not only me, but the memory of my dear mate, Freddie Sansom, who, unlike Barrett, had been a man that day in Albany. I went back downstairs to Barrett's cell.

'Don,' I said.

'What?' he said.

'Here's your bacca.'

And I floored him with one on the hooter.

'Get up,' I said. But it didn't matter. A mass of screws converged on me and I found myself in the chokey again.

The business with Barrett was not over, however, and a couple of days later I was walking round the tiny exercise area with a black guy called Purvis when I decided to break out and give Barrett a seeing to.

'Do me a favour,' I said to Purvis. I pointed to the twelve-foot-high wall surrounding us. 'Give us a lift up.'

'You're joking, man,' he said. 'Where you going to go?'

'I'm going over,' I said.

Purvis shook his head. 'I'm in enough shit as it is.'

'I'm going over,' I repeated.

'Man, don't do this to me!'

'Are you one of us?' I said scornfully. 'Or one of them? Just stand up against the wall and get me over. I'll say I did it on my own.'

Reluctantly, he stood on tiptoe against the wall and gave me a lift onto his shoulders. There was no barbed wire on the wall, just a rounded top, and I dragged myself up onto it. I dropped to the ground and walked quickly towards a working party, which, conveniently, was heading to Medway Wing. I went all over the wing, looking for Barrett, but couldn't find him. All the cons were staring at me as if I was mad. They knew I was supposed to be in the chokey. In the end, I never did get to finish off the business, because half-a-dozen screws piled on me and took me back where I'd come from. Not without a battle, I might add. I never spoke to Barrett again.

That incident was the last straw for Governor Timms. Maidstone had tried to cope with me in every possible way, he said, but I was not ready for a Category C prison yet. I tried to reason with him, saying I was a Christian and had reacted only under extreme provocation.

'How can you say you're a Christian when you use the violence you do?' Timms said. 'You should control your anger.'

'Even the Apostle Peter got angry and cut off a centurion's ear with a sword,' I said. 'And even Jesus could be violent. He turned over the moneychangers' tables.'

It cut no ice with Timms. He said I was being moved immediately.

'Where am I going?' I asked, with a feeling of dread.

'Albany,' he said.

My heart sank. I could have wept. Maidstone was just thirty miles or so from London, and easy for my dad to visit.

Now, he was faced with that gruelling, six-hour round trip to the Isle of Wight once more. I felt sick. I had done it to him yet again.

Albany had changed. When I was there before the screws were in control, but now the cons were running things. There were lots of feuds going on and I was there only three days before someone offered me a knife, saying I'd be well advised to sleep with it, just in case.

I didn't want a big blade. I didn't want to be part of some pointless feud. I didn't want the villainy or the violence any more.

At Maidstone, I felt I'd found something worthwhile, made a few strides forward and seen a little bit of daylight through the thick, grim fog that had been suffocating me for ten years. But, now, I'd gone backwards and was, once again, among losers who didn't give a monkey's and screws who cared even less.

I tried to make the best of it. I read the Bible behind my door, went to church, and wrote children's stories for cons who didn't know how to communicate with their kids. But generally I was sinking deeper and deeper into despair at the sheer hopelessness of my plight.

Sending me back to Albany was a calculated decision. The authorities saw it as part of my humiliation process, to see how I coped back in the gaol where I'd been so badly beaten. It was a game I did not want to play. I was way past it. I'd been there, done it, and was not interested any more.

As the months wore on, I became more and more depressed at the crushing negativity, and knew I would have to do something drastic before the prison robbed me of all I'd found in myself.

I went to the governor and said I didn't want to be on the wing any more: I wanted to be moved. When he told me he could not do that, I said, 'OK, put me down the block on my own.' He couldn't do that either, but I said he'd better, or I would cause him more problems than he would wish for.

Finally, he agreed, thinking, I'm sure, that I'd get bored after a few days and ask to come up. But I didn't get bored. I loved being on my own and catching up on all the reading and writing I'd been unable to do on the wing. There were twenty-five other cells in the chokey block, but I didn't have to see anyone, or talk to anyone, for days, if I wished. I made a little life for myself down there and I loved every solitary second of it.

When I was not reading or writing, I would look out of a tiny, barred window and watch the birds having dust baths in puddles dried by the sun; I felt I almost knew them and gave them names. I found the ringed doves the saddest. Other cons in the chokey would attach cotton to peas and tug at it, getting the doves all tangled up as they fed. I would look at the doves feeling an empathy: like them, I'd been caught in a trap and could see no way out.

One day I asked to see Mr Rutledge, one of the prison's tutors. It was an enlightening experience – for him, not me.

When he walked into my cell and saw my collection of classic literature and books on religion, history and philosophy, he said, 'What are they for? For show, aren't they?'

There was something in his tone I didn't like.

'If you say so,' I said.

He picked up Krishnamurti's *Kingdom of Happiness*. 'This is very interesting.' He gave a sort of smirk, '*If* you can find five minutes to read it.'

I was hurt. He didn't know me, didn't really want to. He was patronizing me, insulting my intelligence.

'I already have,' I said.

He looked at me, disbelieving, so I told him about it. He looked shocked, then impressed. Then we started chatting about the books in general and particularly Oscar Wilde's children's stories, which I'd found moving and compassionate, illustrating how much the great man understood human nature.

After a while, Rutledge lowered his head. 'Mr Lambrianou,' he said, sombrely, 'we have done you the greatest disservice that anyone could to another human being. I'm very, very sorry.'

I don't know if Mr Rutledge had anything to do with it, but a couple of months later I was told I was on the move again, back to Hull for the third time. I was pleased, for my dad's sake. He had managed the long journey to the island five times, but he was now eighty and a mainland prison would be better for him.

In a perverse way, being sent back to Albany had been good for me. It had made me more self-aware and given me a certain amount of pride and self-respect at having made a stand for what was right for me.

The parole system had knocked all the rebellion out of Hull. Everyone, even the long-termers, were reluctant to get involved in any disruption in case it hindered their chances of an early release. From the moment I arrived, in May 1979, I led a quiet life, spent mainly cultivating the soil in the gardens and studying. I'd been interested in gardening since those days at approved school, when I worked in the fields, and I threw myself into it in Hull, finding it a blessed relief being in the open air after the claustrophobia of the chokey.

I would spend nine hours in the garden from 8 a.m., then in the evening I would go on courses, studying English literature, poetry and maths, not to pass examinations, just to challenge myself and prove I could do it. I found it impossible to talk to other cons about the stuff I was learning, but there were academics in authority who realized my brain was expanding, and encouraged me. I was active in the church, encouraging cons to join us in worship, and gradually I began to win some respect. Thankfully, I was regarded as a genuine Christian, not merely a con-artist trying to pull a flanker.

It did surprise me, however, when the governor came to me one day and suggested I took a business studies course.

'I want you to think seriously about it, Lambrianou,' he said. 'I think you would do very well here if you went for a degree. We would give you all the encouragement we possibly could.'

I wanted to be positive, because he was so considerate and well-meaning. But staying at Hull, even for something so beneficial to me, was out of the question. All I wanted was to get out of there, into a gaol nearer London, for the sake of my dad, who came to see me every two weeks without fail.

With Nicky, my youngest brother, now also in prison on the Isle of Wight, it meant Dad had three visits to make.

'Please consider the business course,' the governor said, 'It would be good for you.'

I knew he was right. A business course could lead to all sorts of things, perhaps help me make something of my life and become what Dad had always wanted me to be – a decent, hard-working citizen. Someone successful. Someone to be proud of.

But, at that time, I could not even see myself getting out of prison, let alone into business. Far more important was making things easier for my dad, before it was too late and he wasn't around any more.

'Thanks very much for being so kind,' I told the governor. 'But there's nothing to consider. I just want to be nearer London.'

From that moment, I was under close scrutiny. Reports went to the governor from the teachers, the priest – even the gardener. And then, after I'd been there nine months, I was told the governor wanted to see me.

He said he had some good news. The Home Office had been in touch to confirm that I was being moved to Coldingley Prison, in Surrey, for my father's sake.

Tears filled my eyes. So the Home Office had a heart after all.

CHAPTER TWENTY-TWO

All the way down the line, in every prison, I'd felt weighed down by chains, but the second I went through the electronic gates at Coldingley they fell off me, making me feel lighter, more at ease. It was a modern gaol and there was an air of relative freedom about the place. From my cell, I could even see the sky.

The chief prison officer quickly put me in my place, however. He was a big man, running to fat, in his late fifties, and looked more like someone's favourite uncle than a prison officer. But there was no doubt who was in charge.

'Well, lad, you're in Coldingley, now,' he said in a thick Tyneside accent. 'No bloody nonsense – otherwise you'll be going back. And not down the block either. You'll be off to Albany. So bloody well behave yourself.'

I said nothing. What was there to say? I'd only just arrived. I wasn't looking for trouble. I wanted a quiet life, like I'd had at Hull.

The PO told me I was due to start in the workshop on Monday, but, as I liked gardening, he might have something more suitable for me.

I was given a lovely meal in the dining area, which looked more like a well-kept staff canteen, and was thrilled to learn that, among many other facilities, the prison had an extensive library.

By Monday morning, I was liking the place and looking forward to my stay there. But I got a surprise when I collected my overalls and asked the chief prison officer how to get to the workshop.

'Don't be so bloody hasty, lad,' he barked. 'Wait there. I want to talk to you.'

I wasn't worried. I knew I had not done anything, not put anyone's nose out of joint. But I was still a little paranoid about my reputation. For a moment, I wondered if someone had already started stirring it, to make life difficult for me before I'd got my feet under the table.

The chief looked into my face. 'The idea I had for you has materialized sooner than I expected. You're going out to the gardens today.'

I was so shocked, I didn't know what to say.

He looked at me, sternly. 'Let me down, you bugger, and I'll have your arse for potatoes. Fall down once, lad, and you're in the shit.'

I felt exhilarated. Obviously the reports from Hull had been favourable. Someone must have said I was all right, that I had shown I could be responsible and commit myself to work, given the freedom. I went along to the garden shed to collect my tools, eager to get cracking. But when I asked for a fork, it was broken, and when I asked for a shovel, I was told there wasn't one, and was given a dustpan.

I realized it was a test of my character. Would I use the lack of proper tools as an excuse? Or would I make the best of it? I wasn't going to let the chief down. I wasn't going to let myself down. And, more important, I wasn't going to let God down. I felt Jesus in me, saying, 'Nobody believes you can do this. But you will – even if you have to do it with your bare hands.'

At Hull, I did the gardening in a party, and was always told what to do. But now I was on my own, able to please myself, and I threw myself into it so vigorously the other cons called me the JCB!

After two months or so, priming the roses and generally breaking up the ground so that the winter frost could do its work, I went to the prison governor, Jim Anderson, with the dustpan, broken fork, a broom with no bristles and a hoe that was snapped in half. I told him I was grateful for the freedom he had given me to work in the garden, but I wanted to do a good job, and I couldn't unless I had the proper tools. I had done a certain amount of work first to prove my intentions – and it worked. When I went to the garden shed after lunch, a brand new array of tools was lined up, waiting for me.

I went to work like a lunatic, transforming the whole place on my own. I moved big boulders to form rockeries, replanted a small tree or rose bush in front of every bare wall I could find, and even relaid a lawn that had been ruined by a reversing laundry van. I was told soapy water kills greenfly, so I filled a fifty-six-gallon oil drum with water and detergent and pulled it round the gardens on a four-wheeled trolley, drenching the rose bushes, first with a watering can, then with a stirrup pump.

Every afternoon, I was allowed in the garden shed for fifteen minutes to share a cup of tea with four other cons who took the prison dustbins to the incinerator. One of the cons was Alan Briggs, who was serving ten years for a bank robbery, and he started accusing me of going to church merely to win parole. I let it rub off me at first, but the attacks got so personal I wondered if a screw had been encouraging him to antagonize me. I wasn't stupid; I knew there were a lot of people there who had expected me to cause trouble, and hated me for proving them wrong. I didn't retaliate with Briggs; instead, I started praying for him. 'Lord, take care of

Alan Briggs. The man is messed up. You can deal with him. I can't. I have a job to do and I'm going to do it.' Nothing Briggs said after that touched me.

One Sunday, I went to church and saw him sitting there. I gave him no more than a few days, but two weeks later he had plastered a notice on his cell door: 'I am a Christian. If anyone feels they need someone to talk with, don't be afraid. I will always be available.'

Someone, it seemed, had heard my prayer.

As I worked, Oscar Wilde's story *The Selfish Giant* kept running around my head. An unhappy and morose giant lived in a gloomy castle, where it was always raining or snowing, never sunny. One day, some children break down part of his wall and he chases them away, shouting, 'Get out of my garden. Don't dare come back.' Walking along, he sees a little boy sitting in a tree, bathed in sunlight, and asks what he is doing there. 'I've come to play with you,' says the boy. The giant allows him into the castle and they talk and play, and soon it is always sunny around the castle. The giant becomes happier and asks the boy to stay because of the change he has brought about. Finally, he knocks down the garden walls and lets all the other children in to play.

In a way, I felt I was doing that at Coldingley: knocking walls down and making the scenery more attractive for prisoners and staff alike, brightening the drab surroundings with some sunshine of my own.

Governor Anderson would wander round the garden – sometimes with the chief – looking at the changes I was making. But he never said anything. It was as if he knew that if he did say something, it would spoil everything. He never once said, 'Well done', and I didn't expect him to. I was not working so hard for compliments. That garden was my life, my survival, and I knew I was doing well. I was first in line to go to work in the mornings and often I'd be so engrossed someone would have to come and get me at night.

Sadly, my dad was not allowed to walk in the garden with me, but he was able to see it from the visiting room and it gave us something different to talk about. My life was no longer just about being free and going home, I didn't think of that any more. No, my days were about going out in that garden and getting closer to God. I was like a monk or priest, able to minister to people I met out there. I met God at every turning. And I suppose that was who those people met in me.

With winter setting in, I felt God's labourer could rest and let Him take over until the spring. So, I went to the governor and applied for a job as a church orderly. There was nothing more to do outside, I said, but the church was a mess and I felt I could improve it in the way I'd transformed the garden. I also explained that I planned to make use of the quiet and solitude to begin Bible studies, with the intention of taking a college course later.

At first, there were objections on security grounds: the church was the one weak spot in the prison, vulnerable to an escape attempt. But I convinced Jim Anderson and the chief that I was not planning to go anywhere, and got the job as the chaplain's orderly.

The first thing I did was make a six-foot-high cross out of an old, dead tree and nailed it to a wall in the entrance to the church. Everyone thought I was mad when they saw me carrying in the wood, but then they saw the significance: an old rugged cross – the symbol of suffering and pain.

Then I cleaned up a neglected and dusty upstairs room, where the chaplain entertained guests. I polished the tea urn, cleaned the sink, and put up colourful and symbolic posters on the walls. Downstairs, in the church itself, I polished the pews until I could smell the wood, and smartened up the altar area. I got such pleasure cleaning the altar. I was saying to God, 'This is Yours. This is the way I'm serving You. Like in the garden.'

I wanted the church looking like new for the Christmas Day service, and I managed it. I remember feeling so proud and privileged that morning, sitting there among 300 people – many of them civilians – knowing I had played my part in making the church such a warm, welcoming place. Many said how beautiful it was.

As spring drew near, I had a dilemma: half of me wanted to stay in the church and continue studying for a place at the London Bible College, and the other half wanted to be outside attacking the new challenges of the garden.

The cons were convinced that now I'd got my feet under the table in the church, able to do what I liked in total privacy, I would not give it up to labour for nine hours in the wind and rain. I did a lot of praying about what I should do, but then, overnight, I made my decision. The daffodils were coming up; the buds were on the trees. I thought, 'Throughout the winter, God has been doing His work, and now it is time to do mine.' When I told the chaplain I would like to go back in the garden, he said he knew I would. Governor Anderson told me the same.

The changes in me were becoming so evident, it seemed, that people knew me better than I knew myself.

When I wasn't weeding or redigging the garden, I was reading, praying or writing down my thoughts in my cell. Life had quietened down dramatically. For the first time, I was at peace with myself and could see a future, a point in going forward.

And then, one June night in the middle of my prayers, I was given the one bit of news I always knew would over-shadow everything I might want for myself.

My dad had been taken to hospital. He was desperately ill and might not have long to live.

The next day in the garden, I tried to concentrate on what I was doing, but Dad was all I could think of. I began to pray, asking God to help me understand His will in this terrible situation. I wanted Him to bring Dad through, because I really wanted him. But I accepted that, perhaps, that was not the plan; that, maybe, God had a place for him in Heaven. My mind went back to the time I went to punch my dad after he'd torn a strip off me for the way I treated Carol. God had held back my arm, like a steel band restraining me. 'Was it time,' I wondered, 'for me to give something back to Him?'

My eyes were drawn to a rose. As I looked closer, I could see it had the most perfect raindrop, like a tear on it. My lovely, uncomplaining, dear dad. It was as if God was crying for him, too.

The following morning, I was told Dad's condition was so critical I was being taken, under escort, to see him in St Leonard's Hospital, in Shoreditch, in the East End.

The first thought my dad had was for me, not himself. Was I all right? he wanted to know. Had I escaped? No, I said, I'd just come to see him.

He told me he had wet himself. I picked him up and carried him to a chair. He was so light, it was like lifting a baby. I stripped him down, then asked a nurse to bring some clean pyjamas, while I changed the bed. Some of my family were there, but I wanted to do it, felt I had to.

I told the hospital I wanted Dad to go home with my sisters-in-law, so they could look after him. But they said no:

he had not long to live. He had cancer and only the drugs were keeping him alive.

I went back to Coldingley with mixed emotions. I hoped he would live, and, in a way, believed he would. He had survived so many other crises in our lives that I told myself that this was just another one, and he'd come through it. At the same time, I still prayed that I'd be strong enough to let go and give Dad to God if that was what He wanted.

I was told I'd be taken to the hospital again, should Dad deteriorate. It never happened. He died at 11.30 that night, but no one rang the prison.

When I was told, I felt empty. And more alone than I'd felt in my life. Dad was eighty-three, a good age. But how many of those years had I, more than any of my brothers, filled him with pain and anguish as I rampaged through the garden of my life, damaging all that was beautiful and good and dear to me?

A consolation, one crumb of comfort, is that he lived to see me becoming a better person, battling to put back some beauty in that garden I'd destroyed. I like to think he hung on for that.

CHAPTER TWENTY-THREE

The next day I was coming in from the garden for lunch when I heard someone call out my name. It was a small, funny-looking, much-disliked screw named Kendrick, who had recently been promoted to a senior officer. He was an authoritarian who took his job very seriously.

'We need to talk,' he said.

I had never liked his attitude and did not see why I had to pass the time of day with him. So I said stiffly, 'I don't need to speak to you.'

'I think you will need to talk to me – if you want to go to your father's funeral.'

'No, I won't,' I said. 'I'll go and see the governor.'

'That won't do you any good,' Kendrick said.

'Then I'll see the chief PO,' I said.

'It won't do you any good. *I'm* the man you've got to see.'

Kendrick and I had never liked each other. I could not imagine him doing me any favours, seeing any good in me, and I said so.

'You may not like me,' he said. 'And you may not think you can get along with me. But I am here to help you.'

'*You!*'

'Yes, me. If you want to get what you want, you've got to tell me things. You have to tell me what you're about.'

Suddenly I glimpsed a softer, caring side of him.

'You really mean that, don't you?'

'Yes,' he said. 'Yes, I do.'

That evening, Kendrick came to my cell and sat on the bed. 'Tell me about your dad,' he said.

For the next half-hour or so, he listened, without once interrupting, as I told him what had happened at the hospital, and how I felt about losing my dad. I told him where the funeral was being held and how I was going to deal with it. Kendrick had always seemed so wrapped up in himself and his job, but that evening I realized that he was a deeply compassionate man, who, like many of the cons under his supervision, had learned not to show his true feelings. I could not believe I was talking to the same man I'd disliked so much. He arranged everything to ensure that, from Coldingley's end at least, the funeral was as painless as possible for me.

Three days later, I was handcuffed and taken to the East End in a van, escorted by four prison officers. I had not been a free man for nearly fourteen years, but, amazingly, I still remembered the short cuts, and was able to get us to Queensbridge Road on time, despite the rush-hour traffic. As the driver parked outside Belford House, one officer took off the handcuffs and said, 'Behave yourself and don't give us any problems. We'll do our best to blend into the background and be unobtrusive.'

Me and my four brothers were allowed to talk together on our own in a back room. Unknown to the officers, there was a secret exit from that room and we could all have had it away while they sat drinking tea.

Escape was a thought. After all, Tony and me were lifers and we were still not sure whether we would ever get out. But it was *only* a thought. It was our dad's day and we were not going to let him down and bring more shame on him at his funeral, after shaming him most of our lives.

The hearse arrived and me and my brothers followed it to the Greek Orthodox Church, in Mornington Crescent, in a second funeral car, with the prison officers following behind, in the van.

Inside the majestic church, I walked to the coffin and kissed it. Then I knelt for half a minute, thinking of Dad. I looked at the little card I'd put with the flowers. I'd written: 'Dad, I am in your heart and you're in my heart and we are both in God's heart.' And then I started to cry.

The service was solemn and very moving and then it was time to take Dad on his final journey, to New Southgate Cemetery.

As we neared the cemetery, a friend of ours named Paddy, driving another car, got between us and the van, and deliberately held it up at traffic lights, to give us a chance to make a run for it. We continued following the coffin, aware that we had lost the van and could easily escape. Neither Tony nor I had changed our minds, so we told the driver to signal the hearse to stop by Tufnell Park Underground Station and wait for our escorts.

When they finally caught up and saw the five of us, standing around on the pavement by the hearse, their faces were a picture. I'm sure they thought we had done a bunk.

All I remember about the burial was throwing some soil into the hole in the ground as the coffin was lowered. When my mum died it was as if she herself was going into the ground, but I didn't feel that with Dad. To me, he was not there. All that was inside that coffin was an old suit Dad had taken off. It was as if he had not died and was nearer to me than he'd ever been. I felt that he was a part of me. No more waving goodbye. He would be with me all the time. Forever.

After the funeral, we all went back to my Uncle John's house in Golders Green, where he had laid on a traditional Greek meal. He handed me a bottle of brandy and a large glass, and I sat on the stairs drinking it, thinking about how much I loved my dad.

The prison officers had begun to relax. The worst was over for them. We had had chances to blow it for them, and we had not taken them, hadn't let them down. They allowed me to wander about the house as I pleased, and even let me walk across the street to a newsagent's to buy some cigarettes.

Me and my brothers sat down for dinner – the first time for years we'd all been together. Tony was as overbearing and full of himself as ever, but I did feel a bit of a bond with him, despite our different personalities. We had both survived all the years in prison. At least, we were both alive. And we were both quite sane.

My future was not with Tony, however. It was in the garden, behind Coldingley's electronic gates and high walls. I wanted to be back there, among the flowers and the trees and bushes, to come to terms with what had happened.

The Native Americans have a saying: 'The son is never a man until his father's death.' That day, that sunny Thursday in July 1982, when we buried my dad, was the day I finally grew up. The day I became a man.

Before going before the Parole Review Board in September, I had to be interviewed by Governor Anderson. But the weeks went by, following my dad's funeral, without him asking me to see him, and I started to worry. I had not got my hopes up about parole. Having been involved in a riot and more than one punch up, the chances were that I'd get an extra five or ten years after completing my fifteen anyway. But I had been honourable all the way down the line, never letting anyone down, and I felt I deserved at least an interview with Anderson.

One afternoon in August, he strolled by as I was tending some roses.

'They're particularly good this year, aren't they, Lambrianou?' he said, in an extra friendly tone.

I agreed and we spent a couple of minutes chatting about them. Then he motioned towards the lawns, saying they, too, were in good nick. I nodded, taking it as a compliment. We spoke generally about growth, rebirth and changes in the garden for another minute or so, then he prepared to move on. There would not be a better opportunity to speak to him, so I seized the moment.

'Mr Anderson,' I said, 'with the Parole Board sitting next month, when can I see you to talk about my record?'

He shook his head. 'No need to Lambrianou. We've just done it.' He was a philosophical man, Jim Anderson, and he had decided that what he was going to tell the Parole Board about me was all there in the garden. Our little chat had been symbolic. Like the garden I'd transformed, I had changed, too; like the flowers and plants I cared for so passionately, I was coming into bloom after my own dark winter.

He walked away, then suddenly turned. 'Let me ask you something, Lambrianou,' he said. 'How did you cope with your father's death?'

'I wrote a lot of it down, sir,' I said. 'I was praying one night and I heard the Holy Spirit say, "Don't say this – *write* it." So that's exactly what I did.'

'Would you mind sharing them with me?' he said. 'Would you allow me to intrude into your private thoughts?'

'Why would you want to?' I asked.

'It isn't long since I lost my own father. I'm finding it difficult.'

That evening, I gave him my meditations. To my amazement, he came to me two weeks later and said that not only had they helped him, but he felt they were so good they ought to be published as a book.

One lunchtime, the following month, I was told to report to Mr Anderson's office. I had no idea what it was about. When I'd gone before the Parole Board everyone had been warm and hopeful, but I'd not allowed myself to get excited because an extra sentence on top of the fifteen was always hanging over me.

My friend Kendrick was there, with PO Fitzgerald. They and Anderson were smiling. I wondered why; it could have been anything. I didn't dare think about parole.

Anderson went through the official business, then said, 'The Home Office has sent through a memo, saying that on 15 September 1983 you will be released on licence.'

For a second I could not take it in, perhaps didn't want to, in case it was just a silly joke. But then I took in all the smiling faces and punched the air as if I'd scored the winner at Wembley.

The three of them shook my hand and said how pleased they were for me. 'I'm so delighted for you,' said Anderson. 'Don't let yourself down. You've got it. Now, whatever you do, don't let yourself down.'

All I wanted to do then was get out of that office and go behind the door of my cell and say a prayer of thanks to God. On the way there, other cons asked what had gone on, I tried to pass it off as nothing, but I could not stop smiling. My elation was in my heart and I could not stop it coming out of my mouth.

'I got it,' I said, quietly.

'Got what?' someone asked.

'Parole,' I whispered. 'I got parole.'

'YOU GOT PAROLE,' they all shouted.

And they all threw their arms round me, hugging me, congratulating me.

Later, in the sanctuary of my cell, I closed my eyes and said that prayer. The news I'd just been given was everything – and more. It was the best woman in the world, the best drink in the world, the best holiday in the world. Add them all together a million times and they would not have meant as much as that little piece of Home Office paper.

And I know that I would not have got it if I had not met Jesus in my cell at Maidstone that frightening night four years before.

That was the good news. The bad news was that I would have to leave Coldingley in November and spend ten months at an open prison at Sudbury in Derbyshire. I was gutted: I had my garden, my church, my pals; I was settled and happy, and the thought of leaving the warmth of familiar, friendly surroundings for the bitter cold uncertainty of the unknown filled me with dread.

I did try to fight the decision, but it was no use. The system was shaking the tree one more time, saying, 'Let's see what happens now. Will he stay how he is – or will he fall?' I didn't think I was going to fall, but I was worried at what lay ahead. I'd left the Kray thing behind, but now, meeting totally different people in a new environment, I was going to have to go through it all again. All I wanted was to continue at Coldingley and go out the following September a positive person with a clear idea of where I was going and what I was going to do. But Sudbury changed all that.

From the moment I arrived, they made it clear they didn't want me there. I was the first ex-Category A man they had

had and they feared the worst. I got the message right away: they weren't going to have an ex-Kray man running the gaol. For three days I got the treatment, and then I met a short, grey-haired, warm, super-fit Scouser called Tommy Atherton.

He came up to me as I was walking round a big lake in the fields. 'You're not getting an easy ride here, are you?' he said.

'You noticed, then,' I said.

'I'm a lifer, too,' he said. 'They don't want us lifers. We know too much. We know the system better than them. They don't want us running things.'

'I don't want to run anything,' I told him. 'All I want is to reach the end of my time. I've got ten months to do before I go to the hostel. I just want to make that.'

He said he wanted the same. So, we became a team, walking round the lake together every day, discussing everything that was going on in the prison and who was grassing on who.

I had to be very careful. I was walking on ice and, at times, it became very thin. Grasses would set situations up to get brownie points and the odd extra privilege, or whatever. I knew that certain people did not want me to get out, so I had to watch my back all the time. Tommy helped keep me sane. We were close and solid. No one could crack us.

I wanted the solitude of the church, but when I asked to use it, they refused.

'I am a Christian,' I said. 'That church is there for my use. I have no privacy anywhere else, but in there I can be alone with my thoughts.'

I was told the church had been shut because it had been used for passing drugs and money.

'That could happen anywhere,' I said and went to see the deputy governor, Miss Seamark.

I told her that I had been in prison an awfully long time and no one had ever closed the House of Christ to me.

'Please open the doors,' I said. 'Otherwise it's like going back to when Christians were persecuted.'

She said she would do what she could.

The following day I was called up by the chief prison officer. There had been a conference, he said, and it had been decided to allow me to use the church. But no one else. Again, I went to Miss Seamark.

'The church is God's house. *Everyone* is welcome.'

'Mr Lambrianou,' she said, 'you speak the simple truth most plainly. I understand what you are saying. But just walk through the door yourself.'

I did go in, whether I liked the situation or not and, eventually, other cons started going in too.

Miss Seamark had had a lot of pressure about what was happening in the church. And, being a Christian, she was hurt by it. She was looking for the right reason to open the door – and I provided it.

Just before Christmas, I needed to phone my brother Nicky to check if he was coming to visit me.

I went in the chaplain's office and dialled what I thought was Nicky's home number. A woman answered, and immediately jumped down my throat.

'Nicky doesn't live here. I'm not a secretary. And this isn't a switchboard. I'm not prepared to take messages.'

I was shocked. I apologized and I said I wouldn't ring her again. Then I put the phone down.

A week later, I received a letter from that angry voice.

'Dear Chris,' she wrote, 'I'm terribly sorry to have blasted you the other day. I didn't know where you were at the time. You sounded so nice and polite. Please accept my apology.'

A couple of weeks later, I got a second letter: 'Sometimes you must get very lonely in there. Would you like a visit?'

I wrote back, saying I would, and the following week she travelled up from her home in Oxfordshire to meet me. Her name was Jenny. And what she did for me over the next three years will remain in my heart forever.

In the early summer of 1983, they started talking about which hostel I should stay in to help prepare me for my release in September. I wanted to go to one adjoining Worm-wood Scrubs, but I was told Tony was going there. Then I was offered Pentonville, but I fought that because I'd heard pre-release cons were put back in prison clothes and banged up in the main gaol every night. Winson Green, in Birmingham, was ideal, but they were too frightened to have me. All they were told was that they were getting a Kray man and to them that meant trouble. It sickened and frustrated me. I'd been doing my best to throw off that evil carcase but it was still there after fifteen years. Forget that I'd seen the Light and was a well-meaning Christian. To many, I was still a terrifying gangster who couldn't be controlled. Happily, however, Winson Green relented and in June I moved into a hostel, next to the gaol.

The idea was for me to go out and find a job, but after two weeks I had not found anything, and the chief prison officer thought I had not been trying.

'I knew it,' he said, one Monday evening. 'I knew you didn't want to work. You're one of that Kray Firm. You don't work for anybody.'

I told him I'd been going round Birmingham's job centres every day, but couldn't find anything. It cut no ice.

'If you don't find a job by the end of this week, I'm putting you behind the wall,' he said.

That frightened me; it was the last thing I wanted after coming so far. But I did not know what to do. I'd been trying as hard as I could, but there was no work around – unless you wanted to slave for a pound an hour, which I didn't.

By the end of the week, I was still jobless, and fearing the worst when the chief PO confronted me the following Monday. On Sunday night, however, a young kid named Chris failed to return to the hostel after weekend home leave, and it gave me an idea.

The next day, I confessed to a screw that I still had not found a job, and asked if Chris would be coming back to the hostel. The screw said he would not. He had broken his contract and would be put behind the wall when he was captured.

'So there's a job going,' I said. 'Chris was working as a carpenter for a roofing firm.'

The screw scoffed. 'You'll never get that job. What do you know about carpentry?'

'Just take me there,' I said. 'Let's see.'

The following morning, we arrived at the offices of C & E Roofing and I was told to wait in an outside office while the screw went in to talk to the managing director, Michael Stephenson. I suspected the screw was bad-mouthing me, saying I was a Kray man and did not really want to work, but it did not bother Mike Stephenson. When he called me, he didn't beat about the bush.

'You're not a sex case, are you?'

'No, I'm not,' I replied.

'You don't hurt women or children?'

'No.'

'You don't bother old-age pensioners?'

'No.'

'What you did was a long, long time ago and you've more than paid for it. I'm not going to punish you any more. You can start work here next Monday morning. Eight o'clock, OK?'

'I'll be here,' I said. 'Thank you, very much.'

I walked out into the June sunshine, wondering how on earth I was going to cope, when I hadn't done a second's carpentry in my life.

For the first three days, fortunately, I was given only menial, labouring jobs on a roof. It suited me fine and I would have been happy doing that all the time. However, after those first few days, the foreman gave me a couple of jobs that required some skill and, of course, I made a pig's ear of them. I thought, 'The game's up. They'll realize I conned them and I'll be back behind the wall.'

I was having a cup of tea, thinking it was best if I simply owned up and apologized, when I noticed a guy in a boiler-suit I'd seen standing around, doing nothing, ever since I'd arrived. I was curious, so I went over to him.

'Excuse me,' I said, warmly. 'My name's Chris. What's yours?'

'Joe,' he said.

'What you doing, Joe?' I asked.

'I'm waiting for someone to tell me what to do,' he said.

'But you've been standing around for three days,' I said.

'Yeah, I know,' he said. 'I don't know what to do. They employed me, but they haven't given me any work.'

Joe was coming up to sixty, and black. There was a bit of racism on the site, and I think he was being given the cold shoulder deliberately.

'What do you do, Joe?' I asked.

'I'm a carpenter,' he said.

A quotation from Proverbs came to mind: 'A brother is born to help in time of need.'

'Come with me,' I said, and I took him to the pig's ear of

a job I'd done on a fascia board round the top of a pipe. 'One of the guys here has made a real mess of that. Do you think you can straighten it out?'

'I'll try,' Joe said.

'I'll come back later and see what you've done,' I said, and disappeared.

When I returned, an hour later, Joe had done a perfect job on the fascia board.

'Not bad, Joe,' I said. 'But the guy who did it has made an even worse job of a toilet roof round the corner.'

Joe did a terrific job on that, too. I looked at it, admiringly. 'You really are a carpenter,' I said.

'Yeah, I worked in the TV scenery department at Pebble Mill,' he said. 'But I was made redundant and have to take work where I can find it.'

There he was, a boilersuit done up to the neck, a trilby hat and his tool kit – a real tradesman. I respected him and had to tell him the truth.

'I've just finished a life sentence and it was me who cocked up those two jobs,' I said. 'I'm not a carpenter. But I'm the best labourer in the world.'

'I can't work without you and you can't work without me. We need each other. If we team up, we'll both get our wages and, who knows, we might turn out to be good mates.'

That's precisely what happened. We became a double act, like Morecambe and Wise, Laurel and Hardy. If you saw Joe, I wouldn't be far away. I was the workhorse carrying the timber up onto the roofs and Joe was the craftsman, turning it into something useful.

We were allowed to operate on piece-work rates and, one day, I suggested getting a chainsaw to cut up more timber and, therefore, make more money. But Joe wouldn't hear of it.

'I'm not a chainsaw man, Chris,' he said. 'A chainsaw is for forests. I'm a skilled craftsman. We're doing a proper job.'

I had to admire him. I only saw a way of speeding up the work, but he was a true professional and took a pride in everything he did.

It didn't really matter in the end. The bosses loved our work so much that what we lost not doing piece work, we made up in overtime. We began at five in the morning and worked right through till it got dark, at ten. I loved every minute of it. I was earning my right to a way out of prison. For the first time in my life, there was a purpose to working and I was bursting with enthusiasm for it.

Joe, bless him, was as straight as they come. On one job, I told him we could sell all the slates we didn't break, but he didn't want to know.

'But, Joe, you're half in,' I said.

'I don't care,' he said. 'I don't want you doing it.'

I told him we were allowed to keep the slates, but Joe would need to hear it from the boss himself and, of course, he knew nothing about it.

We would have real rows over things like that, but I never lost my respect for Joe.

I loved him; it was almost as if my dad had come back to life.

I had got to know Jenny really well, and when she invited me to stay at her home in Banbury during my weekend home leave, I accepted gratefully.

Jenny was a lovely lady of forty-two who had had a tragic life. Her husband had died at just thirty-five, and she had a son, Lee, who was not only deaf and dumb, but physically handicapped, too. She had a daughter, Trish, who was in her mid-twenties, and we all got along well. Jenny provided the sort of friendship I needed at that time. She was very supportive, encouraging me to do this or that, and helped restore some of my self-esteem.

She loved surprises – giving them, as well as receiving. And she laid on a spectacular one for me on the day I was released. I'd mentioned that I would love to drive away from the prison gates in a white Rolls-Royce, and she had one waiting for me when I became a free man, on 15 September 1983. She was standing beside it, a bottle of champagne in one hand, a rolling pin in the other, all smiles.

The Roller had a chauffeur, too, and I asked him to drive us to the building site where Joe and the rest of my mates were working.

Joe broke down. 'Chris,' he said, through his tears, 'what can I say? Man, I love you.' And he put his arms round me.

'You're going to be all right, Joe,' I said. And I meant it. He had just won £3,000 on the football pools and was going to buy a little piece of land in Jamaica.

When Jenny and I reached her home, people seemed to be coming from all directions – her family, my family, friends and neighbours – and, on the front of the house, was a huge banner: 'WELL DONE, CHRIS. WELCOME HOME'.

After only a few minutes. I felt an overpowering need to be on my own. It was all happening too quickly. I was choked and wanted to be on my own, to take it all in.

That evening, my brother Jimmy, who owned a company, Countrywide Fabrications, in Banbury, treated Jenny and me, and the rest of our families, to a Greek meal at a restaurant in Stratford-upon-Avon. We had a marvellous meze, about thirty dishes, then started smashing the plates in traditional Greek style. There was the obligatory belly dancer, who had been told by my brothers to make a fuss of me. I was told she was mine if I wanted her, but, no matter how much I needed a woman, I could not do that to Jenny, even though our relationship was only platonic.

I left that restaurant at 1 a.m., quite drunk. Six hours later, after just three hours' sleep, I was on a plane, leaving Heathrow for my dad's beloved homeland, Cyprus.

It was Jenny's idea. She knew that I wanted, more than anything else, to pay my respects to my dad's country, and she arranged the passports through my probation and parole officers.

It was unforgettable. For the first time in fifteen years I was able to be myself, to sit and drink and chat with people who didn't have a clue who I was or what I had done: people who knew nothing about the Kray madness that had destroyed my life. When the Cyprus sun goes down, it is like nothing else on earth, and to sit at an outside bar, talking to total strangers about anything other than crime, was an exhilarating experience for me.

Someone must have known my background, however, because my passport mysteriously disappeared. After much inconvenience, including an 80-mile round trip to the capital, Nicosia, I learned that it was probably the secret police. Why the passport was taken and never returned I don't know, but it seemed to prove that, despite being more than 1,000 miles from home, I was being watched; that who I had been involved with, all those years before, was still of great concern to those in authority.

After an otherwise blissful fortnight, I had to come back to earth in England. I tried for several jobs and finally got one that, given my three years in Coldingley, suited me perfectly – landscaping old people's gardens.

I bought a van and a flamboyant grass cutter with the money I'd saved from my roof work and invested in some business cards, which I distributed around Banbury. Sadly, I was no businessman: I'd get involved listening to the old people's financial problems and if they couldn't pay at the end of the day, I'd let them off.

I'd always been a softie for old ladies. Which is how I came to make a 300-mile round trip to Stockport with one hundred red and white roses in my van.

While I had been in prison, Susie Edge, the redhead I'd met in a Northern club, had tragically died at the age of thirty-two, after suffering multiple sclerosis. Her mother, Nellie, wrote, telling me that Susie had got out of bed one morning, walked downstairs into her kitchen, and keeled over, hitting her head on the floor. She had a brain haemorrhage and never recovered.

Jenny and I had become lovers, not mere friends, and we were lying in bed one morning when I told her how Nellie had written dozens of letters of support while I'd been away. 'She was brilliant,' I said. 'I told her I'd bring her roses one day. I'd love to do that.'

'Don't talk about it, Lambrianou,' Jenny said. 'Do it.' That was how she talked to me.

Nellie, who didn't know I was out of prison, was delighted to hear from me. But she thought I was joking when I said she would be seeing me the next day.

'I've got a surprise for you,' was all I told her.

I bought dozens of roses and put them in five buckets of water, then set off for Stockport. Nellie was gobsmacked, but thrilled, when she saw me at the door, a bucket in each hand.

'I told you, didn't I?' I said. 'I told you that, one day, I'd say thank you with roses, for supporting me all those years.'

She was a lovely lady, Nellie. Just like her dear daughter, Susie.

I gave up the gardening job and went for one as a part-time driver. I was dashing here, there and everywhere without a valid driving licence and, finally, it got too much for Jenny.

'If you really want us to be together, Chris,' she said, 'you have to go and take a proper driving test.'

'I'm a good driver, Jen,' I said. 'I don't need a licence.'

But she would not hear of it and made me sell the van until I'd passed.

I went to a motoring school and told an instructor I knew it all, and needed only one lesson. I took the test in his car – and failed. It was one of the biggest surprises, and disappointments, of my life.

Jenny forced me to go back and enrol for six lessons. It was galling having to fork out money when I could already drive, but Jenny was adamant: I wasn't going back on the road until I had a driving licence in my hand.

I completed six lessons, under the tolerant eye of the instructor, Mr Vale, and got behind the wheel for The Test. I had been in a few hairy situations, but this was unnerving, for all sorts of reasons.

'Good luck, Chris,' said Mr Vale. 'I feel you can do it this time.'

'Go on, Chris, you'll pass, I know it,' said Jenny.

She was right to have bought a congratulations card in advance, because I did, indeed, pass.

I had had my work exhibited at Westminster Cathedral. I had won the coveted Koestler Award for literature while still in prison, and my meditations would eventually be published as a book. But nothing thrilled me more than being told, that morning in February, 1984: 'You've passed.'

For the first time in my life, I felt I'd achieved something worthwhile; something that was down to me and me alone, without someone else getting the recognition.

And I burst into tears.

By the spring of 1985, I felt that Jenny and I had gone as far as we could together. She had built me up, strengthened me, and given me all the encouragement I needed to put the horrors of prison behind me and create a new, worthwhile life. But now I started to feel more and more uncomfortable with her and her friends. Everyone, it seemed, knew my background, and I began to feel an oddity, a showpiece. It irritated me: I didn't feel I fitted in. And my feelings led to tension. We began rubbing each other up the wrong way.

Before we met, Jenny had been a widow, in full control of her life. I'd been like a monk, with almost no control over what happened to me. To join those two contrasting lifestyles and philosophies into a long-lasting, happy unit was, on reflection, an impossibility. We could love each other, go to church together, be there for each other, but, when it came down to it, we belonged in two different places and needed our own space.

There was something else bothering me, too. I wanted to get married and have children, but, while I was in Sudbury, Jenny had had an hysterectomy.

I spent a lot of time wondering how to break it to Jenny that I felt it best if I moved out.

And then she came home unexpectedly from work one February morning, and held me tight and told me about Trish.

And I knew I had to stay.

She walked through the door, her face ashen.

'What's the matter, Jen?' I said.

She walked up to me and put her arms round me and started crying. 'Oh, Chrissie.'

'What on earth's the matter?' I said.

'Trish is dead,' she said.

'What? Don't be silly. I was with her last night.'

'She was killed this morning.'

'No, no. It can't be true.'

'It is, Chrissie,' she said. 'I've just been told. There was an accident.'

It was true. Trish had been driving along a country lane in her car when a Range Rover, coming the other way, skidded and crashed into it, killing her instantly.

Poor Trish. She had just been promoted to manageress at a German computer company in Banbury and was a charming young lady, with everything to live for.

Poor Jenny. Her husband had been killed at just thirty-five. She had a tragically handicapped son. And now her only daughter had been snatched from her in the most tragic circumstances.

Of course, I wouldn't, couldn't, walk out on Jenny. I had to be there for her; to pray for her, support her, encourage her and love her, as she had done for me. I was not meant to leave her. I was where I was meant to be. That was where God had put me, and I was not about to run out, no matter how much I felt we had drifted apart.

Three months or so after the funeral, Jenny had reached the point where she needed to take her pain out on somebody. She came home, one rainswept evening, looking like a drowned rat. I was painting an upstairs room, and called out, 'Jen, did you get that sherry?'

Without saying a word, she put on her coat and walked out the door. Ten minutes later, she came and put the sherry on a table. Then she went to a cupboard and picked up a crowbar. She walked up the stairs and started bashing it against the door of the room I was painting.

I stood behind it, laughing. But it was no joke to Jenny. She was boiling mad. She had snapped.

'I've always been the most gentle little widow you can imagine,' she screamed. 'You are the only one who can stir me up to outright violence.'

Eventually, she calmed down and I apologized for upsetting her and treating her badly. But the incident gave me the perfect opportunity to tell her that I was going to leave as soon as I'd found another place to live. It was not easy, but it had to be done, for her sake as well as mine. She didn't want me to leave, but agreed that if I no longer felt comfortable with her, I should move out. When I did finally leave, I knew that I would never forget Jenny and what she did for me.

And I never have.

CHAPTER TWENTY-FOUR

One evening in April 1985, the phone rang at my flat, in Bicester. The caller was a young woman, named Caroline. I'd met her and her mother seven months before at her brother's house, next door to my brother Nicky in Banbury. He was a painter and decorator, and I was talking to him about work I wanted done in my own home, when Caroline walked in. To be honest, I didn't like her much. There was nothing vulnerable or gentle about her; she was brash, and quite full of herself, to the point of appearing arrogant. And she seemed a bit of a yuppie, with a well-paid promotional job, a new Rover car, a fur coat – and an Arabian stallion called Prince which she rode at weekends.

She re-introduced herself and said she wanted to meet because she had a job that might interest me. We met the following evening at the Moat House Hotel, in Banbury – and both got a shock. She knew my background and expected me to be in the bar, with a couple of drinks already under my belt; but I was sitting quietly in the lounge with a pot of tea. I was defensive, expecting the unlikeable girl-about-town, but Caroline had changed: she was less forceful, much softer. And physically far more attractive than when I'd last seen her.

One of her friends was recruiting people to sell insurance, but I wasn't interested. I'd been approached with a similar proposition several months before and had decided it wasn't for me. So, we started chatting generally, and discovered we liked each other.

Despite looking and sounding like a yuppie, she was a country girl, born and bred in Oxfordshire, and she was interested that I was keen to visit stately homes and beauty spots I'd seen only in magazines in prison.

'Let me take you somewhere wonderful on Saturday,' she said. 'It will take your breath away.'

I was already enchanted by her and accepted immediately.

Caroline took me to Waddesdon Manor, the Rothschild Estate, near Aylesbury. And she was right: it *did* take my breath away. The huge, elegant mansion and sprawling landscaped gardens were like something out of *Country Life* or *Tatler* and, as I marvelled at the splendour, all I could think was, 'If I go blind, or I'm sent back to prison, at least I've got this in my head. I've seen something truly special.'

After that, Caroline took great pleasure showing me other places of great beauty and historical interest. And she would add to my excitement by making each trip a surprise.

'Where are we going this time?' I'd ask.

'You mustn't ask me any questions,' she'd say.

'You've got to let me know.'

'No. Wait till we get there.'

And then we'd drive into Blenheim Palace, or Florence Nightingale's home, Claydon House, near Winslow, in Buckinghamshire, or have a picnic at a renowned beauty spot, like Brill on the Hill, with a spectacular view of the Oxfordshire countryside.

It was as if I had become Caroline's cause, and she was taking my education a step further by making everything I'd only dreamed about a reality. Again, I found myself thinking, 'Well, if this is what it's really about, then I don't want any more than what I can close my eyes and see. If it doesn't last forever, then at least I have it now.'

During that summer of 1985, I was falling in love with Caroline, but I didn't know how to react to her. She was only twenty-five, more than twenty years younger than me, and I was too frightened even to hold her hand.

I went to a priest and explained the problem. He told me his parents had always enjoyed a loving relationship, despite a twenty-five-year age gap, and he encouraged me to tell Caroline my true feelings. But it was easier said than done. The age difference was a barrier I found difficult to come to terms with, mainly because I felt that other people would think of me as a cradle snatcher. Somehow, it was all right sitting down in a restaurant, or driving along in a car, but walking down the street, holding hands or not, filled me with embarrassment.

After a couple of months, however, I conquered my reservations and our love for each other developed into a physical relationship. I moved into Caroline's one-bedroomed cottage in the village of Wendlebury. We both wanted children and three months later, in December, she told me, proudly, that she was pregnant. We decided to get married at Bicester Register Office the following May. One of her friends carried out a test to see whether the baby would be a boy or a girl, with a prophetic result. She dangled a wedding ring from a thread of cotton and said that Caroline would have a boy if the ring swung in a straight line. If the ring went round in circles, she would have a girl.

The ring couldn't make up its mind: it would swing in a straight line, then start going round in circles.

None of us thought for a minute that Caroline might be carrying a boy *and* a girl.

*

I desperately wanted a boy, a son to call Christopher, like my dad. I hadn't been good for him; I hadn't even learned to communicate with him in his native tongue. And I had brought him pain and misery and anguish in his final years. I wanted a son to call Christopher; to give him all the things I never had, and help him grow into a decent Christian-minded citizen. One Christopher Lambrianou who would get it right. That's all I wanted.

One night, late in December, all my hopes for that – or, indeed, for a daughter – looked lost when I went to pick Caroline up from her mother's house and found her distressed and in a state of near-panic because she was bleeding. I had to get Caroline to hospital. Fast.

I drew up at the main entrance to Horton Hospital, in Banbury, and dashed in, leaving Caroline in the car. I grabbed the first trolley I saw and pushed it outside. I picked up Caroline and gently laid her on it. Her face was ashen. I backed in the door, then turned and pushed the trolley down a long, deserted corridor as fast as I could, screaming, 'Help me! Is there a doctor here? Help me!'

A couple of nurses and a doctor ran out of a side ward. One of them said, 'What's the problem?'

'My wife's having a miscarriage,' I gasped.

I waited outside while Caroline was taken into a room and given some tests. Then the doctor came out. His face said it all.

'I'm afraid I have some terrible news,' he said. 'You have lost this baby. I can't find a heartbeat.'

'You have *got* to find a heartbeat,' I told him.

'I'm sorry. I can't. There isn't one.'

I was devastated, a broken man. Everything I'd ever wanted was wrapped up in that woman in that room. I loved her like I'd never loved anybody or anything. She was all I ever really wanted. And I'd believed she was giving me the one gift I never dreamed possible.

If I'd gone to the Social Services and said, 'I've got this wonderful love and I need to share it and I wonder if you could see your way clear to me adopting a son?' they would have taken one look at my record and said, 'You can't be serious.'

Happily, God does not see things that way.

There was an Irish sister there. She was so sorry for us.

I looked into her sad face and said, 'Sister, I am a Christian, and God has never let me down. He took me through Hell and back. And he has never given me a promise he hasn't kept. He doesn't give a baby, then take it away.'

'I know what you're talking about, Mr Lambrianou,' she said. 'I am a Catholic. I, too, believe in God. But I also have to believe a doctor, who is very skilled and trained to do a job. If he cannot hear a heartbeat, you really must accept that and let this child go back to God.'

I told her I could not accept that. I wasn't going to let go.

I went in to see Caroline. She was crying. I held her hands and started crying, too.

'Don't give up,' I said. But it was an empty plea.

The doctor came in and said there was nothing more they could do. But Caroline was being kept in for a 'D and C'.

It was 1 a.m. when I drove away from hospital, tears streaming down my face. I was upset. I was hurt. And I was angry, angrier than I'd ever been in my life.

'If you can hear me, you bastard, you'd better do something,' I screamed into the silence of the car. 'You'd better do something. Quick.'

And I sobbed uncontrollably. 'How can you do this to me?'

When I went to bed I couldn't sleep. I tossed and turned. I got out of bed. I got in again. And I was still crying. I didn't want to believe I'd come all that way to achieving what I truly wanted, only for it to be snatched away. I wanted that baby. I wanted a son I could call Christopher.

Feeling ragged, I got up early and was at the hospital before 8 a.m. Caroline was in a huge, short-stay ward, filled with old women dying of cancer and other illnesses. She was tired and drawn, but she brightened a little when she saw me. 'Chris, I've got some pretty good news,' she said. 'An Indian doctor came in during the night. He said he wasn't happy with the other doctor's opinion, and has arranged for me to have a scan. But there's definitely no heartbeat, so we mustn't be too hopeful.'

When the time came for the scan, I put Caroline in a wheelchair and pushed her along the ward, past all the other, tragic patients. They had all heard the tale of the night before, of the man who Jesus had never let down, and as we passed by their beds, many called out, 'Good luck, son . . . God bless, girl . . .'

I pushed the wheelchair along, saying one prayer after another. Prison was gone; it was as if I'd never done a day. What was happening now was far, far more important. If someone had asked me which I would rather face – that make-or-break scan or prison – I would have said prison. At least, I knew how to deal with that.

The radiographer did not want me present during the scan, but Caroline said, 'I want him here. He was there when the baby was conceived and, if this is to be the end, I want him there, too.'

'I'm not sure Mr Lambrianou will be able to take it,' the radiographer said. 'It's going to be quite difficult. He may find it upsetting.'

Caroline was adamant, and that made me want to be there even more. I was given a gown and a mask and hat, and watched as electrodes were placed on Caroline's tummy, then hooked up to a monitor.

I took Caroline's hand, putting my strength into her, but inside, I was crying because her precious gift to me was disappearing before our eyes.

I could not make much sense out of what was happening on the monitor, but the radiographer pointed at a tiny figure that seemed to be waving.

'That's movement,' she said. 'That's a baby. And it's healthy. There's nothing wrong at all.'

As she leaned forward to measure the baby, a wonderful saying from the Bible came into my head: 'They will go out with tears in their eyes, but in the morning they will wake and rejoice.'

But it was not over yet.

'I think you'd better go and empty your bladder, Mrs Lambrianou,' the radiographer said. 'I can see further movement in there, but the fluid is making it difficult to determine what it is.'

When Caroline came back, she went through the same procedure again and we saw the movement the radiographer thought was there.

'Mr and Mrs Lambrianou,' she said, excitedly. 'You're going to have twins.'

We couldn't believe it. From the despair of thinking we had lost one baby, we were experiencing the elation of there being two.

Chris, I told myself, this is what the Lord does. Twins wrecked your life. Now He is giving you twins to put it back together. I really felt that. I felt all those lost years had been restored to me. He just wiped them away.

I had gone out in the morning crying with grief, but would be going home in the evening with tears of joy. God had not let me down, as I knew He wouldn't. He had kept his promise.

I knew He could be giving me a son I could call Christopher.

We were overjoyed at the thought of having twins in July, but we had to get through the winter first. It was not going to be easy. I'd been doing landscape gardening for a guy at Appleton, but had to quit because of the travelling expenses, and now I was on the dole. To survive, Caroline sold her car and horse, and we kept the cottage warm by burning tarry blocks from railway sleepers, which British Rail staff generously allowed me to load into my battered Cortina.

By the time Caroline was due to go into hospital – after our May wedding – I felt ashamed, because we hardly had a penny, and I was forced to sell my car. Caroline was giving me everything I ever wanted, but, while she was in hospital, I would not be able to give her anything: no food, no clothes for the babies, no presents. I wasn't even sure how I was going to get there.

A week before she was due to go in, I had £20 left out of my dole money.

'Come on, girl,' I said to Caroline. 'Here's some money to get your hair done. You'll want to look nice when you go in.' But my heart was breaking: there was a real struggle going on inside me and I was even considering going back to crime to get some money.

I left Caroline at the hairdresser's in Market Square and carried on walking to get a paper. I didn't go to the newsagent's, however. My feet seemed to have a mind of their own and kept going towards the job centre. I went to the board and saw a notice, saying, 'Quarry Manager wanted. £4 an hour.'

I had been praying for a job, and I had a feeling my prayers had been answered. Several people had shown interest in the job, but the site manager, Ken Haynes, agreed to see me that afternoon.

After the hair-do, I took Caroline back to the house and told her about the interview. She was sure I would get the job. I borrowed a car to drive to see Mr Haynes, at the quarry in Kirtlington, about four miles away. The Lord was smiling on me that afternoon. Ken was a Londoner, who had been evacuated to Oxford in the war, and he took to me straight away. He said he had a lot more applicants to see, but thought I stood a good chance. He said he would be in touch, and I returned home, confident I would not be one of the unemployed much longer.

My faith in myself and Caroline's faith in me was justified. That evening Ken rang, offering me the job, and I started the following Monday.

The man who was actually in charge of the quarry was a big guy, nicknamed Yogi, after the bear. And, sadly, he was a small-time operator with no vision, who thought he could run the quarry on a shoestring; even his old bulldozer didn't work. He did not want to spend money on advertising, and I'd sit around for days with nothing to do and no income coming in through the gate.

I'd been there only a couple of weeks when he gave me some devastating news: he felt the quarry was a waste of time and he was going to shut it during the week and open it only at weekends. My services would no longer be required. I couldn't believe what I was hearing: with twins due in under a month, I could not face being out of work again.

I looked Yogi straight in the eye and said, 'I was employed by Ken Haynes as a full-time site operator. I signed a contract. And I'm going to hold you to it.'

'Tough,' he said. 'I'm shutting the site.'

'No, you're not,' I said. 'That gate's staying open.' And I turned my back on him.

Later, Yogi came down to the quarry with two heavily built guys, in their late twenties, early thirties. They looked at me menacingly. They genuinely thought Yogi was being had over.

'Look,' I said to Yogi, 'if you've brought these two here because I'm giving you a hard time, I'm still not moving. You want to close this site down because you can't support it. You only want it for a bit of pocket money at the weekend. Well, let me tell you something. I've got two little babies about to be born. I've got no money and my chances of finding work are nil. I'm not leaving this job.'

'You've got no choice,' Yogi said. 'I'm closing the site.'

'You're not,' I said, determined to hang on. 'I don't care if I work in the mud and the filth and anything else. If you get in my way, I'm just going to walk all over you, because I got this job in the proper way, and you're playing around with my livelihood and my family's future.'

We had a few hard words, but the two heavies walked away. They weren't frightened of me; they knew nothing of my background. To them I was simply a genuine working bloke, battling for his bread and butter, and they felt I, not Yogi, was in the right. They could identify with me.

In the end, everything worked out well for me. Yogi chucked his job in and James Budget, the actual owner of the land where the quarry was, asked me if I wanted to take it over. I didn't have enough faith in the business, or know enough about it, to borrow money from the bank and set up a company, so I declined the offer. However, I was approached by David Beacroft, a wealthy plant-hire businessman, who I knew wanted to use the quarry as a tip for his lorries. He was excited and said, 'I will give you anything you want if you help me get the site.'

'I want to keep my job,' I said.

'No problem,' he said.

'I'd like a good wage.'

'Yes.'

'And I want all the scrap metal that comes through the gates and any other perks.'

'You've got it,' Beacroft said.

In the end, Messrs Budget and Beacroft did a deal that suited them both, and I became a sort of king in my own castle, running an enterprise of my own within Mr Beacroft's business. Soon, I was making enough money from scrap metal not to have to touch my wages as quarry manager, and I proudly spent it on a pram, cots, baby clothes and other essential items for the twins.

I became a character among the expectant mothers. None of them knew anything about the Krays, or Jack McVitie, or my fifteen years inside. To them, I was just Caroline's crazy husband, who always arrived, full of life and smiling, with loads of bags and silly balloons and all the rest. They couldn't wait to see me; I was far more entertaining than their husbands, who just smoked their fags and bit their fingernails.

Dave Beacroft had given me a mobile phone because the nurses said they might have to induce the birth and would keep me informed. When I finished work on 12 July, I'd heard nothing, so I went straight to the hospital. They had, indeed, decided to induce that evening, and I joined Caroline in the labour suite, where I was given a cup of tea and told to sit quietly in an armchair. I sat there, listening to the piped music, thinking how far I'd come since that day in the Old Bailey when a chunk of my life was taken away. How wonderfully different this genteel, tranquil room was to some of the disgustingly filthy holes I'd been thrown into during my years of incarceration. I'd come a million miles since those crazed, bloody days in the chokey at Albany. I had taken off into orbit and was on another planet. I wasn't that evil, ruthless, conniving, brain-dead loser. I was a good-humoured, easy-going, loving human being, blessed with a woman I loved, who was about to deliver the most priceless of gifts. I was truly home, and about to go through a beautiful experience, one I would recommend to any man.

There was a whole team of medical staff on standby – half-a-dozen nurses, two doctors and an obstetrician. I was holding Caroline's hand as the first baby began its struggle to come into the world.

'Come on, come on now,' I urged Caroline, tightening my grip on her hand, trying to force some of my strength into her. 'We're nearly there. Come on, get it out . . . Come on, we're going to do it.' No football or boxing fan ever called for his team with more heart. Then I broke down.

There she was, a baby girl. A gorgeous little creature, but a girl.

My spirits dropped. I had been expecting a boy: I had convinced myself the first one would be my Christopher. As a nurse put Holly on some scales, I went to the window and looked out, my heart heavy with disappointment. The sun was coming up.

Suddenly, I saw a magpie, then two more, fly on to a tree in the hospital grounds.

'One for sorrow, two for joy, three for a girl . . .'

A second later, a fourth magpie flew down and joined the others.

'. . . four for a boy . . .'

Excitedly, I turned and walked to Caroline. 'The next one

is a boy for sure,' I told her. 'I promise you, the next one is a boy.'

Six minutes later, at 6.43 p.m., I kept that promise. Another, equally lovable, adorable baby emerged from the woman I loved, and he was a boy.

I couldn't contain myself. I jumped up and cheered. And then I hugged the Lebanese obstetrician and danced round the room with him.

Holly was sleeping, in an incubator beside Caroline's bed; she looked great. But Christopher looked more frail, much weaker, and, after weighing him, a nurse almost ran out of the room with him. I couldn't take it in.

'What's going on?' I wanted to know.

I was told Christopher was just three pounds three ounces and his lungs were underdeveloped, which can happen with twins.

Caroline told me not to worry; he was going to be all right. But I couldn't relax; I needed to see him. I was allowed into the Special Baby Care Unit and looked at him in an incubator, a woollen hat on his tiny head, wires and tubes attached to his frail little body. There was a hole in the side of the incubator, so that parents could touch their babies. I squeezed a massive hand through and gently held one of Christopher's. Tears running down my face, I looked at him lovingly, and started to pray. My son, Christopher, was fighting for his life and I was in there fighting with him. I prayed that God would help us win this battle. Thankfully, He did.

Sadly, things started to go wrong between Caroline and me only a few minutes after I picked her up from the hospital.

I'd borrowed a car from someone who owed me a favour, but it was a dilapidated old wreck and Caroline was furious when she saw it. I calmed her down and got the babies in, but no sooner had we set off than Caroline started moaning that I was driving too fast.

I felt dreadful. 'It should not be like this,' I thought. 'Our babies are here. I've got a job and a house to take them all back to. I love Caroline. It should be a big, wonderful adventure, a time to be really happy.' But Caroline was not and, one afternoon, I came home from work to find her and the twins missing.

I finally discovered they were all back in hospital, Caroline in bed, in a tiny, cramped room, the babies in two cots beside her. When I started talking to her, it was like speaking to a complete stranger; she was so remote, so unhappy. I later discovered that she had been seen by a social worker, who told her to end the relationship with me. 'Do you know who he is?' she had said. 'Do you know what he did?'

Caroline was transferred to the Park Hospital, nearby, and I talked to a doctor there, who was aware of all that had happened. He asked me to be patient and tolerant but, quite honestly, I could not understand what he was going on about. I didn't know what I'd done wrong. I hadn't beaten Caroline up. I hadn't got nasty with her, hadn't even sworn at her. I'd supported her all the way through her pregnancy, even held her hand as our tiny bundles of joy had emerged into the world.

Somehow the marriage survived the trauma of the next few months and we had the twins christened by a close friend, the Reverend Chris Handforth, at a lovely church in Wroxton. Even that marvellous occasion had its problems, however. And, of course, I was the culprit.

During the reception for guests in the Wroxton village hall, we ran out of alcoholic drinks, so I nipped round to a nearby off-licence to buy some more.

On the way back, I saw a grubby, dishevelled, miserable-looking old tramp and stopped to chat to him. I was feeling on top of the world, revelling in one of the happiest days of my life, but the tramp told me he had had a rough old day. When he said he was hungry, I took him back to the party and gave him some food and drink. Caroline looked at me as if she was having a fit and her mother looked at me as if I was a mess a dog had left in the middle of the floor.

But, as far as I was concerned, I'd done the right thing. My babies had been dedicated to God and I had met a man who was hungry. What kind of man would I have been if I'd left him out on the street when I had food and drink to give him?

Caroline and her mother did not understand my gesture at all, but there were real Christians at that party who knew what I was expressing and appreciated it. The old tramp marched out, having had a tot or two, and, who knows, maybe he appreciated it. Maybe he felt he had met a decent citizen and understood some of the joy I was feeling.

Caroline made it clear she wanted me to share the responsibility of the children. 'Go on, off you go with them,' she would say at weekends, as she tackled the housework. I didn't mind in the least: I loved the twins and enjoyed taking them out in their double pushchair, and would sing to them as we went along.

A year later, Caroline fell pregnant again and she pushed me into buying a bigger house. I went to Ken Haynes's brother, Ron, who managed Beacroft Plant Hire and asked him for a reference to get a mortgage. He obliged and even assured the building society I was earning enough to meet the repayments. And it was with some pride that, for the first time, I became the owner of a house – a lovely, three-bedroomed property, with garage, on a small estate in Bicester.

Caroline gave birth to another boy, whom we called David.

He was a beautiful kid and should have bonded us closer together, but, sadly, he divided us. In my eyes, he could do no wrong, whereas he and Caroline butted heads. I kind of took him under my wing. Caroline doted on the twins and they had each other. David had me. I became his best friend.

At the same time Caroline and I stopped communicating in the way we should have done. Although we would have two more children – Laura and Rebecca – those years after David was born were the beginning of the end of what had promised to be an idyllic marriage.

I believe there was a lot of pressure put on Caroline from all quarters about my past and our age difference, and once the devil gets a foothold he can soon drive a wedge into a relationship. He did into ours. Caroline found it hard looking after so many young children. Life became difficult and nothing I did pleased her.

We went through three reconciliations, for the sake of our friends as well as our own beliefs, but we were doing the right things for the wrong reasons. We never reconciled because we loved each other. We tried everything – counselling, taking time out with each other – but it seemed only to work for a while. It would paper over the cracks until the inevitable unhappy ending. I kept praying faithfully for the girl I married to come back but she was gone.

CHAPTER TWENTY-FIVE

My job at the quarry lasted three years. David Beacroft did his best to find work for me, but I knew it was time to leave and face a fresh challenge. Thankfully, I found one – again through the job centre – driving a road-sweeping lorry or JCB, for an Irish company, Henley Plant, which was one of the constructors working on the M40 motorway from London to Oxford. The other guys on the firm had no idea of my background: I was just Chris, a decent, reliable bloke, who, like them, got up early and worked a long, hard day. My dear old dad would have been proud of me. I wasn't too displeased either; after all those violent, wasted years, where my self-esteem was at rock bottom, I actually had some respect for myself. OK, it wasn't the most skilled, demanding job in the world, but at least I was facing up to my responsibilities and doing something straight to feed my wife and family. Caroline appreciated it, too; she even drove the kids to a bridge, so that they could look down and see their dad working on top of a mountain of crushed stone with his JCB, filling the crushing machine with large rocks.

That job lasted a year. I was offered more work, but it meant moving to London, and of course I could not leave Caroline and the kids. Throughout that year, my parole officer, Mike Howard, had been dropping hints about the Ley Community, a rehabilitation centre for alcohol and drug abusers, suggesting I went there for a look round. I could not see the point: I didn't have a problem myself and didn't particularly want to meet people who did. But Mike kept on and on, and when the M40 work stopped I agreed to go to the centre, if only to keep him happy.

The Ley Community is set in seven acres on what was Dr David Livingstone's country estate, in the village of Yarnton, a few miles north of Oxford. As Mike Howard turned off Sandy Lane and cruised slowly up a long, tree-lined drive, towards a large house, the Ley's headquarters, I was moved by a feeling of peace and tranquillity. I don't know what I'd expected, but it was not this: I liked the place on sight.

Mike introduced me to Paul Toon, the director, who told me that the Ley was founded in 1970 to teach people to lead purposeful lives, free of their dependence on drugs and/or alcohol. In return, I told him about me, warts and all, and then had a look round the place. When I left, Paul said he would be pleased to have me on the team, if I wanted to do some voluntary work. When I told Caroline, she thought it might be a good idea but, quite honestly, I didn't think working with such damaged people was for me. After all, I'd barely got myself sorted out.

I didn't think I'd ever return to the Ley, but when Mike Howard told me that Paul had asked to see me again, I found myself agreeing to go. I liked Paul even more than I had on first meeting him: he had a way of making me feel good about myself; it was OK that I wasn't perfect, that life had damaged me and put me in the reject bin.

I agreed to do some voluntary work and, over the next couple of months, Paul got me doing all sorts of jobs, such as pulling down buildings, gardening and accompanying him on trips to meetings in London. He was also a local councillor and took me along to meetings at Banbury Town Hall.

Paul is a sort of patron saint of hopeless causes and, basically, he felt that, having come out of prison relatively unscathed after fifteen years, I could be an incentive to the drug addicts and alcoholics sent to the Ley. I could understand his thinking and when he asked me if I would escort one of his charges to London for a court appearance, I said I would. Everything went smoothly, except for the amount of time and aggravation on trains and buses, and when I went back I told Paul I would be happy to help out again, providing I had the use of the community's car.

He agreed and, for the next three months, I travelled backwards and forwards to London and various other places, making sure that people who were due in court actually got there.

And then Paul asked me if I wanted to apply for a permanent job that was coming up, and I found myself in a dilemma. The Ley liked to employ ex-residents and two guys who were applying for the job had just come through the programme. I felt that if I applied and got the job, they might go back to taking drugs, so I said I would stand back and let them fight it out between them. In the event, each was given a job and went on to do well.

My limited involvement had given me a taste for the work and I asked the directors of a Christian trust if they would fund me as a special needs officer at the Ley. The company is an equal opportunities employer, taking on people with all sorts of dubious backgrounds, and my present character and attitude, not my life sentence, was what interested them. They discussed the matter with the management company running the Ley and, several weeks later, I was delighted to hear I was being given a year's trial, at a salary of £12,000.

To be frank, the Ley did not know they needed me until I was there: not only did I drive to courts – as far afield as

Glasgow and Norfolk – but I also got to know the accused person's family and friends, so that I could speak to solicitors and barristers, magistrates and judges, all of whom needed briefing. I also found myself in the bizarre position of going back to gaols where I'd been locked up, and asking for prisoners to be released into my custody. On one occasion I had to pick a man up from Wandsworth Prison, that big forbidding fortress in South London. Looking at it from the outside filled me with horror, and I could imagine the intimidation my dad and other visitors felt going there to see their loved ones: the degradation of a search, being stared at and spoken to like dirt, shepherded into a room filling with smoke, the floor littered with cigarette ends, hearing your name shouted out. We were unaware of what people had to go through to visit us. We were so used to that behaviour inside we never realized how it must have felt to our visitors.

It was not long before the Ley job took hold of me. Steve Walker, the deputy director, despaired of me at times because I allowed myself to be pulled this way and that by anyone I felt in need. Poor Caroline, too. She was seeing less and less of me as I started putting more into the Ley than I did into my home.

And then a nineteen-year-old drug addict named Billy ran away from the Ley and tragically died while I was on holiday.

And the guilt I felt made me even more dedicated to the Ley, putting an even greater strain on my marriage.

I'd spoken up for Billy at Surrey Crown Court, convincing the judge that the boy desperately wanted to kick his habit, and the Ley would help him do so. Billy was doing fine, but then I took some leave due to me and, for some reason, Billy walked out of the Ley and never came back. Two months later, Mike Howard told me that Billy had been found dead from drug-induced asphyxiation.

Something Billy had said on the way back to the Ley from court haunted me. He'd said, 'Chris, I can afford to make some mistakes – I'm only nineteen.' Sadly, he had been proved tragically wrong. I could not get Billy out of my mind. In a way, I blamed myself for his death. I felt I'd abandoned him in his hour of need. If I'd not taken that holiday, I told myself, I would have been there to talk to him, and he would not have felt the need to run away. What Billy's death did to me was to make me feel that I needed to be at the Ley at all hours of the day and night in case someone, like him, needed to talk. Who knows, I convinced myself, I might even be able to save a life.

Whenever I told Caroline I was going, yet again, to the Ley and didn't know when I'd be back, she would scream, 'Perhaps you'd have some time for me if I had a bloody needle sticking out of my arm!' I have to admit she did have a point.

But Caroline was very supportive at times. Once, around 9 p.m., I got a call saying that a resident named Frank had left the Ley and gone to London without getting proper clearance. Caroline immediately filled her car with petrol, handed me the keys, and said, 'You'd better go to London and bring Frank back – otherwise you'll be impossible to live with.'

I drove to South London, got Frank out of a boozer, and took him back to the Ley. But, far from praising me, Paul Toon and his colleagues were critical. 'Get a grip, Chris,' they said. 'You're getting too involved. You're like a one-man crusade. Think of your health. Your marriage. Your children.'

Sadly, I did not take their advice – and, on 7 June 1991, when Caroline was expecting our fifth child, I paid the price, nearly with my life.

Driving back to the Ley, after escorting a young resident to Snaresbrook Crown Court, I felt a severe pain in my back.

It was so bad by the time we reached the Ley that I could not drive, and asked Jane Brogan, a fellow staff member, to take me home. I lay on the sofa, thinking the pain would go away, but it got steadily worse and moved from my back to my stomach, then to my kidneys. Caroline rang our doctor, who took one look at me, asked a few questions, and said he was calling an ambulance.

'You can't be serious,' I said. 'I can't go into hospital. I've got to take someone to London tomorrow.'

The doctor shook his head. 'You're not. You won't be going anywhere for a long time. And if we don't get you into hospital and operate, you'll be beyond help.'

What on earth was wrong with me? I wanted to know. He said the main artery from the heart was bursting in my stomach, and I would die unless I had an operation quickly. The speed with which the ambulance took me to the John Radcliffe Infirmary, in Oxford, blue light flashing, siren wailing, left me in no doubt he was serious. I was on gas and air for the relief of pain throughout the journey.

Strangely, I wasn't afraid of dying; I felt a great sense of peace, as if God was saying, 'Don't worry, Chris. I've got it all under control.'

A medical team was standing by to rush me into the operating theatre. A surgeon looked at me gravely and told me they would do their best, but nothing was guaranteed; he did not know whether he could save me.

'I'm a Christian, doctor,' I told him. 'If it doesn't work out, don't worry – Jesus and my mum and dad are waiting for me on the other side. I'm not afraid. I know you'll do your best.'

He just shook his head and squeezed my hand. And that's the last I remembered, until I came round in intensive care and Paul Toon was holding my hand.

When he had heard I was having an emergency operation,

he had rushed to the hospital and never left. Apparently, the first thing I said when I saw him was, 'What are you doing here? I'm in hell, aren't I?' Then Caroline's worried face came slowly into focus and it dawned on me that I had, indeed, come through it and was alive.

In an odd way, I felt a little let down that I was not in Heaven, about to be reunited with my mum and dad; but I reasoned that God still had work for me to do on earth.

Paul Toon and Steve Walker were marvellous: they arranged for Caroline to have a nanny and a driver, so that she could visit me every day in hospital; they had a collection to help us pay the bills; and they kept me on full salary all the time I was out of action.

The Ley, I discovered, looks after its own. When I left intensive care and went onto a ward, I had so many visitors from the centre that Caroline found it hard to get near me! In the six weeks I was there, I found everything I wanted in those people: loyalty, care, strength and friendship – everything, in fact, that I expected, but didn't get, from the Kray twins. Those wonderful people from the Ley were there for me and my family in my darkest hour, and for no other motive than that they cared about me. I cannot thank them enough. They may have been ex-junkies and alcoholics, but they had become my family in a real time of need and they were there in numbers with their honesty, love and care.

Sadly, the pressures of my brush with death took its toll on my marriage. While I spent six months convalescing, at the lovely home of Lord and Lady Lees, at Lytchett Minster, in Dorset, Caroline, pregnant and alone with our four children in our new home in Bicester, lurched from one crisis to another.

Caroline was my hero, everything I'd ever wanted, and I

admired and respected her. But when I rang her, asking how things were going, she seemed like a stranger. The baby she was expecting worried the hospital, and doctors wanted to admit her for a rest. But, of course, that was impossible. What made matters even more traumatic for Caroline was that her father died. She found it difficult coming to terms with that.

When I returned home I walked into a storm. Caroline made it clear that she was nothing like the gentle, kind girl I'd married; she was strong, single-minded and determined to get me out of her life. She could cope with the children and whatever, but I was just too much. I had to agree to a separation and in June 1992 Caroline filed for divorce.

Waiting for it to come through was a devastating time and I don't know how I would have coped without the support of Steve Walker, who kept me on track during some tough times. He had been there himself, so I listened hard.

After the divorce, in August two years later, Caroline moved to Trowbridge, Wiltshire, with our five children. Every Friday night, Harry Wishart, a friend of mine who lived nearby, would pick the kids up from Caroline and I'd meet him in Trowbridge then drive them home.

All that year, I'd been looking forward to joining more than a hundred college students – and staff parishioners, like myself, from Oxford's St Aldate's Church – for an evangelical mission, in Reading, organized by a former rector of the church, Michael Green. We arrived in the Berkshire town on the last Sunday in September, and spent the week visiting other churches, jobless and homeless people – and even inmates at Reading gaol. It was an uphill task, but hugely rewarding, and we were all enjoying it.

Then, on Friday, at our morning prayer meeting, I felt an overpowering urge – no, a desperate *need* – to leave, to see my children. At the same time something in my head, which even today I can't explain, was compelling me to go home. So, I said my goodbyes to Michael Green and the other organizers and drove to Bicester.

No sooner had I got in when the phone rang. It was Harry.

'I have some bad news, Chris,' he said, his voice heavy with concern. 'Laura's had a terrible accident, a really bad fall. She's been taken to hospital by helicopter.'

I screamed, from so deep inside me I felt I'd tear myself in half. I dropped the phone and wandered about the house, shaking and sobbing: 'NO, NO, NO.'

CHAPTER TWENTY-SIX

I finally pulled myself back into the here and now, and went back to the phone, desperate to know what had happened. But Harry couldn't give me any further information, apart from the fact that Laura was in the Frenchay Hospital, Bristol. I told him I was leaving right away.

Tears streaming down my face, I picked up a large Good News Bible. I wanted something from God. I had given of myself on the mission; I wanted the promise that they who honour God, He will also honour. His reply came in the silence of my soul: 'Be still and know that I am God.'

I set off for Bristol. I knew I had to make for the M4, which I would pick up somewhere near Swindon. I don't know how I made it, driving through the tears. All I could whisper was, 'Not yet, Lord! Just let me see her before You take her, if that is to be Your will.'

My legs and the rest of my body were shaking. You can't have love like Laura Ashley's (as Holly had named her) in your life, and not want it forever! We all loved that little bossy, curly haired moppet in our own special way; we all called her, 'Your Majesty, the Baby'. I knew what Abraham felt like when he came so near to losing his beloved son Isaac, and just how God must have felt as a father when he lost his Jesus. It's not anger, it's not bitterness, it's not hatred – it's emptiness, loneliness, as if a light has been turned out in your life. A part of you dies too.

I got to Bristol early that evening, but I didn't know how to get to the Frenchay. I saw a church with lights on, so I turned off the motorway and drove round until I found it. I went inside, finding a youth club in progress. I saw two men speaking together and I explained my predicament about my daughter and the Frenchay Hospital. One of the chaps, Peter, said, 'Don't worry, I'll take you there.'

He got in his car and I followed. I knew the Lord was working in my life and I could trust him to bring order out of confusion, as he had so often in the past. We travelled about six miles and came to the Frenchay. I didn't know what to expect but Peter stayed with me until I was taken over to intensive care by a nurse. He grasped my hand tightly, and quietly said, 'Brother, our prayers are with you and your family.'

Walking down the long corridor leading to intensive care, the icy fingers of fear gripped at my emotions. Yet the hospital seemed to be a place of tranquillity. The nurse ushered me into a waiting room, and after a few moments the door opened and Caroline came in, the strain was showing clearly on her face. I broke down in tears and told her I couldn't face looking at Laura's broken body. I still didn't know the extent of her injuries or what had happened to her.

Caroline took me by the hand and led me into the ward, past the rows of beds where people on life-support machines were fighting for their lives.

She led me to the end of the ward, where there was a small room, and there, lying wrapped up in bandages, was my precious little angel, being kept alive by wires and drips and monitors. The floodgates broke again as I held her hand, oblivious to anything going on in that darkened room. I said the prayer of my life: 'Please, Lord, if it is possible, regardless of what she may be, bring her back, and don't turn out the light on us. We will love her regardless, even if she can move only one finger.'

A doctor came in, Dr Aziz, and told us not to be hopeful. Laura was between life and death, and if she made it through the night there might be some hope, but after such a fall we should be aware that she could be a living vegetable. The horror of this struck right at my heart. Our beautiful little Laura Ashley, so full of life and vigour, this little chatterbox who could take you down or make you do her bidding with just one look. What would we be able to do for her? How would her little sister Rebecca cope? They were just like twins, and Laura was so protective of Becka.

Caroline and I stayed by Laura's bedside right through the night, watching the slightest change in the monitor, heart pressure and heart rate. We became quite expert at reading what was going on with our little girl. We were told that because of the extensive swelling inside her brain it would be a long wait to find out what was going on. If we coughed or sneezed, we would reach four on a monitor, Laura Ashley's heart rate was nearing forty, with high blood pressure to contend with as well. We did actually lose Laura in the course of that long harrowing night, but doctors brought her round.

I believe sincerely that the lowest point in my whole life must have been the desperate lonely hours I spent at the Frenchay in intensive care. We were told that, even if Laura survived, she might take years and years to get back any movement in her limbs. We were to expect a long, long painful process of rehabilitation. She might not even recognize us.

Caroline and I prayed our hearts out. She felt she was to blame. I hadn't heard what had really happened, so Caroline explained. Laura, her sister Becka and another little girl had been playing in an upstairs room. The little girl started to throw dolls out of the window. Laura was looking out of the window, trying to see what had happened to her dolls, when she fell twenty-eight feet down onto the concrete paving slabs.

Our other children were staying with neighbours so, on the third day, I felt it right to go and get some clean clothes and make the Ley aware of the situation. I was a little worried about how I was going to ask for a long time off. I had already had two weeks off to go to the mission in Reading. I left the Frenchay at about four in the afternoon and got home about six, packed all the things I needed and went and found Steve Walker, who had become a good friend.

'Steve,' I said, 'I've got to tell you that I've just come from the Frenchay Hospital in Bristol where my little girl is in intensive care. She might not make it out of there because things look very bad. I just want your blessing so I can go there and forget about work for the time being.'

I can still remember his words: 'Chris, I'm not worried about Laura Ashley, because she's in the best hands possible, but I am worried about you. When did you last sleep or eat or get some rest?'

'Three days ago,' I said.

'Go home and go to the hospital tomorrow,' he told me. 'Don't worry about work, come back when it's sorted. You won't be any good to us with your head down at the hospital all the time, so get it out of the way.'

With that, this tough guy with a heart of gold put his arms round me and gave me the kind of hug only one brother can give to another. I took off for Bristol and the Frenchay with his words ringing in my ears: 'We'll ring every day just in case you need us.'

When I got down to the Frenchay, Paul Toon was on the

phone. It was all I could do to keep him away. As I've already said, the Ley is like a family. We've all been in the reject bin of life, and we've helped each other out. We're the real rag dolls; we're not perfect – we've been broken, hurt, damaged, cast aside – but we are real human beings, and we understand the significance of the term 'wounded healers'.

When I returned, things were pretty much the same in the intensive care ward with Laura holding her own. Caroline and I had spoken about getting all the children back under one roof as soon as possible instead of farming them out to other people. We were well into the crisis now and it was time to get organized. Caroline would go home every evening for the other children and I would stay at the hospital.

We were getting messages from the churches in Reading and Oxford that there were large numbers of people praying for Laura to make a complete recovery. We were very moved by all this support. I had made friends with other families of people whose kin were in intensive care. The Frenchay had supplied us with a self-contained flat which three families could share at the same time. Adversity binds people together. I hope those that I met have gone on to rejoice at the departure of that long dark night of tears we all shared together.

We were into our fifth day in the intensive care ward, feeling frustrated that no real progress was being made, when, looking up, who should I see strolling towards us but my friend Steve Clark and his wife Judith. His face and smile, I swear, lit up that intensive care ward. This giant of a man came up, put his arms around me and said in his Australian drawl, 'Brother, have I got a message for you.'

He started to explain that what was going on in our lives was like looking at the back of a tapestry. It was all knots and loose ends but that God was even now building a beautiful picture for us which we would see when it was completed, and we would have to trust him, have faith and be justified.

'Steve,' I said, 'I knew you were coming because the Lord has told me! I want to say that you might have been invited to England by Michael Green, but the Lord really brought you all this way just to be here right now just for Laura and us and we praise Him for that.'

I asked Steve and Judith if they would lay hands with us on Laura and pray the prayer of faith, believing that we had sincerely received what we had asked for. When they said goodbye it was with great sadness, because they were leaving for Australia within a few days and we would not see them again. I sincerely believe that that was the turning point in our long, dark night of tears.

Two days later Laura started to improve. She was very weak initially but once she was taken off the drip and the tubes came out, her strength returned and a miraculous healing was taking place, baffling the doctors, nurses and physiotherapists.

Laura came out of intensive care and went into the children's ward. Caroline stopped coming during the week, but on Friday nights she would bring the other children to the Frenchay. Then I would take them home for the weekend and she would stay at the hospital.

Laura began to grow stronger and eventually got some coordination back in her limbs. I would have her reaching for toys, stretching muscles that had not been used for weeks. I was testing her all the time; some things were quite easy but others hard. We had our successes and our disappointments but at least we were not standing still.

Then one day I had her taking a couple of steps towards me and before too long she started to walk to the toilet across the room. She was finally getting her independence back.

The Frenchay became a beautiful, happy place for me. Laura Ashley and I had lots of friends. I was allowed to sleep beside her on a put-you-up in the children's ward. I promised her that when she could walk properly I would take her to McDonald's. So one day, when I knew that she was strong enough, we went for a walk, got into the car and went into Bristol for a wonderful outing. We were away for about three hours in which we bought clothes and toys from a store. Laura rode on my shoulders like a queen, still Her Majesty, the Baby!

A couple of days later came the news that Laura would be allowed to go home. I dreaded saying goodbye to her and didn't want even to think about it. I just wished we could stay as we were forever. But it was not to be. The day that should have been the happiest was also the saddest.

I got Laura Ashley fed, bathed, dressed and ready. The doctors came round and said their goodbyes. Caroline came with some friends and we put all Laura's stuff into the car. I kissed Laura goodbye. Caroline said she would be in touch and through the driving rain my little angel went out of sight. That was the last I saw or heard of Laura Ashley or the other children for about a month. The miracle completed, Laura was fully healed.

I would like to offer my sincere, heartfelt thanks to the emergency services who reacted so swiftly. They got the call at 2.40 p.m. and Laura was in the operating theatre at 3 p.m. Almost unbelievable! Those guys helped save my daughter's life and I shall be eternally grateful.

I must also thank the thousands of Christians who prayed for Laura while she lay in a coma. Caroline's Evangelical Church in Trowbridge and mine in Oxford, St Aldate's, spread the need for prayer during those six dark days and hundreds of churches throughout the country responded.

No one will ever convince me that Laura would have made it without those prayers. The doctors said the pressure on her brain was so intense, she needed a miracle to survive.

And a miracle is what all those prayers gave her.

CHAPTER TWENTY-SEVEN

Six months later, on 17 March 1995, I heard on the news that Ronnie Kray was dead; he'd been taken from Broadmoor to Heatherwood Hospital, in nearby Ascot, after collapsing. When his condition worsened he was transferred to Wexham Park Hospital where he died from a heart attack. I had no reason to shed any tears; after all, he'd refused to help me when I needed him most. But, you know, I was sad that he'd gone; I felt it was a waste of a life. It might sound strange to some people, but I genuinely feel Ron was someone who, despite his dreadful, self-damaging illness, could have achieved so much. He, like his twin, wanted something, but didn't know how to get it. With their charisma and power, they should have been professional, conducting serious, legal business. But they lacked that vital ingredient – intelligence – and allowed themselves to become obsessed with money and misguided fame. There was only one way they were going to end up.

I didn't go to the ludicrous circus that was Ronnie's funeral, near the family's East End home. I chose instead to be on the other side of the river, at Southwark Crown Court, pleading with a judge to give a young thief with a drug problem the chance to join the Ley Community and change his life. I'm pleased to say I succeeded, because that young man ended up going straight. Dreams can come true, if you want them enough. I wonder what Ronnie Kray's dreams were in the quiet of his mind.

That summer, Caroline remarried and, despite all the heartache we'd gone through, I was pleased for her; I sincerely hoped she would find the happiness and contentment I'd been unable to provide. For myself, it was going to take time for all the hurts and disappointments to heal, and I found it hard coping with close relationships. Then, in 1997, I retired from the Ley and, to my great delight, was given custody of all my children. They came to live with me, in Bicester, and I spent the next two years trying to strengthen the bonds that had been damaged by my divorce.

I was not looking for a long-term relationship, but then in 1999 I met a lovely Yorkshire lass, named Sharon, who had written to me at the Ley, saying she would love to meet up. We did and clicked immediately: she was very family orientated, which was important to me, and I could see us spending our lives together. Sharon did, too, and we got married and had a son, in January 2000 – the year Reggie and Charlie Kray died.

Charlie went first, in April. He died from pneumonia in hospital on the Isle of Wight, three years after being jailed for twelve years for offering to supply cocaine. I liked Charlie, as did everyone who met him. He was everything the twins were not: warm, friendly, charming – and always obliging. He wanted to go straight, but his brothers trapped him, too: another person they destroyed. I don't think Charlie had an enemy in the world. And, unlike Ron and Reg, he thought of others, not just himself. When Laura fell out of the window, he was quick to write me a lovely letter, offering to help in any way he could.

As much as I liked Charlie, and valued him as a friend, I

resisted the temptation to visit him in gaol, after his sentence: as a former Category A prisoner, it would have been bad for me, and bad for him. I didn't go to his funeral for the same reason.

Six months after Charlie's death, Reggie also died – from bladder cancer. He was in a Norfolk prison when diagnosed, but, like Charlie, was allowed out to die. In his case, though, he was in the honeymoon suite of the Beefeater Town House Hotel in Norwich. By his side was a young woman he'd recently married, and Bradley Allardyce, a young man he'd befriended in prison.

As with Ronnie, I felt sad at Reggie's demise: in Frances, he'd found the love he was looking for, and her tragic death devastated him: he was never the same man again. As one might expect from a respected gangster, Reg kept his grief under wraps: he might have let out his feelings to his mum at home in Vallance Road, but in the pub, surrounded by fawning heavies, he never talked about Frances. One night – a night I've never forgotten – I spotted him walking away from the Carpenters Arms and he struck me as one of the saddest men I'd ever seen. He was on his own, and hunched, like he had the woes of the world on his shoulders. Which, given what had happened to the young woman he adored, and what was going on with Ronnie, was probably true: the police were busy on the Cornell case and he must have sensed the net closing in.

As with Ronnie and Charlie, a huge crowd turned out for Reggie's funeral, but, again, I wasn't there.

Unfortunately, Sharon and I couldn't make our marriage work: she longed for the village life, near her parents and siblings, and I didn't want to move to Yorkshire. We lived together for only four months and were divorced in 2005 –

the year after my brother Tony died, at the relatively young age of sixty-two.

When Tony and I were freed from prison, I was still angry that we got mixed up in the McVitie murder because he had not listened to me and insisted on going to the Regency, all those years ago. But I did not harbour a grudge: he was my brother, after all, and I could never, *would* never, turn my back on him. His lifestyle was a world apart from mine: he loved the gangland culture and couldn't wait to embrace it again, but that was his choice. He had a big heart, Tony, and would march into dangerous situations, fearlessly, whereas I was more cautious and tried to look out for him.

When I think of him now, I often smile, because he had a dry sense of humour and, no matter how bleak a situation might look, he was always optimistic; he never saw anything as the end, only the beginning. There was a huge turnout for his funeral, illustrating how many people – even those he'd met only a few times – cared about him. Tony wasn't blessed with much fortune in his life, but he did strike lucky on a trip to Las Vegas with his wife, Wendy. Tony didn't gamble all the time they were there, but for some reason, on their last day, he asked Wendy for a dollar to put in a slot machine. He won the jackpot!

In spite of three failed marriages, I never gave up on finding a woman I could be happy with, and I'm thrilled to say I did – the year Sharon and I divorced. Her name is Helen, a lovely, honest, straightforward lady, who works for Children's Services, in a hospital. We were introduced by a mutual friend in Nottingham, where I was giving a talk, and we liked each other. She wanted to get married on the London Eye. I didn't know if that was possible, but anyway I kicked the idea into touch because I don't like heights. Helen then said she'd love a proper, old-fashioned East End wedding – so that's what we did. On 20 June 2006, we were married at Bow Register Office, blessed in St Matthew's Church, and celebrated the occasion at Kelly's Pie and Mash shop on Bethnal Green Road.

That day, we were in the heart of where Ronnie and Reggie had reigned supreme, but, as I enjoyed one of the happiest times of my life, they – and all the horrors they'd put me through – could not have been further from my mind. The past was buried. Or so I thought.

Eight years later, I got that call from Brian Helgeland and found myself agreeing to help him research his movie. I could understand why he wanted to make it: having read the books by and about the twins, and seen that ludicrously inaccurate film with the Kemp brothers, he could see that the Kray story had all the makings of a big-budget Hollywood blockbuster. And, thanks to a mesmerizing tour-de-force by Tom Hardy, as Ronnie and Reggie, that's what he produced. I went to the premiere, met Hardy, and was generally impressed with how the twins were portrayed.

By all accounts, the film did well, even in the US, where the Kray twins were barely known; and, in this country, all those who went expecting a lot of blood and gore were not disappointed. For me, however, the story lacked authenticity: it majored not so much on the frightening fearlessness of the twins, but Reggie's doomed Romeo and Juliet-type love affair with Frances, sister of my friend Frankie. I knew little about Frances, except that she killed herself with a drugs' overdose, but from what I'd heard she was mentally unbalanced all her life, and had tried suicide several times. This was a significant fact missing from the film, presumably because Hollywood preferred to tell what audiences wanted to happen, not what actually did.

The McVitie murder, too, was inaccurate in an important aspect: the movie made it appear that Tony and I lured Jack The Hat to a harmless Saturday night knees-up, with young women as well as men enjoying themselves in that basement flat. But there were no women there that night, only men. And they weren't there for a shindig.

Generally, though, the movie was far too stylized and glitzy for me. Yes, the twins had a larger-than-life charisma about them – Frank Sinatra and Damon Runyon wrapped up in one – but, apart from a brief period mixing with wealthy high society in Knightsbridge, their story was a dark and gritty one, played out in grim East End surroundings. And this was not conveyed on screen.

In the end I still hold the words of Martin Luther King in my heart. 'We will remember not the words of our enemies but the silence of our friends.' The Twins, who could have taken responsibility for their actions and spared their associates long prison sentences, were not legends. For me, the real legends were Tony's wife Pat and his children, who waited fifteen years. Ronnie Bender's wife Buddy and their children who waited twenty years. Ian Barrie, Freddie Foreman and Charlie Kray's families who also waited.

Today, I'm enjoying my retirement. Life is good, and now that all the ballyhoo of the film is over, I rarely think of the Kray madness that all but destroyed me. When I do, I still find it hard to come to terms with the fact that, in the biggest crisis of my life, I was not strong enough to stand up and do what was right, not only for myself but for my loved ones.

The thought makes me cringe now, but, in 1968 and 1969, my love for the code of the underworld was greater than it was for anything else: I put it before my wife, Carol, my lovely little daughter, Angela, and even before my dear old dad and my brothers.

Why? For God's sake, why?

Several trusted members of the Kray Firm were secretly telling all to the police, and it would have been easy for me to do the same: I would have been kept away from the twins until the court appearances, with only my conscience, not my safety, to worry about.

It was my conscience that was bothering me. That, and the image I had of myself as an honourable and loyal pal whom the twins could rely on when the chips were down.

As the police turned up the heat, I was no longer the bubble-and-squeak kid my friends' parents did not want to know, the outcast they didn't want at their children's parties. I was a real man, a Resistance fighter. And, like those brave Greeks who defied the Germans in wartime, I was going to stand shoulder to shoulder with the Krays against the police. No one was going to call me a coward or, worse, a grass.

For some reason I don't fully comprehend, I wanted to be a true good friend in the twins' eyes and, by doing so, be rewarded with a heartfelt thank you and perhaps a nod of respect, acknowledging that, when it mattered, Chris Lambrianou was an OK bloke who stood up and was counted, who didn't break the East End code.

How misguided. How naive. How downright stupid.

The Kray twins never gave a monkey's about me or any of the others caught up in the madness of that Saturday night in Stoke Newington. The sense of honour and decency and straightness I'd detected after being summoned to the Widow's pub went out the window. When it came to the crunch, all the twins displayed was the most astounding single-minded arrogance towards the police, and sneering contempt for those innocently implicated in their crimes.

For nearly two years, they had strutted around the East End, cocksure that no one had the bottle to say it was Ronnie who blew George Cornell's brains out. It was the same with McVitie. They believed their own firm were too loyal to tell the truth, and, when they discovered they were wrong and that even their own cousin had put them in the frame, they still refused to think of anyone but themselves.

They had shown their disregard for people close to them on the night of the murder itself. Having butchered the poor soul, they hurried away into the night, leaving the luckless Ronnie Bender, not only to clean up their bloody mess on his own, but to heave the remains of it over a railway bridge. Then, after I'd taken charge of the unsavoury operation, ensuring McVitie's body was transported safely away, they had the arrogance to complain it had been taken to the wrong location.

I had been led to believe that the Krays were leaders of a highly professional outfit, but the truth is that they were egomaniacs, too short-sighted to appreciate what they had achieved and where it could take them.

Why else did they even begin to think of such a senseless scenario as the one they instigated in Evering Road? If shooting a man in a pub at 8.30 p.m. was risky, luring a well-known local character from a crowded club for a humiliation in front of so many witnesses was mind-blowingly stupid. Even today, nearly fifty years on, I still can't understand it.

And I have to say that I still don't believe Reggie Kray set out to murder Jack McVitie that October night. Think about it. Reggie has a problem with the man, so he orders someone to go and get him from a place, teeming with more than a hundred people, and bring him to a little room, where, firstly, he puts a gun to McVitie's head, then plunges a knife into him in front of witnesses.

I swear on the Bible I hold so dear that I did not believe, in a million years, that such a blatantly stupid incident could happen. It defies logic, doesn't it?

If Reggie did, indeed, want McVitie out of the way, all he had to do was give two henchmen a few quid and a shooter and leave the rest to them. Then it would be: 'We're going for a little drive, Jack. OK, old son, pull over here in this dark side street.' Then – *bosh*. Two bullets in the nut, and it was all over. Leave the car. Get rid of the shooter. Burn the clothes and car. It could have been as simple as that, the cost of a gallon of petrol and a bullet.

There was no need for the Krays to have any connection with the killing, no need to perform the massacre in front of an audience, two or more of whom were total strangers with no allegiance to them at all.

Why they did beggared belief then, and still does today.

My sons and daughters are not impressed by the Krays, or the part I played in their story. I'm just their dad – their rock – and I'm proud of all of them, with, perhaps, the exception of David who became surrounded by the wrong people. I blame myself; I should have seen it from a distance.

Holly graduated from Southampton University in 2010, with a degree in media studies, and now works as a customer services manager at a large company in Oxford. Her twin brother, Christopher, works in travel insurance, and Laura Ashley is a social worker at the Ley, while also studying sociology at Buckinghamshire New University. Becky is a sales executive for a company in Oxfordshire. Charlie is fifteen and still in school in Doncaster. He wants to work in I.T. Angie continues to thrive

I'm deeply disappointed how David has turned out: he

went down the wrong road early in life. I did my best to persuade him to change his ways, but he wouldn't listen and, to my regret, we didn't speak for two years. Sadly, at the time of writing, he is in gaol for violence and as it was his second offence he was given an IPP. He has been moved around the prison system, but I visit him as much as I can. No matter how much I disapprove of how he has turned out, I'll always be there for him; for, when all's said and done, it's not how much money or possessions you've acquired that's important, is it? It's the love of people around you.

My family is everything to me and I do hope they're proud of how I turned my life around. I'm living proof that if you're honest with yourself, admit your mistakes and failings – no matter how terrible they are – you *can* change. Thankfully, I did: I escaped the Kray madness and emerged into the sunlight of the real world, with a sense of values for the first time.

I really did see the Light. And, for that, I give thanks to God.

EPILOGUE

I had to be persuaded to write this book.

It had to be about two people: one, a selfish, arrogant thug, who put the Kray twins before everything – even his own father; the other, a compassionate, caring Christian, trying his damndest to be a decent citizen.

I wasn't sure I wanted anybody to see the first one. Revealing what he did, how he thought, and the people he hurt and abused, would be like unlocking the door on a madman, and I wasn't sure I'd have the courage to do it; at least, not until I'd achieved something worthwhile.

Well, after a lifetime of failure, of being told what a worthless waster I was, I feel I *have* achieved something to be proud of. And, more important, earned the respect of people, who once would not have wanted to know me. No longer am I the Kray gangster, unable to communicate without the threat of violence, the thug who'd reach for a gun to solve a problem. Now, I use words to make my point, often in courtrooms where I once stood, accused, in the dock.

I was in the prime of my life when my association with the Kray twins slammed the door on my liberty. But, you know, I'm not in the least bitter about those fifteen lost years. For they changed my life in a way no amount of freedom could have.

Bizarrely, perhaps, I believe my imprisonment was inevitable.

Having swaggered round the edges of the underworld for nearly twenty years, caring for no one but myself, I passionately believe I had to do those fifteen years to get rid of the madman in me and come out, the real Chris Lambrianou. I've read some of the world's most enlightening literature, lived fantastic lifetimes through such great men as Gandhi, Kipling and Shakespeare, and am much, much richer for it.

My only regret – and it's an overpowering one, even now – is shaming my family's name, and putting my dad through years of crushing torment. When me and my brothers were young, he said we were the fingers on one of his hands; that when any of us got in trouble with the police, it was like one of those fingers breaking off. Well, me and Tony and Nicky broke three fingers. And that hurts me, still.

While banged up, I had plenty of time to consider why I turned out so badly. And though it will sound naive, coming from someone who was robbing West End stores at eight years old, I honestly don't believe I was born bad.

I was dearly loved by my parents, but when four brothers came along – three in quick succession – I was forced, encouraged almost, to go out and entertain myself. I can't remember ever feeling downright miserable, but I *did* feel left out, and I'm sure I turned to crime to make myself seem important; be the centre of attention. I wasn't wicked: my thieving, I'm convinced, was no more than a cry for help.

If there was a thread that ran through everything I experienced in those early years, it was the racial prejudice: I was as cockney as jellied eels, but treated as an outcast by people I was supposed to respect. Custody could – and possibly *should* – have brought out the qualities I knew I possessed, to make something better of my life. But nobody taught me the skills to go and get a job and hold it down: the system for young guys like me was geared to get us fit for gaol, and nothing else.

I was taken from a loving home environment at a young, crucial, stage and thrown into a tough, male-dominated world, where my ability to take the blows was, it seemed, all anyone understood. I needed somewhere to run; and some-body to run *to*. But there was no one; I was on my own, trapped.

The Approved School and borstal, then the prisons, kept me away from society. But the self-protecting walls I was building round myself formed another impenetrable fortress altogether. My hurt and pain had to come out sooner or later, and when it did, it was in the form of violence: my revenge on a society I felt had let me down.

It might have helped if I'd been strong, but I wasn't. I was hard, but not strong. And there is a world of difference, as my dear old dad never stopped trying to explain, as he trekked from one prison to another, consoling and comforting me after my losing battles against society, and the injustices I felt it was inflicting on me.

Even now, I remember his anguish, staring at my battered face after that terrible Albany tear-up: he was so heartbroken, he could hardly speak. Finally, he said, in that adorable broken English I still miss so much: 'Chrissie, you're too *hard*.'

I had no idea what he meant, and said so.

'There's good and bad in the world, boy, but you see only the bad,' he said. 'You don't see both sides; you don't bend.'

I sneered at that. 'If the world kicks me, I kick it back – harder,' I said. 'That's what the world understands.'

'But that's not the way, boy,' he sighed. 'You can break hard things all the time, but you'll never break something strong.'

He must have seen that I still didn't get it, because he went on: 'The fiercest wind can flatten a cornfield, but the corn is so strong it comes back up. The stalks will never be broken because they bend. Chrissie, you're hard – very hard. But you're not strong. You don't bend.'

Dad was no orator or poet, but he had an almost primitive way of speaking that had its own charm, and I got the drift: when anything went wrong in my life, I always confronted it head on, using violence to get my way. I didn't have an inner strength, a moral fibre, if you like, to make my point any other way. As a result, in his eyes, I'd always be a loser.

I had many, many long, lonely days and months and years to dwell on Dad's philosophy; to agonize over the flaw in my character that, in 1969, made me a sheep, not a shepherd; that, in the biggest crisis of my life, I was not strong enough to do what was right, not only for myself, but for my loved ones.

The shame and humiliation I brought on my dad all those years, after my arrest in 1968, choke me with guilt. My misplaced, incomprehensible loyalty to the Kray twins forced him on a treadmill of misery when all he should have had was happiness. The journeys he should have been making, in the winter of his life, were perhaps to watch his grandchildren grow up; but I subjected him to hundreds of hours and miles, traipsing to depressing places he had no wish to see, bringing him face to face, time and again, with the person he never wished me to be. He walked away from those prisons miserable, when he should have been somewhere pleasant and good, enjoying himself.

No one would have blamed him if he'd disowned me, left me to stew in my own foul juice for disappointing him so dreadfully. But he was too fine a father not to forgive, or stop loving, me. This is why it's so important to me, late as it is, to be the son he wanted – that decent, law-abiding citizen he would be proud of. It was all he ever asked of me, and I didn't deliver, didn't give a monkey's, until Jesus came to me in that cell and told me there was a different way to live.

I can't erase my ugly, grotesque past, pretend the man I didn't want the world to see didn't exist. But I can make sure, for my dear father's memory, that the madman is back behind that door.

Locked away forever.

Chris Lambrianou: A Personal View
by his Probation Officer,
Mike Howard

Chris Lambrianou is a bear of a man, of powerful physique and compelling personality. He can dominate any situation or conversation, and often does. Though mellowed by time and experience, and his deep cockney growl more often than not a chuckle, it is easy to visualize the figure he cut in the criminal culture of the sixties, at the peak of his physical strength and explosive energy.

Those were the years of the London gang wars, the ascendancy of the notorious Krays who chose the two Lambrianou brothers to be their henchmen. By then Chris had served prison sentences, a spell in the Army, borstal, a detention centre – and three years at an Approved School, from the age of eleven. There the sensitivities of the child were stunted and brutalized by a regime of barbaric discipline and corporal punishment. The unruly behaviour which put him there had been generated amid the poverty, deprivation and racial prejudice endured by a working-class immigrant family in the social setting of the time. His parents' high standards and values were rejected, though his remorse at failing them never left him. His adolescent confusions and resentments were reinforced, not resolved, by the various sentences, the desire to retaliate burned ever deeper into him, the seeds of his future adult criminality nurtured and nourished. The resentments were reinforced, not resolved, by the various sentences, the desire to retaliate burned ever deeper into him, the seeds of his future adult criminality nurtured and nourished. The lessons he learned were: the harder you're hit, the harder you hit back, might is right. Such is the impact of punishment on people, contrary to popular belief.

Chris emerged from his early prison experiences in his twenties. He was well qualified to make his mark in a vicious criminal underworld where no quarter was given and none expected. He is a natural storyteller and the vivid picture he paints of ruthless brutality is chilling in both its detachment and detail. He simply tells it as it was, with no elaboration or exaggeration, revealing himself at his worst, as part of 'his story'. This has taken a long time coming. Over the many years I have known him, he has always been reluctant to talk of that era unless there was good reason to do so. Certainly he has resisted media pressure from time to time to make money by selling his story. 'I have no wish to glamorize my criminal past.' Rather, if there is any lesson or message at all, it is in the old adage: crime doesn't pay. For a brief period he achieved his ambition of life in the fast lane, easy money, fast cars, fast women, style and status. But his success was short-lived, ending with his conviction for murder and sentence of life imprisonment.

Chris always regarded both his conviction and sentence as unjust, his fifteen years in prison as excessive. But he reckons that, for all his misdeeds, he probably deserved ten. Whenever his feelings have spilled over in an outburst of anger, it has ended abruptly, in a characteristic chuckle, 'But I came out a very much better man than I went in, I might add!'

What did he mean? Several years into his life sentence, an extraordinary thing began to happen. From reading the writings of great authors and religious teachers, he found himself drawn increasingly to the person of Christ: first by a simple poster a fellow prisoner stuck on his cell wall; then by a popular song which went round and round in his head; finally by a vision which sealed his conversion. That was no sudden emotional experience but one which took place slowly over a long period of time 'drawing on a well of spirituality inside me, so far untapped'. It transformed his life, thinking, attitudes, behaviour and made him a model prisoner. He found a physical outlet in tending prison gardens, and expression in his writings. Of these, the prayers he wrote around the time of his father's death are the most moving. Published much later as *Meditations of a Lifer* they reveal, not a religious crank, but a man described by one reviewer as 'with hardly an ounce of religion in his body. Thank God for that! Instead he is filled with a burning desire to know and be known by his creator . . . has experienced rage, despair and darkness, as not many of us have, is determined to be real, to be himself, equally determined to walk with Jesus, the toughest and most genuinely loving master of them all.'

Anyone might think prison is as good or bad a place as any to live out one's faith, to practise one's beliefs. It is not. For all the difficulties and deprivations, prison is a protected, unreal world. It has an ordered, predictable routine and the necessities of life are assured. There are no great decisions to be made, uncertainties over employment, tensions of family life, conflicts between work, home and personal interests, the weekly worries of making ends meet. For Chris, the real test of his Christian faith came after his discharge from prison. He had served the minimum fifteen years recommended by the judge at his sentence, demonstrated good behaviour, and was released on life licence: subject to recall if he failed to comply with the numerous requirements.

When we first met he had had two years at liberty, married the lovely Caroline, fathered two beautiful babies (the twins) and was in charge of an old quarry near Bicester, Oxfordshire. I was his new parole officer, fortunate to take over from Roy Watkins of Banbury who had earned his trust and respect. My responsibilities were to supervise his licence, record every contact, report to the Home Office and recommend if necessary his recall to prison. That was the framework we never forgot. If it ever seemed important to remind him, he would reply, as I knew he would: 'No one could be more aware of that than me.' Within that framework developed the deepest of friendships. For over seven years, it would be rare for a week to pass without some kind of contact.

Chris always worked immensely long hours. The quarry was followed by pipe-laying, building sites, driving jobs, gardening and construction of the M40 motorway. With his family commitments as well, he had no time to see me in my office. Instead we would meet in all kinds of unlikely places: huddling round a fire of burning timbers at the quarry in winter; sitting on a roadside verge in summer; the cab of a motorway construction vehicle; over pots of tea at Oxford's Randolph Hotel. I was welcomed by Caroline into the home, to the children's birthday parties, listened to their bedtime stories, splashed with them through puddles at the Cotswold Wildlife Park. There was much happiness being with them all. Those were the best of times – and the worst of times.

The births of three more children in rapid succession increased the tensions between Chris and Caroline to breaking point. Both tried so hard to make their marriage work, and so did others. Chris could not accept that, finally, it was over. He seemed to feel he could still put it together, by sheer force of will, and I feared for his future. He was a soul in torment, I was his confidante and confessor, sounding board and safety valve. But his heart ruled his head, he would promise me one thing – then do another. Thank God he had other supports by then, as important to him or more so than I: the people and place where he worked. This was the Ley Community, a few miles north of Oxford.

Some seven years into his licence, five after we first met, Chris became unemployed and could not find work. Always abounding with energy, Chris frustrated was fearsome! I had always believed his experience, insights and wisdom were wasted in manual work, as had Caroline. He had so much more to offer, as we often discussed, but what organization or agency could contain so rugged an individual, so forceful a personality? Now with time on his hands, he was ready and willing to find out. Together we toured the hostels and night shelters of Oxford and talked to staff, in the hope something would click. Nothing did. The last resort was where I myself worked as liaison probation officer, a drug rehabilitation centre, the Ley Community. I had sometimes talked to Chris about this inspirational place which enables drug users and serious offenders to turn their lives round. But I was anxious over taking him there lest it, too, seemed somehow not right.

When we first went together, it was to see the member of staff responsible for voluntary work placements and ask her advice. It just happened that the director, Paul Toon, was free, met Chris and subsequently decided to take him on. He knew that it was a risk, he could have a loose cannon on his hands. But it was a risk that paid off. At the Ley Community, Chris found his niche. From beginning as a volunteer, he was employed with the main task of collecting remand prisoners from London courts and escorting them back to the Ley for bail assessments. They are then at their most anxious, most likely to abscond. Who better then to meet them, listen to and reassure them, than one such as Chris Lambrianou, ex-criminal, ex-con? Have they suffered injustice, imprisonment, deprivation, poverty, prejudice, abused drugs, made a mess of their lives? So has he. With his uncanny gift for knowing people's feelings and fears, no one could do it better. Chris gave all he could to the Ley Community. He still does. When he needed them, they were there for him.

For Chris now, life revolves around his children, his work, his church and his friendships. Through all runs the thread of his Christian faith. That has not made him perfect, far from it. But the church is for sinners, of which Chris would say, like St Paul, that he is the chief. In his own words, 'I have made many dreadful messes in my life, but I am closest to reality when I am on my knees.' If there is anything which best fits how he is and feels, it is the prayer about coming to the master-carpenter of Nazareth rough-hewn, and being fashioned to a truer likeness. I once borrowed some words from the old *Reader's Digest* series to describe Chris as 'The most unforgettable character I have ever met'. He still is.

PICTURE ACKNOWLEDGEMENTS

All photographs are from the author's collection
with the exception of the following:

Page 1 bottom © Hulton Deutsch Collection

Page 2 top © Pat Larkin/Daily Mail/REX/Shutterstock

Page 2 bottom, page 5 top right and page 4 and 5 bottom
© Mirrorpix

Page 3 top and page 5 top left © John Twine/
Associated Newspapers/REX/Shutterstock

Page 3 bottom photo by Bentley Archive/Popperfoto/Getty Images

Page 4 top © PA/PA Archive/Press Association Images